STYLE

Ten Lessons
in Clarity and Grace

STYLE

Ten Lessons in Clarity and Grace

EIGHTH EDITION

Joseph M. Williams
The University of Chicago

PEARSON
Longman

New York Boston San Francisco
London Toronto Sydney Tokyo Singapore Madrid
Mexico City Munich Paris Cape Town Hong Kong Montreal

Senior Sponsoring Editor: Virginia Blanford
Senior Supplements Editor: Donna Campion
Executive Marketing Manager: Megan Galvin-Fak
Managing Editor: Bob Ginsberg
Production Manager: Joseph Vella
Project Coordination, Text Design,
    and Electronic Page Makeup: Thompson Steele, Inc.
Senior Cover Design Manager: Nancy Danahy
Cover Design Manager/Designer: John Callahan
Manufacturing Manager/Buyer: Mary Fischer
Printer and Binder: R.R. Donnelley & Sons, Inc.
Cover Printer: Phoenix Color Corp.

For permission to use copyrighted material, grateful acknowledgment is made to the copyright holders on p. 269, which are hereby made part of this copyright page.

Library of Congress Cataloging-in-Publication Data
Williams, Joseph M.
    Style : ten lessons in clarity and grace / Joseph M. Williams.—8th ed.
    p. cm.
    Includes bibliographical references and index.
    ISBN 0-321-28831-9
    1. English language—Style. 2. English language—Technical English.
3. English language—Business English. 4. English language—
Rhetoric. 5. Technical writing. 6. Business writing. I. Title.
PE1421.W545 2005
808'.042—dc22

                                                                2004021740

Please visit our website at http://www.ablongman.com

ISBN 0-321-28831-9

1 2 3 4 5 6 7 8 9 10—DOH—07 06 05 04

To my mother and father

*. . . English style, familiar but not coarse,
elegant, but not ostentatious . . .*
—SAMUEL JOHNSON

CONTENTS

PREFACE

Most people won't realize that writing is a craft.
You have to take your apprenticeship in it like anything else.
—KATHERINE ANNE PORTER

THE EIGHTH EDITION

What's New

In this eighth edition of *Style*, I've reorganized parts of some lessons to make them flow more logically and imposed on most of the lessons a three-part structure of *Understanding, Diagnosis and Revision,* and *Summing Up*. Both changes should help readers move through those lessons more easily.

I have also done a good deal of line editing (by this time, you'd think there would be nothing to edit, but there always seems to be). I've replaced examples in Lessons Five and Six and have almost completely rewritten the Epilogue on coherence and divided it in two. Epilogue One focuses on coherence and includes a generalization that links clarity in sentences with coherence in paragraphs, sections, and whole documents. So far as I know, it is a principle new in the literature on clear and readable prose. In Epilogue Two, I focus on how to motivate readers to read attentively.

What's the Same

This eighth edition aims at answering the same questions I asked in the seven earlier ones:

- What is it in a sentence that makes readers judge it as they do?
- How can we diagnose our own prose to anticipate their judgments?
- How can we revise a sentence so that readers will think better of it?

The standard advice about writing ignores those questions. It is mostly truisms like "Make a plan" and "Think of your audience"—advice that most of us ignore as we wrestle ideas out onto the page. When I first drafted this paragraph, I wasn't thinking about you; I was struggling to get my own ideas straight. What I did know was that I would come back to this paragraph again and again, and that it was likely to be only then—as I revised—that I could think about you and discover the plan that fit my draft. I also knew that as I did so, there were some principles I could rely on. This book explains them.

PRINCIPLES, NOT PRESCRIPTIONS

Those principles may seem prescriptive, but that's not how I intend them. I offer them as ways to help you predict how readers will judge your prose and then help you decide whether and how to revise it. As you learn all those principles, you may find that you write more slowly. That's inevitable. Whenever we reflect on what we do as we do it, we become self-conscious, sometimes to the point of paralysis. It passes. You can avoid some of that paralysis if you remember that these principles have little to do with how you draft, much to do with how you revise. If there is a first principle of drafting, it's to forget advice about how to do it.

Some Prerequisites

To learn how to revise efficiently, though, you have to know a few things:

- You should know a few grammatical terms: SUBJECT, VERB, NOUN, ACTIVE, PASSIVE, CLAUSE, PREPOSITION, and COORDINATION. All key terms are capitalized the first time they appear and are defined in the text or in the Glossary.

- You will have to learn new meanings for two familiar words: TOPIC and STRESS.

- You will need five terms that you probably don't know. Two are important: NOMINALIZATION and METADISCOURSE; three are useful: RESUMPTIVE MODIFIER, SUMMATIVE MODIFIER, and FREE MODIFIER.

Finally, if you are reading this book on your own, go slowly. It is not an amiable essay to read in a sitting or two. Take the lessons a few pages at a time, up to the exercises. Do the exercises, edit someone else's writing, then some of your own written a few weeks ago, then something you've written that day.

An *Instructor's Manual* is available for those who are interested in some of the scholarly and pedagogical thinking that has gone into *Style*. It also provides suggested revisions for exercises that are not listed on pages 257–268.

ACKNOWLEDGMENTS

So many have offered support, suggestions, and criticisms over the last twenty-five years, that I cannot thank you all. But again I begin with those English 194 students who put up with faintly dittoed pages (that tells you how many years ago this book was born) and with a teacher who at times was at least as puzzled as they. I remain grateful to you all.

I have learned from undergraduate, graduate and professional students, and post-docs who have gone through the Little Red Schoolhouse writing program at the University of Chicago (a.k.a. Advanced Academic and Professional Writing). I am equally grateful to the graduate students who taught these principles and offered important feedback.

I have intellectual debts to those who broke ground in psycholinguistics, text linguistics, and functional sentence perspective. Those who keep up with such matters will recognize the influence of Charles Filmore, Jan Firbas, Nils Enkvist, Michael Halliday, Noam Chomsky, Thomas Bever, Vic Yngve, and others. The work of Eleanore Rosch has provided a rich explanation for why verbs should be actions and characters should be subjects. Her work in prototype semantics is a powerful theoretical basis for the kind of style urged here.

I am indebted to colleagues who have taken time to read the work of another. For their thoughtful reviews of this edition, I wish to acknowledge Christopher Buck, Michigan State University; Richard Grande, Pennsylvania State; Craig Kleinman, City College of San Francisco; Brij Lunine, University of California Santa Cruz; Richard McLain, Binghamton University; Ed Moritz, Indiana University–Purdue University Fort Wayne; Janice Neuleib, Illinois State University; Matthew Parfitt, Boston University; and Wendy Wayman, University of Nevada, Reno.

For reading earlier versions of this book, I thank Randy Berlin, Ken Bruffee, Douglas Butturff, Donald Byker, Bruce Campbell, Elaine Chaika, Avon Crismore, Constance Gefvert, Maxine Hairston, George Hoffman, Ted Lowe, Susan Miller, Neil Nakadate, Mike Pownall, Peter Priest, Margaret Shaklee, Nancy Sommers, Mary Taylor, Stephen Witte, John Ruszkiewicz, Bill Vande Kopple, Margaret Batschelet, Theresa Ammirati, Yvonne Atkinson, Cheryl Brooke, Jeanne Gunner, Rebecca Moore Howard, Richard Jenseth, Elizabeth Bourque Johnson, Patricia Murray, John Taylor, Joseph Wappel, Alison Warriner, Kevin S. Wilson, Nancy Barendse, Darren Cambridge, Mark Canada, Paul Contino, Jim Garrett, Jill Gladstein, Karen Gocsik, Julie Kalish, Bernadette Longo, Joel Margulis, Linda Mitchell, Ellen Moody, Ann Palkovich, Donna Burns Philips, and Laura Bartlett Snyder. I am grateful for the feedback from the class taught by Stan Henning at the University of Wisconsin, Madison, and for the error in usage caught by Linda Ziff. I am particularly indebted to an exchange with Keith Rhodes about Lesson Ten.

I am indebted to Christina Devlin for the Wesley quotation in Lesson Seven and to James Vanden Bosch for the Montaigne quotation in the Glossary. I gratefully acknowledge Frederick C. Mish, editorial director, G. & C. Merriam Company, for locating the best examples of three citations in Lesson Two, and Charles Bazerman, for leading me to the first paragraph of Crick and Watson's DNA paper. I am still profoundly indebted to the person who urged me to write this book, Harriett Prentiss.

For several years, I have had the good fortune to work with two people who have been both good colleagues and good friends and whose careful thinking has helped me think better about many matters, both professional and personal: Don Freeman and Greg Colomb. Don's careful readings have saved me from more than a few howlers; I am indebted to him for the quote from William Blake in Lesson Eight. For more than twenty-five years now, Greg has put up with more than most friends would, and I have benefited from both his scrupulous critical thinking and our intemperate shouting matches. We developed together much of the material in the two Epilogues. It has been a pleasure and a privilege to work with him and to travel and hang out with him and Sandra.

And again, those who contribute more to my life than I let them know: Oliver, Chris, and Ingrid; Dave, Patty, Owen, and Matilda; Megan, Phil, and Lily; Joe, Christine, Nicholas, and Katherine. And at beginning and end still, Joan, whose patience and love still flow more generously than I deserve.

JOSEPH M. WILLIAMS

PART ONE

Style as Choice

*Have something to say,
and say it as clearly as you can.
That is the only secret of style.*
—MATTHEW ARNOLD

Understanding Style

Essentially style resembles good manners.
It comes of endeavouring to understand others,
of thinking for them rather than yourself—or thinking,
that is, with the heart as well as the head.
—SIR ARTHUR QUILLER-COUCH

The great enemy of clear language is insincerity.
—GEORGE ORWELL

In matters of grave importance,
style, not sincerity, is the vital thing.
—OSCAR WILDE

PRINCIPLES AND AIMS

This book rests on two principles: it is good to write clearly, and anyone can. The first is self-evident, especially to those who have to read a lot of writing like this:

> An understanding of the causal factors involved in excessive drinking by students could lead to their more effective treatment.

But that second principle may seem optimistic to those who try to write more clearly, but can't get close to this:

> We could more effectively treat students who drink excessively if we understood why they do.

Of course, writing fails for reasons more serious than unclear sentences. We bewilder readers when we can't organize complex ideas coherently (an issue I address in the two Epilogues), and we can't expect their assent when we ignore their reasonable questions and objections. But once we've formulated our claims, organized supporting reasons, and grounded them on sound evidence, we must still express it all in clear, direct sentences, a difficult task for most writers and a daunting one for many.

It is a problem that has afflicted generations of writers who have hidden their ideas not only from their readers, but sometimes even from themselves. When we read that kind of writing in government regulations, we call it *bureaucratese;* when we read it in legal documents, *legalese;* in academic writing that inflates small ideas into gassy abstractions, *academese*. Written deliberately or carelessly, it's a language of exclusion that a democracy can't tolerate. It is a problem with a long history.

A SHORT HISTORY OF UNCLEAR WRITING

The Past

It wasn't until about the middle of the sixteenth century that writers of English decided that our language was eloquent enough to replace Latin and French in serious discourse. But their first efforts were written in a style so complex that it defeated easy understanding:

> If use and custom, having the help of so long time and continuance wherein to [re]fine our tongue, of so great learning and experience

which furnish matter for the [re]fining, of so good wits and judgments which can tell how to refine, have griped at nothing in all that
time, with all that cunning, by all those wits which they won't let go
but hold for most certain in the right of our writing, that then our
tongue has no certainty to trust to, but write all at random.

—Richard Mulcaster, *The First Part of the Elementary,* 1582

Within a century, a complex style had spread to the writing of
scientists (or, as they were called, *natural philosophers*). As one
complained,

Of all the studies of men, nothing may sooner be obtained than this
vicious abundance of phrase, this trick of metaphors, this volubility
of tongue which makes so great a noise in the world.

—Thomas Sprat, *History of the Royal Society,* 1667

When this country was settled, our writers could have established a new, democratic prose style, not viciously voluble, but
simple and direct. In fact, in 1776, the plain speaking of Thomas
Paine's *Common Sense* helped inspire our Revolution:

In the following pages I offer nothing more than simple facts, plain
arguments, and common sense.

Sad to say, he sparked no revolution in our style of writing.

By the early nineteenth century, James Fenimore Cooper was
complaining about our turgid language:

The love of turgid expressions is gaining ground, and ought to be cor-
rected. One of the most certain evidences of a man of high breeding,
is his simplicity of speech: a simplicity that is equally removed from
vulgarity and exaggeration. . . . Simplicity should be the firm aim, after one is removed from vulgarity. . . . In no case, however, can one
who aims at turgid language, exaggerated sentiments, or pedantic utterances, lay claim to be either a man or a woman of the world.

—James Fenimore Cooper, *The American Democrat,* 1838

Unfortunately, in abusing that style, Cooper adopted it. Had
he followed his own advice, he might have written,

We should discourage those who love turgid language. A well-bred
person speaks simply, in a way that is neither vulgar nor exaggerated.
After we rid our language of vulgarity, we should aim at simplicity.
No one can claim to be a man or woman of the world who exagger-
ates sentiments or deliberately speaks in language that is turgid or
pedantic.

About fifty years later, Mark Twain wrote what we now think is classic American prose—easy, clear, and direct. He said this about Cooper's style:

> There have been daring people in the world who claimed that Cooper could write English, but they are all dead now—all dead but Lounsbury [an academic who praised Cooper's style]. . . . [He] says that *Deerslayer* is a "pure work of art." . . . [But] Cooper wrote about the poorest English that exists in our language, and . . . the English of *Deerslayer* is the very worst tha[t] even Cooper ever wrote.

We still admire Twain's directness, but few of us consistently emulate it.

The Present

In the best-known essay on modern English style, "Politics and the English Language," George Orwell anatomized the pretentious language of politicians and academics:

> The keynote [of a pretentious style] is the elimination of simple verbs. Instead of being a single word, such as *break, stop, spoil, mend, kill*, a verb becomes a phrase, made up of a noun or adjective tacked on to some general-purposes verb such as *prove, serve, form, play, render*. In addition, the passive voice is wherever possible used in preference to the active, and noun constructions are used instead of gerunds (*by examination* of instead of *by examining*).

But as Cooper did, in abusing that style Orwell adopted it. He could have written more concisely:

> Pretentious writers eliminate simple verbs. Instead of using one word, such as *break, stop, kill*, they turn a verb into a noun or adjective, then tack it on to a general-purpose verb such as *prove, serve, form, play, render*. Wherever they can, they use the passive voice instead of the active and noun constructions instead of gerunds (*by examination* instead of *by examining*).

If the best-known critic of a turgid style could not resist it, we shouldn't be surprised that politicians and academics embrace it. On the language of the social sciences:

> A turgid and polysyllabic prose does seem to prevail in the social sciences. . . . Such a lack of ready intelligibility, I believe, usually has little or nothing to do with the complexity of thought. It has to do

almost entirely with certain confusions of the academic writer about his own status.

—C. Wright Mills, *The Sociological Imagination*

On the language of medicine:

It now appears that obligatory obfuscation is a firm tradition within the medical profession. . . . [Medical writing] is a highly skilled, calculated attempt to confuse the reader. . . . A doctor feels he might get passed over for an assistant professorship because he wrote his papers too clearly—because he made his ideas seem too simple.

—Michael Crichton, *New England Journal of Medicine*

On the language of law:

In law journals, in speeches, in classrooms and in courtrooms, lawyers and judges are beginning to worry about how often they have been misunderstood, and they are discovering that sometimes they can't even understand each other.

—Tom Goldstein, *New York Times*

On the language of science:

There are times when the more the authors explain [about ape communication], the less we understand. Apes certainly seem capable of using language to communicate. Whether scientists are remains doubtful.

—Douglas Chadwick, *New York Times*

Most of us first confront that kind of unclear writing in textbook sentences like this one:

Recognition of the fact that systems [of grammar] differ from one language to another can serve as the basis for serious consideration of the problems confronting translators of the great works of world literature originally written in a language other than English.

In about half as many words, that means,

When we recognize that languages have different grammars, we can consider the problems of those who translate great works of literature into English.

Generations of students have struggled with dense writing, many thinking they were not smart enough to grasp a writer's deep ideas. Some have been right about that, but more could have blamed the writer's inability (or refusal) to write clearly. Many students, sad to say, give up; sadder still, others learn not only to read that style but to write it, inflicting it on the next generation of readers, thereby sustaining a 400-year-old tradition of opaque prose.

SOME PRIVATE CAUSES OF UNCLEAR WRITING

But if unclear writing has a long social history, it also has private causes. Michael Crichton mentioned one: some writers plump up their prose to impress those who confuse a difficult style with deep thinking. And when we don't know what we're talking about (or have no confidence in what we do know) we typically throw up a tangle of abstract words in long, complex sentences.

Others write graceless prose not deliberately but because they are seized by the idea that writing is good only when it's free of errors only a grammarian can explain. They approach a blank page not as a place to explore new ideas, but as a minefield to cross gingerly. They creep from word to word, concerned less with their readers' understanding than with their own survival.

Others write unclearly because they just freeze up, especially when they are learning to think and write in a new academic or professional setting. Those afflicted include not just undergraduates taking their first course in economics or psychology, but graduate students, businesspeople, doctors, lawyers—anyone writing on a new topic for unfamiliar and therefore intimidating readers. As we struggle to master new and complex ideas, most of us write worse than we do when we write about things we understand better. If that sounds like you, take heart. You will write more clearly once you more clearly understand your subject and readers.

But the biggest reason we write unclearly is our ignorance of how others read our writing. What we write always seems clearer to us than it does to our readers, because we can read into it what we want readers to get out of it. And so instead of revising our writing to meet their needs, we send it off as soon as it meets ours.

In all of this, of course, there is a great irony: we are likely to confuse others when we write about a subject that confuses us. But when we also read about a complex subject written in a complex style, we too easily assume that such complexity signals deep thought, and so we try to imitate it, compounding our already confused writing.

This book shows you how to avoid that, how to read your own writing as others will, and, when you should, how to make it better.

ON WRITING AND REWRITING

A warning: if you think about these principles *as you draft,* you may never draft anything. Most experienced writers get something down on paper or up on the screen as fast as they can, just to have something to revise. Then as they rewrite an early draft into something clearer, they more clearly understand their ideas. And when they understand their ideas better, they express them more clearly, and when they express them more clearly, they understand them even better . . . and so it goes, until they run out of energy, interest, or time.

For a fortunate few, that moment comes weeks, months, even years after they begin. (Over the last twenty-five years, I've wrestled this book through dozens of drafts, and there are still parts I can't get right.) For most of us, though, the deadline is closer to tomorrow morning. And so we have to settle for prose that is less than perfect, but as good as we can make it. (Perfection is the ideal, but the enemy of done.) So use what you find here not as rules to impose on every sentence *as* you draft it, but as principles to help you identify sentences likely to give your readers a problem, and then to revise those sentences quickly.

As important as clarity is, though, some occasions call for more:

> Now the trumpet summons us again—not as a call to bear arms, though arms we need; not as a call to battle, though embattled we are; but a call to bear the burden of a long twilight struggle, year in and year out, "rejoicing in hope, patient in tribulation," a struggle against the common enemies of man: tyranny, poverty, disease and war itself.
>
> —John F. Kennedy, Inaugural Address, January 20, 1961

Few of us are called upon to write a presidential address, but in even our modest prose, some of us take a private pleasure in writing a shapely sentence, regardless of whether anyone will notice, like the cabinetmaker who sands the back of a drawer. Those who enjoy not just writing a sentence but crafting it will find suggestions in Lesson Nine. Writing is also a social act that might or might not serve the best interests of readers, so in Lesson Ten, I address some ethical issues of style. In the two Epilogues, I go beyond the clarity of individual sentences to discuss the coherence of a whole document. In an Appendix, I discuss styles of punctuation.

Many years ago, H. L. Mencken wrote this:

> With precious few exceptions, all the books on style in English are by writers quite unable to write. The subject, indeed, seems to exercise a special and dreadful fascination over school ma'ams, bucolic college professors, and other such pseudoliterates. . . . Their central aim, of course, is to reduce the whole thing to a series of simple rules—the overmastering passion of their melancholy order, at all times and everywhere.

Mencken was right: no one learns to write well by rule, especially those who can't feel or think or see. But I know that many who do see clearly, feel deeply, and think carefully can't write sentences that make their thoughts, feelings, and visions clear to others. I also know that the more clearly we write, the more clearly we see and feel and think. Rules help no one do that, but some principles can.

Here they are.

2

Correctness

*God does not much mind bad grammar, but He does not take
any particular pleasure in it.*
—ERASMUS

*No grammatical rules have sufficient authority to control the firm
and established usage of language. Established custom, in speaking
and writing, is the standard to which we must at last resort for
determining every controverted point in language and style.*
—HUGH BLAIR

*English usage is sometimes more than mere taste, judgment,
and education—sometimes it's sheer luck,
like getting across the street.*
—E. B. WHITE

UNDERSTANDING CORRECTNESS

To a careful writer, nothing is more important than choice, but in some matters, we have none—we can't put *the* after a NOUN, as in *street the* (capitalized words are defined in the Glossary). But we choose when we can. For example, which of these sentences would you choose to write if you wanted readers to think you wrote clearly?

1. Lack of newspaper support caused our loss of the election.
2. We lost the election because newspapers didn't support us.

Both are grammatically "correct," but most of us choose (2).

Unlike clarity, though, correctness seems a matter not of choice, but of obedience. When the *American Heritage Dictionary* says that *irregardless* is "never acceptable" (except, they say, for humor), our freedom to choose it seems at best academic. In matters of this kind, we choose not between better and worse, but between right and utterly, irredeemably, unequivocally Wrong, which is, of course, no choice at all.

But that lack of choice does seem to simplify things: "Correctness" requires not good judgment but only a good memory. If we remember that *irregardless* is always Wrong, it ought not rise to even a subconscious level of choice. Some teachers and editors think we should memorize dozens of other such "rules":

- Don't begin a sentence with *and* or *but*.
- Don't use double negatives.
- Don't split INFINITIVES.

Unfortunately, it's more complicated than that. Some rules are real rules: we must obey them or be labeled at least unschooled. But a handful of other often repeated rules are less important than many think (some are based on a grammarian's whim). If you obsess over them, you will keep yourself from writing quickly and clearly. In fact, that's why I address "correctness" now, before clarity, because I want to put it where it belongs—behind us.

Rules of Grammar and Their Sources

Opinion is split on the social role of grammatical rules. To some, they are just another trick of the Ins to control the Outs by stigmatizing their language and thereby discourage their social and political aspirations. To others, the rules of Standard English have been refined by generations of educated speakers, rules that are now observed by all the best writers of English—or at least should be.

Correctness as Historical Accident

Both views are correct, but only partly. For centuries, those governing our affairs have used grammatical "errors" to screen out those unwilling or unable to acquire the habits of the schooled middle class. But they are wrong to claim that they were *devised* for that end. Standard forms of a language always originate in accidents of geography and economic power. When a language has different regional dialects, that of the most influential speakers usually becomes the most prestigious and the basis for that nation's "correct" form of writing.

Thus if some geographical accident had put Scotland closer to the European continent than is London, and its capital, Edinburgh, had been the center of Britain's economic, political, and literary life, we would write and speak less like Shakespeare and more like the Scottish poet Bobby Burns:

A ye wha are sae guid yourself	(All you who are so good yourselves
Sae pious and sae holy,	So pious and so holy,
Ye've nought to do but mark and tell	You've nothing to do but talk about
Your neebours' fauts and folly!	Your neighbors' faults and folly!)

Correctness as Unpredictability

Conservatives, on the other hand, are right that many rules of Standard English did originate in useful efficiencies of expression. For example, we no longer use the complex verb endings that English required a thousand years ago. We now omit present tense endings in all but one context (and we don't need it there):

	1ST PERSON	2ND PERSON	3RD PERSON
Singular	I know + Ø.	You know + Ø.	She know + **S.**
Plural	We know + Ø.	You know + Ø.	They know + Ø.

But critics on the right are wrong when they claim that what refined Standard English was the superior logic of educated speakers and writers, and so their language must be superior to that of their alleged social inferiors. True, many rules of Standard English do reflect an evolution toward logical efficiency. But if by logical we mean regular and therefore predictable, then Standard English is in some ways less "logical" than nonstandard English.

For example, the person who says *I **knowed*** makes the same "mistake" as the person who first said *I **climbed*** *the tree* instead of the originally "correct" *I **clum**.* Both speakers logically smooth out an irregularity, an act usually taken as a sign of intelligence.

We could cite a dozen more examples where the violation of a rule reflects a logical mind making English grammar more regular. But it is, of course, the very *ir*regularity of Standard English that makes its rules so useful to those who would use them to discriminate: to speak and write Standard English, we must either be born into it or invest a lot of time learning its idiosyncrasies (along with the values of its speakers).

> ***Here's the point:*** Those determined to discriminate will use any difference. But since our language seems to reflect our quality of mind more directly than do our ZIP codes, it's easy for those inclined to look down on others to think that grammatical "errors" indicate mental or moral deficiency. But we must reject the notion that observing the rules of Standard English testifies to someone's intellectual or moral superiority. That belief is not just factually wrong; in a diverse democracy like ours, it's destructive. Yet even if logic predicts *knowed*, so much greater is the power of social convention that we still avoid it if we want to be taken seriously when we write for serious purposes.

THREE KINDS OF RULES

These corrosive social attitudes about correctness have been encouraged by generations of grammarians who, in their zeal to codify "good" English, have confused three kinds of "rules":

1. Some rules—call them the "Real Rules"—define what makes English—ARTICLES precede nouns: *the book,* not *book the.*

Speakers born into English don't think about these rules at all and violate them only when they are distracted or tired.

2. A few other rules—call them "the rules of Standard English"—distinguish the standard dialect from nonstandard ones: *He doesn't have any money* versus *He don't have no money.* Schooled writers observe these rules as naturally as they observe the Real Rules and think about them only when they notice others violating them. The only writers who *self-consciously* follow them are those who were not born into Standard English and are striving to join the educated class.

3. Finally, some grammarians have invented a handful of rules that they think we all *should* observe—call them "Folklore." These are the rules that too many well-educated writers obsess over. Most date from the last half of the eighteenth century:

   > Don't split infinitives, as in *to **quietly** leave.*
   >
   > Don't end a sentence with a preposition.

   A few date from the twentieth century:

   > Don't use *hopefully* for *I hope,* as in ***Hopefully,** it won't rain.*
   >
   > Don't use *which* for *that,* as in *a car **which** I sold.*

For 250 years, grammarians have accused the best writers of violating these invented rules, and for 250 years those writers have ignored them. Which is lucky for the grammarians, because if writers did obey all their rules, the grammarians would have to keep inventing new ones, or find another line of work. The fact is, none of these invented rules reflects the consensus of unself-conscious usage of our best writers.

In this lesson, we focus on this third kind of rule, the handful of invented ones, because only they vex those who already write Standard English.

Observing Rules Thoughtfully

It is, however, no simple matter to deal with these rules if you want to be thought of as someone who writes both clearly and "correctly." You could choose the worst-case policy: follow all the rules all the time because sometime, someone will criticize you for something—for beginning a sentence with *and* or ending it with *up.* But if you mindlessly obey all the rules all the time, you surrender a measure of choice. Worse, you risk becoming so obsessed with rules that you tie yourself in knots. And sooner or later, you will impose those rules—real or not—on others. After all, what good is learning a rule if all you can do is obey it?

The alternative to blind obedience is selective observance. But then you have to decide which rules to ignore. And then if you do ignore some rule, you may have to deal with those whose passionate memory for "good" grammar seems to endow them with the ability to see in a split infinitive a symptom of moral corruption and social decay.

If you want to avoid being accused of "lacking standards," but refuse to submit to whatever "rule" someone can dredge up from ninth-grade English, you have to know more about these invented rules than the rule-mongers do. The rest of this lesson helps you do that.

TWO KINDS OF INVENTED RULES

We can sort most of these invented rules into two groups: Folklore and Elegant Options.

1. *Folklore.* When you violate "rules" like these, few careful readers notice, much less care. So they are not rules at all, but folklore you can ignore (unless you are writing for someone with the power to demand even the folklore).

2. *Elegant Options.* When you ignore these rules, few readers notice. But paradoxically, some do when you observe them, because when you do, they detect signals of special care. So you can observe these rules or not, depending on how you want your readers to respond.

1. Folklore

These rules include those that most careful readers and writers ignore. You may not have heard of some of these "rules," but even if you have not yet had one inflicted on you, chances are that one day you will. In these examples, the quotations "violating" these rules are from writers of intellectual and scholarly stature or who, on matters of usage, are reliable conservatives (some are both). A check mark indicates those sentences that are acceptable Standard English, despite what some grammarians claim.

1. **"Don't begin sentences with *and* or *but*."** This passage ignores the "rule" twice:

   ✓ **But,** it will be asked, is tact not an individual gift, therefore highly variable in its choices? **And** if that is so, what guidance can a manual offer, other than that of its author's prejudices—mere impressionism?

   —Wilson Follett, *Modern American Usage: A Guide,*
   edited and completed by Jacques Barzun et al.

   On this matter, it's useful to consult the guide used by conservative writers: the *second* edition of H. W. Fowler's *A Dictionary of Modern English Usage* (first edition, Oxford University Press, 1926; second edition, 1965; third edition, 1997, considered too permissive by archconservatives). The second edition was edited by Sir Ernest Gowers, who, to Fowler's original entry for *and* in the first edition, added this:

   That it is a solecism to begin a sentence with *and* is a faintly lingering superstition. (p. 29)

   To the original entry for *but,* he added "see *and.*" Some inexperienced writers do begin too many sentences with *and,* but that is an error not in grammar but of style.

   Some insecure writers also think they should not begin a sentence with *because.* Not this:

   ✓ **Because** we have access to so much historical fact, today we know a good deal about changes within the humanities which were not apparent to those of any age much before our own and which the individual scholar must constantly reflect on.

   —Walter Ong, S. J., "The Expanding Humanities and the Individual
   Scholar," *Publication of the Modern Language Association*

   This folklore about *because* appears in no handbook, but it's gaining currency. It probably stems from advice aimed at avoiding sentence FRAGMENTS like this one:

   The plan was rejected. **Because** it was incomplete.

2. **"Use the RELATIVE PRONOUN *that*—not *which*—for RESTRICTIVE clauses."** Allegedly, not this:

   ✓ Next is a typical situation **which** a practiced writer corrects "for style" virtually by reflex action.

   —Jacques Barzun, *Simple and Direct* (p. 69)

Yet just a few sentences earlier, Barzun himself (one of our most eminent intellectual historians and critics of style) had asserted,

> Us[e] *that* with defining [i.e. restrictive] clauses except when stylistic reasons interpose.

(In the sentence in question, no such reasons interposed.)

A rule can have no force when someone as eminent as Barzun asserts it on one page and unself-consciously violates it on the next, and his "error" is never caught, not by his editors, not by his proofreaders, not even by Barzun himself.

This "rule" is relatively new. It first appeared in 1906 in Henry and Francis Fowler's *The King's English* (Oxford University Press; reprinted as an Oxford University Press paperback, 1973). The Fowlers thought that the random variation between *that* and *which* to begin a restrictive clause was messy, so they just asserted that writers should (with some exceptions) limit *which* to nonrestrictive clauses.

A nonrestrictive clause, you may recall, describes a noun that you can identify unambiguously without the information in that clause. For example,

✓ ABCO Inc. ended its bankruptcy, **which** it had filed in 1997.

A company can have only one bankruptcy at a time, so we can unambiguously identify the bankruptcy mentioned without the information in the clause. We therefore call that clause *nonrestrictive*, because it cannot "restrict" or narrow the meaning of the noun phrase *its bankruptcy* any more than it already is. We put a comma before the modifying clause and begin it with *which*. That rule is based on historical and contemporary usage.

But the Fowlers claimed that for *restrictive* clauses, we should use not *which* but only *that*: For example,

✓ ABCO Inc. sold a product **that** [*not* **which**] made millions.

Since ABCO presumably makes many products, the clause "restricts" the product to only the one that made millions, and so, said the Fowlers, it should begin with *that*.

Francis died in 1918, but Henry continued the family tradition with *A Dictionary of Modern English Usage*. In that landmark work, he discussed the finer points of *which* and *that*, then added this:

Some there are who follow this principle now; but it would be idle to pretend that it is the practice either of most or of the best writers. (p. 635)

That wistful observation was kept in the second edition and again in the third. (For another *which*, see the passage by Walter Ong on p. 17.)

Having said that, I confess I follow Fowler's advice, not because a restrictive *which* is an error, but because *that* is softer. I do choose a *which* when it's within a word or two of a *that*, because I don't like the sound of two *that*s close together:

✓ We all have **that** one rule **that** we will not give up.

✓ We all have **that** one rule **which** we will not give up.

3. **"Use *fewer* with nouns you count, *less* with nouns you can't."** Allegedly not this:

✓ I can remember no **less** than five occasions when the correspondence columns of *The Times* rocked with volleys of letters . . .

—Noel Gilroy Annan, Lord Annan, "The Life of the Mind
in British Universities Today," *American Council
of Learned Societies Newsletter*

No one uses *fewer* with mass nouns (*fewer sand*) but educated writers often use *less* with countable plural nouns (*less resources*).

4. **"Use *since* and *while* to refer only to time, not to mean *because* or *although*."** Most careful writers use *since* with a meaning close to *because* but with an added sense of "What follows I assume you already know":

✓ **Since** asbestos causes lung disease, avoid it.

Nor do most careful writers restrict *while* to its temporal sense (*We'll wait while you eat*), but also use it with a meaning close to "I assume you know what I state in this clause, but what I assert in the next will qualify it":

✓ **While** we agree on a date, we disagree about the place.

On the other hand, you might observe the advice to avoid *as* to signal causation, because it does so weakly:

As the expenses are minor, we need not discuss them.

Use *since*.

Here's the point: If writers we judge competent regularly violate some alleged rule, then the rule can have no force. In those cases, it's not writers who should change their usage but grammarians who should change their rules.

2. Elegant Options

These next "rules" complement the Real Rules: call them *Elegant Options*. Most readers do not notice when you observe a Real Rule, but do when violates you it (like that). On the other hand, few readers notice when you violate one of these optional rules, but some do when you observe it, because doing so adds a note of formality.

1. **"Don't split infinitives."** Purists condemn Dwight MacDonald, a linguistic archconservative, for this sentence (my emphasis in all the examples that follow).

   ✓ One wonders why Dr. Gove and his editors did not think of labeling *knowed* as substandard right where it occurs, and one suspects that they wanted **to slightly conceal** the fact . . .

   —"The String Untuned," *The New Yorker*

   They would require

   . . . they wanted **to conceal slightly** the fact . . .

   Infinitives are now split so commonly that when you avoid splitting one, careful readers may think you are trying to be especially correct, whether you are or not.

2. **"Use *whom* as the OBJECT of a verb or preposition."** Purists would condemn William Zinsser for this use of *who:*

   ✓ Soon after you confront this matter of preserving your identity, another question will occur to you: "**Who** am I writing for?"

   —*On Writing Well*

   They would insist on

   . . . another question will occur to you: "For **whom** am I writing?"

   Most readers take *whom* as a sign of self-conscious correctness, so when a writer uses it incorrectly, that choice is probably a sign of insecurity, as in this sentence:

The committee must decide **whom** should be promoted.

In that sentence, *whom* is the subject of the verb *should be promoted*, so it should be *who*. Here is an actual rule: Use *who* when it's the subject of a verb *in its own clause*; use *whom* only when it's an object in its own clause.

3. **"Don't end a sentence with a preposition."** Purists would condemn Sir Ernest Gowers, editor of Fowler's second edition, for this:

> ✓ The peculiarities of legal English are often used as a stick to beat the official **with.**

> —*The Complete Plain Words*

and insist on this:

> . . . a stick **with which** to beat the official.

The first is correct; the second more formal. (Again, see the Ong passage on p. 17.) And when you choose to shift both the preposition and its *whom* to the left, that sentence seems even more formal. Compare:

> ✓ The man I met with was the man I had written **to.**
> ✓ The man **with whom** I met was the man **to whom** I had written.

A final preposition can, however, end a sentence weakly (see pp. 158–159). George Orwell may have chosen to end this next sentence with *from* to make a sly point about English grammar, but I suspect it just landed there (and note the "incorrect" *which* six words from the end):

> [The defense of the English language] has nothing to do with . . . the setting up of a "standard English" **which** must never be departed **from.**

> —George Orwell, "Politics and the English Language"

This would have been less awkward and more emphatic:

> We do not defend English just to create a "standard English" whose rules we must always obey.

4. **"Use the singular with *none* and *any*."** *None* and *any* were originally singular, but today most writers use them as plurals. Therefore, if you use them as singular, some readers will notice. The second is a bit more formal than the first:

✓ **None** of the reasons **are** sufficient to end the project.

✓ **None** of the reasons **is** sufficient to end the project.

When you are under the closest scrutiny, you might choose to observe these optional rules. Ordinarily, though, they are ignored by most careful writers, which is to say they are not rules at all, but rather stylistic choices to signal a bit of formality. If you adopt the worst-case approach and observe them all, all the time—well, private virtues are their own reward.

Hobgoblins

For some reason, a handful of items has become the object of particularly zealous abuse. There's no explaining why; none of them interferes with clarity or concision.

1. **"Never use *like* for *as* or *as if*."** Not this:

   These operations failed **like** the earlier ones did.

   But this:

   These operations failed **as** the earlier ones did.

   Like became a SUBORDINATING CONJUNCTION in the eighteenth century when writers began to drop *as* from the phrase *like as*, leaving *like* as the conjunction. This process is called *elision* and is a common linguistic change. It is telling that the editor of the second edition of Fowler (the one favored by conservatives) deleted *like* for *as* from Fowler's list of "Illiteracies" and moved it into the category of "Sturdy Indefensibles."

2. **"Don't use *hopefully* to mean 'I hope.'"** Not this:

   ✓ Hopefully, it will not rain.

   But this:

   ✓ It is hoped that it will not rain.

   This "rule" dates from the twentieth century; it has no basis in logic or grammar. It parallels the usage of other words that no one abuses, words such as *candidly, frankly, sadly,* and *happily:*

   ✓ Candidly, we may fail. (That is, *I am candid when I say we may fail.*)

   ✓ Seriously, we must go. (That is, *I am serious when I say we must go.*)

3. **"Don't use *finalize* to mean 'finish' or 'complete.'"** But *finalize* doesn't mean just "finish." It means "to clean up the last few details," a sense captured by no other word. Moreover, if we think *finalize* is bad because *-ize* is ugly, we would have to reject *nationalize, synthesize,* and *rationalize,* along with hundreds of other useful words.

4. **"Don't use *impact* as a verb, as in *The survey impacted our strategy*. Use it only as a noun, as in *The survey had an impact on our strategy*."** *Impact* has been used as a verb since the seventeenth century, but on some people, historical evidence has none.

5. **"Don't modify absolute words such as *perfect, unique, final,* or *complete* with *very, more, quite,* and so on."** That rule would have ruled out this familiar sentence:

   ✓ We the People of the United States, in order to form a **more perfect** union . . .

   (Even so, this is a rule worth following most of the time.)

6. **"Never ever use *irregardless* for *regardless* or *irrespective*."** However arbitrary this rule is, it's one you should follow.

Some Words That Attract Special Attention

A few words are so often confused with others that careful readers are likely to note your care when you correctly distinguish them—*flaunt* and *flout* for example. When you use them correctly, those who think the difference matters are likely to note that at least *you* know that *flaunt* means "to display conspicuously" and that *flout* means "to scorn a rule or standard." Thus if you chose to scorn the rule about *flaunt* and *flout,* you would not flout your flaunting it, but flaunt your flouting it. Here are some others:

   aggravate means "to make worse." It does not mean to **annoy.** You can aggravate an injury but not a person.

   anticipate means "to prepare for a contingency." It does not mean just **expect.** You anticipate a question when you prepare its answer before it's asked; if you know it's coming but don't prepare, you only expect it.

   anxious means "uneasy" not **eager.** You're eager to leave if you're happy to. You're anxious about leaving if it makes you nervous.

blackmail means "to extort by threatening to reveal damaging information." It does not mean simply **coerce.** One country cannot blackmail another with nuclear weapons when it only threatens to use them.

cohort means "a group who attends on someone." It does not mean a single accompanying person. If Prince Charles marries his friend she will become his **consort;** his hangers-on will still be his *cohort.*

comprise means "to include all parts in a single unit." It does not mean **constitute.** The alphabet is not comprised by its letters; it comprises them. Letters constitute the alphabet; it is constituted by them.

continuous means "without interruption." It is not synonymous with **continual,** which means an activity through time, with interruptions. If you continuously interrupt someone, that person will never say a word because your interruption will never stop. If you continually interrupt, you let the other person finish a sentence from time to time.

disinterested means "neutral." It does not mean **uninterested.** A judge should be disinterested in the outcome of a case, but not uninterested in it. (Incidentally, the original meaning of *disinterested* was "to be uninterested.")

enormity means "hugely bad." It does not mean **enormous.** In private, a belch might be enormous, but at a state funeral, it would also be an enormity.

fortuitous means "by chance." It does not mean **fortunate.** You are fortunate when you fortuitously pick the right number in the lottery.

fulsome means "sickeningly excessive." It does not mean just "much." All of us enjoy full praise, except when it becomes fulsome.

notorious means "well known for bad behavior." It does not mean **famous.** Frank Sinatra was a famous singer but a notorious bully.

These days only a few readers care about these distinctions, but they may be just those whose judgment carries special weight when it matters most. It takes only a few minutes to learn to use these words in ways that testify to your precision, so it may be worth doing so, especially if you also think their distinctions are worth preserving.

On the other hand, you get no points for correctly distinguishing *imply* and *infer, principal* and *principle, accept* and *except, capi-*

tal and *capitol, affect* and *effect, proceed* and *precede, discrete* and *discreet.* That's just expected of schooled writers. Most careful readers also notice when a Latinate or Greek plural noun is used as a singular, so you might want to keep these straight, too:

Singular	datum	criterion	medium	stratum	phenomenon
Plural	data	criteria	media	strata	phenomena

A Problem: Pronouns and Gender Bias

Pronouns and Their Referents

We expect literate writers to make verbs agree with subjects:

✓ Our **reasons** ARE based on solid evidence.

We also expect their pronouns to agree with antecedents. Not this:

Early **efforts** to oppose the hydrogen bomb failed because **it** ignored political issues. **No one** wanted to expose **themselves** to anti-Communist hysteria.

But this:

✓ Early **efforts** to oppose the hydrogen bomb failed because **they** ignored political issues. **No one** wanted to expose **himself** to anti-Communist hysteria.

There are, however, two problems.

First, do we use a singular or plural pronoun when referring to a noun that is singular in grammar but plural in meaning? For example, when we refer to a *group, committee, staff, administration,* and so on, do we use *it* or *they?* And do we use a singular or plural verb? Some writers use a singular verb and pronoun when the group acts as a single entity:

✓ The **committee has** met but has not yet made **its** decision.

But they use a plural verb and pronoun when its members act individually:

✓ The **faculty have** the memo, but not all of **them** have read it.

These days plurals are irregularly used in both senses (but the plural is the rule in British English).

Second, what pronoun do we use to refer to *someone, everyone, no one* and to singular nouns that signal no gender: *teacher, doctor, student?* We casually use *they:*

> **Everyone** knows **they** must answer for **their** actions.
>
> When **a person** is on drugs, it is hard to help **them**.

More formal usage requires a singular pronoun:

> ✓ **Everyone** realizes that **he** must answer for **his actions.**

But the formal rule raises the problem of biased language.

Gender and Biased Language

Common sense demands that we not gratuitously offend readers, but if we reject *he* as a generic pronoun because it's biased and *they* because some readers consider it ungrammatical, we are left with a lot of bad choices. Some writers choose a clumsy *he or she;* others choose a worse *he/she* or even *s/he.*

> If **a writer** ignores the ethnicity of **his or her** readers, **s/he** may respond in ways **the writer** would not expect to words that to **him or her** are innocent of bias.

Some writers substitute plurals for singulars:

> ✓ When **writers** ignore **their** readers' ethnicity, **they** may respond in ways **they** might not expect to words that are to **them** innocent of bias.

But in that sentence, *they, their,* and *them* are confusing, because they can refer to two different referents, and to the careful ear, a sentence with singular nouns and pronouns seems a shade more precise than one with plural nouns and pronouns. Compare the sentence above with this one:

> If **a writer** ignores the ethnicity of **his** reader, his reader might respond to a word in a way that the writer would not expect.

We can try a first person *we,*

> ✓ If **we** ignore the ethnicity of **our** readers, they may respond in ways **we** would not expect to words that to **us** are innocent of bias.

But *we* can also be ambiguous. We could also try impersonal abstraction, but that creates its own problem:

> Failure to consider ethnicity may lead to an unexpected response to words considered innocent of bias.

Finally, we can alternately use *he* and *she,* as I have. But that's not a perfect solution, because some readers find a *she* as intrusive as *he/she*. A reviewer in the *New York Times*, for example, wondered what to make of an author whom the reviewer charged with attempting to

> right history's wrongs to women by referring to random examples as "she," as in "Ask a particle physicist what happens when a quark is knocked out of a proton, and she will tell you . . . ," which strikes this reader as oddly patronizing to women.

(We might wonder how it strikes women particle physicists.)

For years to come, we will have a problem with singular generic pronouns, and to some readers, any solution will be awkward. I suspect that eventually we will accept the plural *they* as a correct singular:

✓ **No one** should turn in **their** writing unedited.

Some claim that in such compromises we cave in to lazy imprecision. Whatever the future holds, we have a choice now, and that's not entirely a bad thing, because our choices define who we are.

SUMMING UP

We must write correctly, but if in defining correctness we ignore the difference between fact and folklore, we risk overlooking what is important—the choices that make our writing wordy and dense or clear and concise. We are not being precise when we merely get right the *which*es and *that*s and eradicate *finalize* and *hopefully*. Many who obsess on such details are oblivious to this more serious kind of imprecision:

> Too precise a specification of information processing requirements incurs the risk of overestimation resulting in unused capacity or inefficient use of costly resources or of underestimation leading to ineffectiveness or other inefficiencies.

That means,

✓ When you specify too precisely the resources you need to process information, you may overestimate. If you do, you risk having more capacity than you need or using costly resources inefficiently.

Both are grammatically precise, but who would choose to read more of the first?

I suspect that those who observe all the rules all the time do so not because they want to protect the integrity of the language or the quality of our culture, but because they want to assert a style of their own. Some of us are straightforward and plain speaking; others take pleasure in a bit of elegance, in a touch of fastidiously self-conscious "class." It is an impulse we should not scorn, so long as it's not a pretext for discrimination, and includes a concern for the more important matters to which we now turn—the choices that define not "good grammar," but clarity and grace.

PART TWO

Clarity

Everything that can be thought at all
can be thought clearly.
Everything that can be said can be said clearly.
—LUDWIG WITTGENSTEIN

Whatever is translatable in other
and simpler words of the same language,
without loss of sense or dignity, is bad.
—SAMUEL TAYLOR COLERIDGE

It takes less time to learn to write nobly than to
learn to write lightly and straightforwardly.
—FRIEDRICH NIETZSCHE

use when revising

Actions

Suit the action to the word, the word to the action.
—WILLIAM SHAKESPEARE, *HAMLET*, 3.2

I am unlikely to trust a sentence that comes easily.
—WILLIAM GASS

Understanding the Principles of Clarity

Making Judgments

We have words enough to praise writing we like: *clear, direct, concise,* and more than enough to abuse writing we don't: *unclear, indirect, abstract, dense, complex.* We could use those words to distinguish these two sentences:

> 1a. The cause of our schools' failure at teaching basic skills is not understanding the influence of cultural background on learning.
>
> 1b. Our schools have failed to teach basic skills because they do not understand how cultural backgrounds influence the way children learn.

Most of us would call (1a) a bit complex, (1b) clearer and more direct. But those words don't refer to anything *in* either sentence; they describe how those sentences make us *feel.* When we say that (1a) is *unclear,* we mean that *we* had a hard time understanding it; when we say it is *dense,* we mean that *we* struggled through it.

The real problem is to understand what it is about those two sentences that makes us feel as we do. Only then can you predict when your readers will think your sentences are dense and unclear so that you can revise them. To do that, you have to understand what counts as a well-told story.

Telling Stories about Characters and Their Actions

It is easy to state the general principle of clarity: match the important actions in your sentences to VERBS, and make the characters in your story their SUBJECTS. (To get the most out of this lesson and the next, you should be able to identify verbs, SIMPLE SUBJECTS, and WHOLE SUBJECTS. See the Glossary.)

Here's a story with a problem:

> 2a. Once upon a time, as a walk through the woods was taking place on the part of Little Red Riding Hood, the Wolf's jump out from behind a tree occurred, causing her fright.

We prefer something closer to this:

> ✓2b. Once upon a time, Little Red Riding Hood was walking through the woods, when the Wolf jumped out from behind a tree and frightened her.

Most readers think (2b) tells its story more clearly than (2a), because it follows those two principles I stated: its main characters are subjects, and its verbs express specific actions. Those two principles seem simple enough, but they need some explanation.

Principle of Clarity 1: Make Main Characters Subjects   Look at the subjects in (2a). The simple subjects (boldfaced) and main characters (italicized) are different words:

> 2a. Once upon a time, as a **walk** through the woods was taking place on the part of *Little Red Riding Hood, the Wolf's* **jump** out from behind a tree occurred, causing *her* fright.

Subjects are not characters; they are actions expressed as abstract NOUNS, *walk* and *jump:*

SUBJECT	VERB
a **walk** through the woods	was taking place
the *Wolf's* **jump** out from behind a tree	occurred

The whole subject of *occurred* has a character *in* it: *the **Wolf's** jump,* but *the Wolf* is only attached to the simple subject *jump;* it is not *the* subject.

   Contrast those abstract subjects with the short, specific subjects (boldfaced) in (2b).

> 2b. Once upon a time, ***Little Red Riding Hood*** was walking through the woods, when ***the Wolf*** jumped out from behind a tree and frightened her.

The subjects and the main characters are now the same words:

SUBJECT/CHARACTER	VERB
Little Red Riding Hood	was walking
the Wolf	jumped

Principle of Clarity 2: Make Important Actions Verbs   Now look at how the actions and verbs differ. In (2a), the actions are not verbs but abstract nouns (actions are boldfaced; verbs are capitalized):

2a. Once upon a time, as a **walk** through the woods WAS TAKING place on the part of Little Red Riding Hood, the Wolf's **jump** out from behind a tree OCCURRED, causing her **fright**.

And note the vague verbs: *was taking, occurred.*

In (2b), the clearer sentence, the verbs are specific because the actions and verbs are the same words:

✓2b. Once upon a time, Little Red Riding Hood WAS WALKING through the woods, when the Wolf JUMPED out from behind a tree and FRIGHTENED her.

Here's the point: In the sentence that seems wordy and indirect, its two main characters, Little Red Riding Hood and the Wolf, are *not* subjects, and their actions—*walk, jump,* and *fright*—are *not* verbs. In the more direct version, (2b), those two main characters *are* subjects and their main actions *are* verbs. In short, in (2a), the story and the grammar of the sentence don't match; in (2b), they do. That's why we prefer (2b).

Fairy Tales and Academic Writing

Fairy tales may seem a long way from writing in college or on the job, but even there, sentences tell stories. Compare these two:

3a. The Federalists' argument in regard to the destabilization of government by popular democracy was based on their belief in the tendency of factions to further their self-interest at the expense of the common good.

✓3b. The Federalists argued that popular democracy destabilized government, because they believed that factions tended to further their self-interest at the expense of the common good.

We can analyze those two sentences as we did the ones about Little Red Riding Hood.

Sentence (3a) feels dense for two reasons. First, its characters and subjects are different words. The simple subject is *argument,* but the main characters are *Federalists, popular democracy,* and *factions* (the characters are italicized; the simple subject is boldfaced):

3a. *The Federalists'* **argument** in regard to the destabilization of *government* by *popular democracy* was based on *their* belief in the tendency of *factions* to further *their* self-interest at the expense of the common good.

Second, most of the actions (boldfaced) are not verbs (capitalized), but rather abstract nouns (also boldfaced):

3a. The Federalists' **argument** in regard to the **destabilization** of government by popular democracy WAS BASED on their **belief** in the **tendency** of factions to FURTHER their self-interest at the expense of the common good.

Notice in particular how long the whole subject of (3a) is and how little meaning is expressed by its main verb *was based:*

WHOLE SUBJECT	VERB
The Federalists' argument in regard to the destabilization of government by popular democracy	was based

Readers think (3b) is clearer, first because its characters (italicized) *are* subjects (boldfaced):

3b. The ***Federalists*** argued that ***popular democracy*** destabilized government, because ***they*** believed that ***factions*** tended to further *their* self-interest at the expense of the common good.

And second, all the actions (boldfaced) are verbs (capitalized):

3b. The Federalists ARGUED that popular democracy DESTABILIZED government, because they BELIEVED that factions TENDED to FURTHER their self-interest at the expense of the common good.

Note that all those subjects are short and specific and that the verbs express specific actions:

WHOLE SUBJECT/CHARACTER	VERB/ACTION
the Federalists	argued
popular democracy	destabilized
they	believed
factions	tended to further

In the rest of this lesson, we look at actions and verbs; in the next, at characters and subjects.

Verbs and Actions

Our principle is this: *A sentence seems clear when its important actions are in verbs.* Look at how sentences (4a) and (4b) express their actions. In (4a), actions (boldfaced) are not verbs (capitalized); they are nouns:

> 4a. Our **lack** of data PREVENTED **evaluation** of UN **actions** in **targeting** funds to areas most in **need** of **assistance.**

In (4b), on the other hand, the actions are almost all verbs:

> ✓4b. Because we LACKED data, we could not EVALUATE whether the UN had TARGETED funds to areas that most NEEDED **assistance.**

Your readers will think your writing is dense if you use lots of abstract nouns, especially ones derived from verbs and ADJECTIVES, nouns ending in -*tion, -ment, -ence,* and so on, *especially when those nouns are subjects of verbs.*

Such nouns have a technical name: *nominalization.* The word illustrates its own meaning: When we nominalize *nominalize,* we create the nominalization *nominalization.* Here are a few examples:

VERB → NOMINALIZATION		ADJECTIVE → NOMINALIZATION	
discover	→ discovery	careless	→ carelessness
resist	→ resistance	different	→ difference
react	→ reaction	proficient	→ proficiency

We can also nominalize a verb by adding -*ing* (making it a GERUND):

> She flies → her flying   We sang → our singing

Some nominalizations and verbs are identical:

> hope → hope   result → result   repair → repair

> We REQUEST that you REVIEW the data.

> Our **request** IS that you DO a **review** of the data.

(Some actions can also hide in adjectives: *It is applicable → it applies* Some others: *indicative, dubious, argumentative, deserving.*)

No feature of style more characterizes abstract, indirect, difficult academic and professional writing than lots of nominalizations, especially when they are subjects of verbs.

Here's the point: In grade school, we learned that subjects *are* characters (or "doers") and that verbs *are* actions. That's true in a sentence like this:

> subject   verb   object
> We   discussed the problem.
> doer   action

But it's not true for this almost synonymous sentence:

> subject   verb
> The problem   was   the topic   of our discussion.
>   doer   action

We can move characters and actions almost wherever we want in a sentence, and subjects and verbs don't have to be any particular thing at all. But readers prefer that most subjects be characters and most verbs be actions. When you match them up in most of your sentences, your readers are likely to think your prose is clear and direct.

Exercise 3.1

Analyze the subject/character and verb/action patterns:

> There is opposition among many voters to nuclear power plants based on a belief of their threat to human health.

> Many voters oppose nuclear power plants because they believe that such plants threaten human health.

Exercise 3.2

If you are uncertain that you can distinguish verbs, adjectives, and nominalizations, turn the verbs and adjectives below into nominalizations and nominalizations back into adjectives and verbs. Remember that some verbs and nominalizations have the same form:

> Poverty predictably CAUSES social problems.
> Poverty IS a predictable **cause** of social problems.

analysis	believe	attempt	conclusion	evaluate
analysis	believe	attempt	conclusion	evaluate
suggest	approach	comparison	define	discuss
expression	failure	intelligent	thorough	appearance
decrease	improve	increase	accuracy	careful
emphasize	explanation	description	clear	examine

Exercise 3.3

Create sentences using verbs and adjectives from Exercise 3.2. Then rewrite them using the corresponding nominalizations (keep the meaning the same). For example, using *suggest, discuss,* and *careful,* write:

> I **SUGGEST** that we **DISCUSS** the issue in a **CAREFUL** manner.

Then rewrite that sentence into its nominalized form:

> My **suggestion** is that our **discussion** of the issue be done with **care**.

Only when you see how a clear sentence can be made unclear will you understand why it seemed clear in the first place.

DIAGNOSIS AND REVISION

You can use the principles to explain why your readers will judge your prose as they do. But more important, you can also use them to identify sentences that your readers would want you to revise, and then to revise them. Revising is a three-step process: diagnose, analyze, revise.

1. **Diagnose.** To predict how a reader will judge your style, do this:

   a. Ignoring short (four- or five-word) introductory phrases, underline the first seven or eight words in each sentence.

   b. Look for two things:
      • You have underlined abstract nouns as simple subjects.
      • You read at least six or seven words before you get to a verb.

2. **Analyze.** If you find such sentences, do this:
   a. Decide who your main characters are, particularly flesh-and-blood characters (more about this in the next lesson).
   b. Look for the actions that those characters perform, especially in nominalizations, those abstract nouns derived from verbs.
3. **Revise.**
   a. If the actions are in nominalizations, change them into verbs.
   b. Make the characters the subjects of those verbs.
   c. Rewrite the sentence with conjunctions like *because, if, when, although, why, how, whether,* or *that.*

For example, let's diagnose and revise this sentence:

> The outsourcing of high-tech work to Asia by corporations means the loss of jobs for many American workers.

Diagnose: Underline the first seven or eight words:

> <u>The outsourcing of high-tech work to Asia</u> by corporations means the loss of jobs for many American workers.

We do not see a character *as* a subject or a verb expressing an important action.

Analyze: Who are the characters and what are their actions?

Characters: *American workers, corporations*
Actions: *outsourcing, loss*

Revise: Turn the actions into verbs and make the characters their subjects:

> *Many middle-class American workers* **are losing** their jobs, because *corporations are outsourcing* their high-tech work to Asia.

Some Common Patterns

You can quickly spot and revise three common patterns of nominalizations.

1. **The nominalization is the subject of an empty verb:**

   > The **intention** of the committee IS to audit the records.

a. Change the nominalization to a verb:

intention → intend

b. Identify the character that would be the subject of that verb:

The intention of **the committee** is to audit the records.

c. Make that character the subject of the verb:

The committee **INTENDS** to audit the records.

2. **A nominalization follows *there is* or *there are*:**

There IS no **need** for *our* further **study** of this problem.

a. Change the nominalization to a verb:

need → need   study → study

b. Identify the character that should be the subject of the verb:

There is no need for **our** further study of this problem.

c. Make that character the subject of the verb:

no need → we need   our study → we study

We **NEED** not **STUDY** this problem further.

3. **One nominalization is a subject and a second appears after an empty verb like *be, seems, has,* etc.:**

Our **loss** in sales WAS a result of their **expansion** of outlets.

a. Revise the nominalizations into verbs:

loss → lose   expansion → expand

b. Identify the characters that would be the subjects of those verbs:

Our loss in sales was a result of **their** expansion of outlets.

c. Make those characters subjects of those verbs:

we lose   they expand

d. Link the new clauses with a logical connection:

- To express simple cause: *because, since, when*
- To express conditional cause: *if, provided that, so long as*

- To contradict expected causes: *though, although, unless*

Our **loss** in sales	→	*We* **LOST** sales
was the result of	→	**because**
their **expansion** of outlets	→	*they* **EXPANDED** outlets

Two other patterns invite you to look for nominalizations after verbs. In these cases, the subject is often a character.

4. **A nominalization follows an empty verb:**

The *agency* CONDUCTED an **investigation** into the matter.

a. Change the nominalization to a verb:

investigation → investigate

b. Replace the empty verb with the new verb:

conducted → investigated

✓ The *agency* **INVESTIGATED** the matter.

5. **Two or three nominalizations in a row are joined by prepositions:**

We did a **review** of the **evolution** of the brain.

a. Turn the first nominalization into a verb:

review → review

b. Either leave the second nominalization as it is or turn it into a verb in a CLAUSE beginning with *how* or *why:*

evolution of the brain → how the brain evolved

First, *we* **REVIEWED** the **evolution** of the *brain.*

✓ First, *we* **REVIEWED** how *the brain* **EVOLVED.**

Some Happy Consequences

When you consistently rely on verbs to express key actions, your readers benefit in many ways:

1. Your sentences are likely to be more concrete, because they will have concrete subjects and verbs. Compare:

There WAS an affirmative **decision** for **expansion.**

✓ *The Director* **DECIDED** to **EXPAND** the program.

2. Your sentences are more concise. When you use nominalizations, you have to use articles like *a* and *the* and prepositional phrases such as *of, by,* and *in.* You don't need them when you use verbs and conjunctions (italicized):

> A **revision** *of* the program WILL RESULT *in* **increases** *in* our **efficiency** *in the* **servicing** *of* clients.

> ✓ *If* we REVISE the program, we CAN SERVE clients more EFFICIENTLY.

3. The logic of your sentences is clearer. When you nominalize verbs, you link actions with fuzzy prepositions and phrases such as *of, by,* and *on the part of.* But when you use verbs, you can link clauses with precise SUBORDINATING CONJUNCTIONS such as *because, although,* and *if:*

> Our more effective presentation of our study resulted in our success, despite an earlier start by others.

> ✓ **Although** others started earlier, we succeeded **because** we presented our study more effectively.

4. Your sentences tell a more coherent story. This next sequence of actions distorts their chronology. (The numbers refer to the real sequence of events.)

> Decisions[4] in regard to administration[5] of medication despite inability[2] of an irrational patient appearing[1] in a Trauma Center to provide legal consent[3] rest with the attending physician alone.

When we revise those actions into verbs and reorder them, we get a more coherent narrative:

> ✓ When a patient appears[1] in a Trauma Center and behaves[2] so irrationally that he cannot legally consent[3] to treatment, only the attending physician can decide[4] whether to medicate[5] him.

A Common Problem Solved

Most of us can identify unclear writing when we read it, unless it's our own. You've probably had this experience: you write something you think is great, but your reader thinks otherwise. You wonder whether that person is just being difficult, but you bite your tongue and try to fix what should be clear to anyone who can read Dr. Seuss. When that happens to me (regularly, I might add), I almost always realize—eventually—that my readers are right, that they see where my writing needs work better than I can.

How can we be right about the writing of others, and so wrong about our own? It is because we all read into our own writing what we want readers to get out of it. That explains why two readers can disagree about the clarity of the same passage: a reader who knows its content better is likely to think the passage is more clearly written than is a reader who knows less about it. Both are right.

That's why we need a way to look at our own writing in a way that is almost mechanical, that sidesteps our too-good understanding of it. The quickest way is to underline the first seven or eight words of every sentence. If you don't see in those words a character as a subject and a verb as a specific action, you have a candidate for revision.

A final tip about diagnosis and revision: Look first at passages where you struggled to express yourself. We all tend to write badly when we're unsure about what we want to say.

Exercise 3.4

One sentence in each of these pairs is clear, expressing characters as subjects and actions as verbs; the other is indirect, with actions in nominalizations and characters often not in subjects. First, identify which is which. Then circle nominalizations and highlight verbs. If you are good at grammar, underline subjects. Then put a "c" over characters that seem to perform actions.

1a. Some people argue that atmospheric carbon dioxide does not elevate global temperature.

1b. There has been speculation by educators about the role of the family in the improvement of educational achievement.

2a. Smoking during pregnancy may cause fetal injury.

2b. When we write concisely, readers understand easily.

3a. Researchers have identified the AIDS virus but failed to develop a vaccine to immunize those at risk.

3b. Attempts by economists at defining full employment have been met with failure.

4a. Complaints by editorial writers about voter apathy rarely offer suggestions about dispelling it.

4b. Although critics claim that children who watch a lot of television tend to become less able readers, no one has demonstrated that to be true.

5a. The loss of market share to Japan by domestic automakers resulted in the disappearance of hundreds of thousands of jobs.

5b. When educators discover how to use computer-assisted instruction, our schools will teach complex subjects more effectively.

6a. We need to know which parts of our national forests are being logged most extensively so that we can save virgin stands at greatest risk.

6b. There is a need for an analysis of library use to provide a reliable base for the projection of needed resources.

7a. Many professional athletes fail to realize that they are unprepared for life after stardom because their teams protect them from the problems that the rest of us adjust to every day.

7b. Colleges have come to an understanding that yearly tuition increases are no longer possible because of strong resistance from parents to the soaring cost of higher education.

Exercise 3.5

Now revise the nominalized sentences in Exercise 3.4 into sentences with verbs. Use its paired verbal version as a model. For example, if the verbal sentence begins with *when*, begin your revision with *when:*

Sentence to revise: 2a. **Smoking** during pregnancy may lead to fetal **injury.**

Model: 2b. When we WRITE concisely, readers UNDERSTAND more easily.

Your revision: 2a. When pregnant women SMOKE . . .

Exercise 3.6

Revise these next sentences so that the nominalizations are verbs and characters are their subjects. In (1) through (5), characters are italicized and nominalizations are boldfaced.

1. *Lincoln's* **hope** was for the **preservation** of the Union without war, but the *South's* **attack** on Fort Sumter made war an **inevitability.**

2. **Attempts** were made on the part of the *president's aides* to assert *his* **immunity** from a *congressional* subpoena.

3. There were **predictions** by *business executives* that the *economy* would experience a quick **revival.**

4. *Your* **analysis** of my report omits any data in **support** of *your* **criticism** of my **findings.**

5. The *health care industry's* **inability** to exert cost **controls** could lead to the *public's* **decision** that *congressional* **action** is needed.

In sentences 6 through 10, the agents are italicized; find the actions and revise.

6. A *papal* appeal was made to the rich *nations of the world* for assistance to those facing the threat of *African* starvation.

7. Attempts at explanations for increases in *voter* participation in this year's elections were offered by *several candidates.*

8. The agreement by the *class* on the reading list was based on the assumption that there would be tests on only certain selections.

9. There was no independent *business-sector* study of the cause of the sudden increase in the trade surplus.

10. An understanding as to the need for controls over drinking on campus was recognized by *fraternities.*

In 11 through 15, only the nominalizations are boldfaced; find or invent the characters and revise.

11. There is **uncertainty** at the CIA about North Korean **intentions** as to **cessation** of missile **testing.**

12. Physical **conditioning** of the team is the **responsibility** of the coaching staff.

13. **Contradictions** among the data require an **explanation.**

14. The Dean's **rejection** of our proposal was a **disappointment** but not a **surprise** because our **expectation** was that a **decision** had been made.

15. Their **performance** of the play was marked by **enthusiasm** but lacked intelligent **staging.**

Exercise 3.7

Revise these sentences. At the end of each is a hint. For example:

> Congress's **reduction** of the deficit resulted in the **decline** of interest rates. [because]
>
> ✓ Interest rates DECLINED because Congress REDUCED the deficit.

1. The use of models in teaching prose style does not result in improvements of clarity and directness in student writing. [Although we used . . .]

2. Precision in plotting the location of building foundations enhances the possibility of its accurate reconstruction. [When we precisely plot . . .]

3. Any departures by the members from established procedures may cause termination of membership by the Board. [If members . . .]

4. A student's lack of socialization into a field may lead to writing problems because of his insufficient understanding about arguments by professionals in that field. [When . . . , . . . , because . . .]

5. The successful implementation of a new curriculum depends on the cooperation of faculty with students in setting achievable goals within a reasonable time. [To implement . . . , . . .]

Two Qualifications

Useful Nominalizations

I have so relentlessly urged you to turn nominalizations into verbs that you might think you should never use one. But in fact, you can't write well without them. The trick is to know which to keep and which to turn into verbs. Keep these:

1. A nominalization as a short subject refers to a previous sentence:

    ✓ **These arguments** all depend on a single unproven claim.

    ✓ **This decision** can lead to positive outcomes.

    Those nominalizations link one sentence to another in a cohesive flow.

2. A short nominalization replaces an awkward *The fact that:*

    The fact that she ACKNOWLEDGED the problem impressed me.

    ✓ Her **acknowledgment** of the problem impressed me.

    But then, why not this:

    ✓ *She* IMPRESSED me when *she* ACKNOWLEDGED the problem.

3. A nominalization names what would be the object of the verb:

    I accepted *what she* REQUESTED.

    ✓ I accepted her **request.**

    This kind of nominalization feels more concrete than an abstract one. However, contrast *request* above with this next sentence, where *request* is more of an action:

    Her **request** for **assistance** CAME after the deadline.

    ✓ She REQUESTED **assistance** after the deadline.

4. A nominalization refers to a concept so familiar to your readers that to them, it is a character (more about this in the next lesson):

    ✓ Few problems have so divided us as **abortion** on **demand.**

    ✓ The Equal Rights **Amendment** was an issue in past **elections.**

    ✓ **Taxation** without **representation** did not spark the American **Revolution.**

Those nominalizations name concepts familiar to us all: *abortion* on *demand, amendment, election, taxation, representation, revolution.* You have to develop an eye for the nominalization that expresses a common idea and one that you can revise into a verb:

> There is a **demand** for a **repeal** of the **inheritance** tax.
>
> ✓ We **DEMAND** that the government **REPEAL** the **inheritance** tax.

Clarity, Not Simplemindedness

Your readers want you to write clearly, but not in Dick-and-Jane sentences. This was written by a student aspiring to academic sophistication:

> After Czar Alexander II's emancipation of Russian serfs in 1861, many freed peasants chose to live on communes for purposes of cooperation in agricultural production as well as for social stability. Despite some communes' attempts at economic and social equalization through the strategy of imposing low economic status on the peasants, which resulted in their reduction to near poverty, a centuries-long history of social distinctions even among serfs prevented social equalization.

In his struggle to write clearly, he revised that paragraph into something that sounds like it was written by a 12-year-old:

> In 1861, Czar Alexander II emancipated the Russian serfs. Many of them chose to live on agricultural communes. There they thought they could cooperate with one another in agricultural production. They could also create a stable social structure. The leaders of some of these communes tried to equalize the peasants economically and socially. As one strategy, they tried to impose on all a low economic status. That reduced them to near poverty. However, the communes failed to equalize them socially. This happened because even serfs had made social distinctions among themselves for centuries.

In Lessons Eight and Nine we look at ways to revise too-short, too-simple sentences into a style that is readable but still complex enough to communicate complex ideas. When that student applied those principles to his primer-style passage, he revised again:

> After the Russian serfs were emancipated by Czar Alexander II in 1861, many chose to live on agricultural communes, hoping they could cooperate in working the land and establish a stable social

structure. At first, those who led some of the communes tried to equalize the new peasants socially and economically by imposing on everyone a low economic status, a strategy that reduced them to near poverty. But the communes failed to equalize them socially because the serfs had for centuries been observing their own social distinctions.

Those sentences are long but clear, because the writer consistently aligned major characters with subjects and actions with verbs.

SUMMING UP

We can represent these principles graphically. As we read, we integrate two levels of sentence structure. One is a relatively fixed grammatical sequence of subject and verb (the empty box is for everything that follows the verb):

Fixed	Subject	Verb	———

The other level of sentence structure is based on its characters and their actions. They have no fixed order, but readers prefer them matched to subjects and verbs. We can graphically combine those principles:

Fixed	Subject	Verb	———
Variable	Character	Action	———

Keep in mind that readers want to see characters not just *in* a subject, as in these two:

The *president's* veto of the bill infuriated Congress.

The veto of the bill by *the president* infuriated Congress.

Instead, they want to see the character *as* the subject, like this:

✓ When *the president*$_{subject}$ VETOED$_{verb}$ the bill, *he*$_{subject}$ INFURIATED$_{verb}$ Congress.

When you frustrate those expectations, you make readers work harder than they should have to. So keep these principles in mind as you revise:

1. Express actions in verbs:

    The **intention** of the committee IS improvement of morale.

    ✓ The committee INTENDS to improve morale.

2. Make the subjects of those verbs the characters associated with those actions.

    A decision by **the dean** in regard to the funding of the program by **the department** IS necessary for adequate **staff** preparation.

    ✓ If **the staff** IS TO PREPARE adequately, **the dean** MUST DECIDE whether **the department** WILL FUND the program.

3. Don't revise these nominalizations:

    a. They refer to a previous sentence:

        ✓ **These arguments** all depend on a single unproven claim.

    b. They replace an awkward "The fact that":

        The fact that she strenuously objected impressed me.

        ✓ **Her strenuous objections** impressed me.

    c. They name what would be the object of a verb:

        I do not know **what she INTENDS.**

        ✓ I do not know **her intentions.**

    d. They name a concept so familiar to your readers that it is a character:

        ✓ Few problems have so divided us as **abortion** on **demand.**

        ✓ The Equal Rights **Amendment** was an issue in past **elections.**

Lesson

4

Characters

There is no artifice as good and desirable as simplicity.
—St. Francis de Sales

When character is lost, all is lost.
—Anonymous

UNDERSTANDING THE IMPORTANCE OF CHARACTERS

Readers judge writing to be clear and direct when they see crucial ACTIONS in VERBS. Compare (1a) with (1b):

1a. The CIA feared the president would recommend to Congress that it reduce its budget.

1b. The CIA had fears that the president would send a recommendation to Congress that it make a reduction in its budget.

But while sentence (1a) is a third shorter than (1b), some readers don't sense a big difference in their clarity.

But now compare (1b) and (1c):

1b. The CIA had fears that the president would send a recommendation to Congress that it make a reduction in its budget.

1c. The fear of the CIA was that a recommendation from the president to Congress would be for a reduction in its budget.

Every reader thinks that (1c) is much less clear than either (1a) or (1b).

The reason is this: In both (1a) and (1b), important characters are short, specific subjects of verbs:

1a. **The CIA** FEARED **the president** would RECOMMEND to Congress that **it** REDUCE its budget.

1b. **The CIA** HAD fears that **the president** would SEND a recommendation to Congress that **it** MAKE a reduction in its budget.

But the two subjects in (1c) are not specific characters, but abstractions.

1c. **The fear of the CIA** WAS **that a recommendation from the president to Congress** WOULD BE for a reduction in its budget.

The main characters (the CIA, the president, and Congress) are not subjects, but OBJECTS of PREPOSITIONS:

1c. The fear *of* **the CIA** was that a recommendation *from* **the president** *to* **Congress** would be for a reduction in its budget.

The different verbs in (1a) and (1b) make some difference, but the different subjects in (1c) make a bigger difference.

Here's the point: Readers want actions in verbs, but even more they want characters as their subjects. We give readers a big problem when for no good reason we do not name characters in subjects, or worse, delete them entirely, like this:

> 1d. There was fear that there would be a recommendation for a budget reduction.

Who fears? Who recommends? Who reduces? It is important to express actions in verbs, but the *first* principle of a clear style is this: Make the subjects of most of your verbs short, specific, and concrete.

DIAGNOSIS AND REVISION

Finding and Relocating Characters

To get characters into subjects, you have to know three things:

1. when you haven't done that
2. if you haven't, where you should look for characters
3. what you should do when you find them (or don't)

For example, this sentence feels indirect and impersonal.

> Governmental intervention in fast changing technologies has led to the distortion of market evolution and interference in new product development.

Let's diagnose that sentence:

1. **Skim the first seven or eight words:**

   > <u>Governmental intervention in fast changing technologies has led</u> to the distortion of market evolution and interference in new product development.

   In those first few words, readers want to see characters as the subjects of verbs. But in that example, they don't.

2. **Find the main characters.** They may be POSSESSIVE PRONOUNS attached to NOMINALIZATIONS, objects of prepositions, particularly *by* and *of*, or only implied. In that sentence about

governmental intervention, one main character is in the ADJECTIVE *governmental;* the other, *market,* is in the object of a preposition: *of market evolution.*

3. **Skim the passage for actions involving those characters, particularly actions buried in nominalizations; then make them verbs and the relevant characters their subjects.** The question to ask is "Who's doing what?"

governmental **intervention**	→	*government* **intervenes**
distortion	→	*[government]* **distorts**
market **evolution**	→	*markets* **evolve**
interference	→	*[government]* **interferes**
development	→	*[market]* **develops**

Now reassemble those new subjects and verbs into a sentence, using CONJUNCTIONS such as *if, although, because, when, how,* and *why:*

✓ **When** a *government* INTERVENES in fast changing technologies, *it* DISTORTS how *markets* EVOLVE or INTERFERES with their ability to DEVELOP new products.

Be aware that just as actions can be in adjectives (*reliable* → *rely*), so can characters:

Medieval *theological* debates often addressed issues considered trivial by modern *philosophical* thought.

When you find a character implied in an adjective, revise in the same way:

✓ *Medieval theologians* often debated issues that *modern philosophers* consider trivial.

Here's the point: The first step in diagnosing your style is to look at your subjects. If you do not see your main characters there, your next step is to look for them. They can be in objects of prepositions, in possessive pronouns, or in adjectives. Once you find them, look for actions they are involved in. Then make those characters the subjects of verbs naming their actions.

Reconstructing Absent Characters

Readers have the biggest problem with sentences devoid of *all* characters:

> A decision was made in favor of doing a study of the disagreements.

That sentence could mean either of these, and more:

> We decided that I should study why they disagreed.
> I decided that you should study why he disagreed.

The writer may know who is doing what, but readers might not and so usually need help.

Sometimes we omit characters to make a general statement.

> Research strategies that look for more than one variable are of more use in understanding factors in psychiatric disorder than strategies based on the assumption that the presence of psychopathology is dependent on a single gene or on strategies in which only one biological variable is studied.

But when we try to revise that into something clearer, we have to invent characters, then decide what to call them. Do we use *one* or *we*, or name a generic "doer"?

> ✔ If *one/we/researchers* are to understand what causes psychiatric disorder, *one/we/they* should use research strategies that look for more than one variable rather than assume that a single gene is responsible for psychopathology or adopt a strategy in which *one/we/they* study only one biological variable.

To most of us, *one* feels stiff, but *we* may be ambiguous because it can refer just to the writer, or to the writer and others but not the reader, or to the reader and writer but not others, or to everyone.

But if you avoid both nominalizations and vague pronouns, you can slide into PASSIVE verbs (I'll discuss them in a moment):

> To understand what makes patients vulnerable to psychiatric disorders, strategies that look for more than one variable SHOULD BE USED rather than strategies in which it IS ASSUMED that a gene causes psychopathology or only one biological variable IS STUDIED.

In some cases, characters are so remote that you just have to start over:

> There are good reasons that account for the lack of evidence.
> ✔ I can explain why I have not found any evidence.

Abstractions as Characters

So far, I've discussed characters as if they had to be flesh-and-blood people. But you can tell stories whose main characters are abstractions, including nominalizations, so long as you make them the subjects of a series of sentences that tell a coherent story. Here's a story about a character called "freedom of speech," two nominalizations.

> ✓ No right is more fundamental to a free society than **freedom of speech. Free speech** served the left in the 1960s when it protested the Vietnam War, and **it** is now used by the right when it claims that speech includes political contributions. **The doctrine of free speech** has been embraced by all sides to protect themselves against those who would silence unpopular views. As a legal concept, **it** arose . . .

The phrase *freedom of speech* (or its equivalents *free speech* and *it*) is a virtual character because it's the subject of a series of sentences and involved in actions such as *served, is used, has been embraced,* and *arose.* Free speech is the central character in the story told by that paragraph.

But when you do use abstractions as characters, you can create a problem. A story about an abstraction as familiar as *free speech* is clear enough, but if you surround an abstract character with a lot of other abstractions, readers may feel that your writing is dense and complex.

For example, few of us are familiar with the concepts of "prospective and immediate intention," so most of us are likely to struggle with a story about them, especially when that word *intention* is surrounded by lots of other abstractions (actions are boldfaced; human characters are italicized):

> The **argument** is this. The cognitive component of **intention** exhibits a high degree of **complexity**. **Intention** is temporally divisible into two: prospective **intention** and immediate **intention**. The cognitive function of prospective **intention** is the **representation** of a *subject*'s similar past **actions**, *his* current situation, and *his* course of future **actions**. That is, the cognitive component of prospective **intention** is a **plan**. The cognitive function of immediate **intention** is the **monitoring** and **guidance** of ongoing bodily **movement**.
>
> —Myles Brand, *Intending and Acting*

We can make that passage clearer if we tell it from the point of view of flesh-and-blood characters (they are italicized; "denominalized" verbs are boldfaced and capitalized):

✓ *I* ARGUE this about intention. It has a complex cognitive component of two temporal kinds: prospective intention and immediate intention. *We* use prospective intention to REPRESENT how *we* have ACTED in our past and present and how *we* will ACT in the future. That is, *we* use the cognitive component of prospective intention to help *us* PLAN. *We* use immediate intention to MONITOR and GUIDE *our* bodies as *we* MOVE them.

But have I made this passage say something that the writer didn't mean? Some argue that any change in form changes meaning. In this case, the writer might offer an opinion, but only his readers could decide whether the two passages have different meanings, because at the end of the day, a passage means only what careful readers think it does.

Here's the point: Most readers want the subjects of verbs to name the main characters in a story, and those main characters to be flesh-and-blood. But often, you must write about abstract concepts. If you do, then turn them into virtual characters by making them the subjects of verbs that tell a story. If readers are familiar with your abstractions, no problem. But when they are not, avoid using lots of other abstract nominalizations around them. When you revise an abstract passage, you may have a problem if the hidden characters are "people in general." You can try *we* or a general term for whoever is doing the action, such as *researchers, social critics, one,* and so on. But the fact is, the English language has no good solution for this problem—that of naming a generic "doer."

Exercise 4.1

Before you revise these next sentences, diagnose them. Look at the first six or seven words (ignore short introductory phrases). Then revise so that each has a specific character as subject of a specific verb. To revise, you may have to invent characters. Use *we, I,* or any other word that seems appropriate.

1. In recent years, the appearance of new interpretations about the meaning of the discovery of America has led to a reassessment of Columbus's place in Western history.

2. Decisions about forcibly administering medication in an emergency room setting despite the inability of an irrational patient to provide legal consent is usually an on-scene medical decision.

3. Tracing transitions in a well-written article provides help in efforts at improving coherence in writing.

4. Resistance has been growing against building mental health facilities in residential areas because of a belief that the few examples of improper management are typical.

5. With the decline in network television viewing in favor of cable and rental DVDs, awareness is growing at the networks of a need to revise programming.

Characters and Passive Verbs

More than any other advice, you probably remember "Write in the active voice, not in the passive." That's not bad advice, but it has exceptions.

When you write in the active voice, you typically put

- a character as the agent of an action in the subject
- the goal or receiver of an action in a DIRECT OBJECT:

	subject	verb	object
Active:	I	lost	the money.
	character/agent	action	goal

The passive differs in three ways:

1. The subject names the goal of the action.
2. A form of *be* precedes a verb in its PAST PARTICIPLE form.
3. The agent of the action is in a *by*-phrase or dropped entirely:

	subject	be + verb	prepositional phrase
Passive:	The money	was lost	[by me].
	goal	action	character/agent

The terms *active* and *passive*, however, are ambiguous, because they can refer not only to those two grammatical constructions but also to how a sentence makes us *feel*. We call a sentence passive if it feels flat, regardless of whether its verb is actually in the passive voice. For example, compare these two sentences.

We will succeed if we can effectively control costs.

Success will depend on cost control effectiveness.

Grammatically, both sentences are in the active voice, but the second *feels* passive, for three reasons:

- Neither of its actions—*success* and *control*—are verbs; both are nominalizations.
- The subject is *success,* an abstraction.
- The sentence lacks flesh-and-blood characters.

We have to distinguish the literal meanings of *active* and *passive* from their figurative meanings before we can understand why we respond to those two sentences as we do.

We make sentences seem and be really passive when we combine passives with nominalizations:

Active-verbal:	*We* **INVESTIGATED** why *they* **INTERVIEWED** so few minority applicants.
Active-nominalized:	*We* CONDUCTED an **investigation** into why *they* DID so few **interviews** of minority applicants.
Passive-nominalized:	An **investigation** WAS CONDUCTED into why so few **interviews** WERE DONE.

Choosing between Active and Passive

Some critics of style relentlessly urge us to avoid the passive because it adds a couple of words and often deletes the agent, the "doer" of the action, usually a main character. But in fact, the passive is often the better choice. To choose between active and passive, you have to answer three questions:

1. **Must your readers know who is responsible for the action?** Often, we won't say who does an action, because we don't know or readers won't care. For example, we naturally choose the passive in these sentences:

   ✓ The president **WAS RUMORED** to have considered resigning.

   ✓ Those who **ARE FOUND** guilty can **BE FINED.**

   ✓ Valuable records should always **BE KEPT** in a safe place.

   If we do not know who spread rumors, we cannot say, and no one doubts who finds people guilty or should keep records safe. So those passives are the right choice.

Sometimes, of course, writers use the passive when they don't want readers to know who did an action, especially when the doer is the writer. For example,

> Because the test was not done, the flaw was uncorrected.

I will discuss the issue of deliberate impersonality in Lesson Ten.

2. **Would the active or passive verb help your readers move more smoothly from one sentence to the next?** We depend on the beginning of a sentence to give us a context of what we know before we follow the sentence to read what's new. A sentence confuses us when it starts with information that is new and unexpected. For example, in this next short passage, the subject of the second sentence gives us new and complex information (boldfaced) before we read more familiar information that we recall from the previous sentence (italicized):

> We must decide whether to improve education in the sciences alone or to raise the level of education across the whole curriculum. **The weight given to industrial competitiveness and the value we attach to the liberal arts**$_{\text{new information}}$ WILL INFLUENCE$_{\text{active verb}}$ *our decision*$_{\text{familiar information}}$.

In the second sentence, the verb *influence* is in the active voice. But we could follow the sentence more easily if it were passive, because the passive would put the short, familiar information first and the new and complex information last, the order we all prefer:

> ✓ We must decide whether to improve education in the sciences alone or raise the level of education across the whole curriculum. *Our decision*$_{\text{familiar information}}$ WILL BE INFLUENCED$_{\text{passive verb}}$ **by the weight we give to industrial competitiveness and the value we attach to the liberal arts**$_{\text{new information}}$.

I discuss the issue of old and new information in detail in the next lesson.

3. **Would the active or passive give your readers a more consistent and appropriate point of view?** The writer of this next passage reports the end of World War II in Europe from the point of view of the Allies. In so doing, she uses active verbs to make the Allies a consistent sequence of subjects:

> ✓ By early 1945, *the Allies* HAD essentially DEFEATED$_{\text{active}}$ Germany; all that remained was a bloody climax. *American, French, British, and*

Russian forces HAD BREACHED_{active} its borders and WERE BOMBING_{active} it around the clock. But *they* HAD not yet so DEVASTATED_{active} Germany as to destroy its ability to resist.

But if she had wanted us to understand history from the point of view of Germany, she would have used passive verbs to make Germany the subject/character:

✓ By early 1945, *Germany* HAD essentially BEEN DEFEATED_{passive}; all that remained was a bloody climax. *Its borders* HAD BEEN BREACHED_{passive}, and *it* WAS BEING BOMBED_{passive} around the clock. *It* HAD not BEEN SO DEVASTATED_{passive}, however, that *it* could not RESIST.

I'll discuss this issue again in the next lesson.

Here's the point: Many writers depend on the passive verb too much, but it has important uses. Use it when

- you don't know who did an action, your readers don't care, or you don't want them to know;

- you want to shift a long and complex bundle of information to the end of its sentence, especially when it also lets you move to its beginning a chunk of information that is shorter, more familiar, and therefore easier to understand;

- you want to focus your readers' attention on one or another character.

Exercise 4.2

In the following, change all active verbs into passives, and all passives into actives. Which sentences improve? Which do not? (In the first two, active verbs that could be passive are italicized; verbs already passive are boldfaced.)

1. Independence is **gained** by those on welfare when skills are **learned** that the marketplace *values*.

2. Different planes of the painting are **noticed,** because their colors are **set** against a background of shades of gray that are **laid** on in layers that cannot be **seen** unless the surface is **examined** closely.

3. In this article, it is argued that the Vietnam War was fought to extend influence in Southeast Asia and was not ended until it was made clear that the United States could not defeat North Vietnam unless atomic weapons were used.

4. Science education will not be improved in this nation to a level sufficient to ensure that American industry will be supplied with skilled workers and researchers until more money is provided to primary and secondary schools.

5. The first part of Bierce's "An Occurrence at Owl Creek Bridge" is presented in a dispassionate way. In the first paragraph, two sentinels are described in detail, but the line, "It did not appear to be the duty of these two men to know what was occurring at the center of the bridge" takes emotion away from them. In paragraph 2, a description is given of the surroundings and spectators, but no feeling is betrayed because the language used is neutral and unemotional. This entire section is presented as devoid of emotion even though it is filled with details.

The "Objective" Passive

Some scholarly writers claim that by deleting a first-person subject, the passive voice creates an objective point of view, something like this:

> Based on the writers' verbal intelligence, prior knowledge, and essay scores, their essays **WERE ANALYZED** for structure and evaluated for richness of concepts. The subjects **WERE** then **DIVIDED** into a high- or low-ability group. Half of each group **WAS** randomly **ASSIGNED** to a treatment group or to a placebo group.

Contrary to that claim, academic and scientific writers use the active voice and the first-person *I* and *we* regularly. These next passages come from articles in respected journals:

✓ This paper is concerned with two problems. How can **we** best handle in a transformational grammar certain restrictions that . . . , To illustrate, **we** may cite . . . , **we** shall show . . .

✓ Since the pituitary-adrenal axis is activated during the acute phase response, **we** have investigated the potential role . . . Specifically, **we** have studied the effects of interleukin-1 . . .

Here are the first few words from several consecutive sentences from *Science,* a journal of considerable prestige:

✓ **We** examine . . . **We** compare . . . **We** have used . . . Each has been weighted . . . **We** merely take . . . They are subject . . . **We** use . . . Efron and Morris describe . . . **We** observed . . . **We** might find . . .

—John P. Gilbert, Bucknam McPeek, and Frederick Mosteller, "Statistics and Ethics in Surgery and Anesthesia," *Science*

Passives, Characters, and Metadiscourse

When academic writers do use the first person, however, they use it in certain ways. Look at the verbs in the passages above. There are two kinds:

- One kind refers to research activities: *study, investigate, examine, observe, use.* These verbs are usually in the passive voice: *The subjects* WERE OBSERVED . . .

- The other kind of verb refers not to the subject matter or the research, but to the writer's own writing and thinking: *cite, show, inquire.* These verbs are often active and in the first person: **We** WILL SHOW . . . These verbs represent what is called METADISCOURSE.

  You use metadiscourse when you refer to ~~writing about writing~~

- your thinking and act of writing: *We/I will explain, show, argue, claim, deny, suggest, contrast, add, expand, summarize* . . .

- your certainty: *it seems, perhaps, undoubtedly, I think* . . .

- the logic and form of what you have written: *first, second; to begin; therefore, however, consequently* . . .

- your readers' actions: *consider now, as you recall, look at the next example* . . .

Metadiscourse appears most often in introductions, where writers announce their intentions: *I claim that* . . . , *I will show* . . . , *We begin by* . . . , and again at the end, when they summarize: *I have argued* . . . , *I have shown* . . .

On the other hand, scholarly writers use the first person less often to describe specific actions performed as *part* of the research. We rarely find passages like this:

To determine if monokines elicited an adrenal steroidogenic response, **I** ADDED preparations of . . .

The writer of the original sentence used a passive verb to name the action of adding because anyone can do that, not just the writer:

> To determine if monokines elicited a response, **preparations** . . .
> WERE ADDED . . .

But a special problem lurks with a passive sentence: as did that writer, you can dangle a modifier. You dangle a modifier when you create an introductory phrase whose *implied* subject differs from the *explicit* subject in the following or preceding CLAUSE. In that example, the implied subject of the INFINITIVE VERB *determine* is *I* or *we: I determine* or *we determine.*

> [So that **I** could] determine if monokines elicited a response, **preparations** . . . WERE ADDED . . .

But that implied subject differs from the *explicit* subject of the clause it introduces—*preparations*, as in *preparations were added.* When that happens, the modifier dangles. Writers of scientific prose use this pattern so often, however, that it has become standard usage in their community.

We might note that this impersonal "scientific" style is a modern development. In his "New Theory of Light and Colors" (1672), Sir Isaac Newton wrote this charming first-person account of an experiment:

> I procured a triangular glass prism, to try therewith the celebrated phenomena of colors. And for that purpose, having darkened my laboratory, and made a small hole in my window shade, to let in a convenient quantity of the sun's light, I placed my prism at the entrance, that the light might be thereby refracted to the opposite wall. It was at first a very pleasing diversion to view the vivid and intense colors produced thereby.

Here's the point: Some writers and editors resolutely avoid the first person by using the passive everywhere, but deleting an *I* or *we* doesn't make a scientist's thinking more objective. We know that behind those impersonal sentences are flesh-and-blood researchers doing, thinking, and writing. The first-person *I* and *we* are common in scholarly prose when used with verbs that name actions unique to the writer. Some critics frown on the expressions *I think . . . , I feel . . . ,*

I believe . . . because inexperienced writers use those words too often to introduce baseless opinion. But when used appropriately, the first person is entirely correct.

Exercise 4.3

The verbs in 1 through 4 below are passive, but two could be active because they are metadiscourse verbs that would take first-person subjects. Revise the passive verbs that should be changed into active verbs. Then go through each sentence again and revise nominalizations into verbs where appropriate.

1. It is believed that a lack of understanding about the risks of alcohol is a cause of student bingeing.

2. The model has been subjected to extensive statistical analysis.

3. Success in exporting more crude oil for hard currency is suggested here as the cause of the improvement of the Russian economy.

4. The creation of a database is being considered, but no estimate has been made in regard to the potential of its usefulness.

The verbs in 5 through 8 are active, but some of them should be passive because they are not metadiscourse verbs. Revise in other ways that seem appropriate.

5. In Section IV, I argue that the indigenous peoples engaged in overcultivation of the land leading to its exhaustion as a food-producing area.

6. Our intention in this book is to help readers achieve an understanding not only of the differences in grammar between Arabic and English but also the differences in worldview as reflected by Arabic vocabulary.

7. To make an evaluation of changes in the flow rate, I made a comparison of the current rate with the original

rate on the basis of figures I had compiled with figures that Jordan had collected.

8. We performed the tissue rejection study on the basis of methods developed with our discovery of increases in dermal sloughing as a result of cellular regeneration.

Exercise 4.4

In these sentences, change passive verbs into actives only where you think it will improve the sentence. If necessary, invent a rhetorical situation to account for your choice of active or passive. (Different answers are correct for this one.)

1. Your figures were analyzed to determine their accuracy. Results will be announced when it is thought appropriate.

2. Home mortgage loans now are made for thirty years. With the price of housing at inflated levels, those loans cannot be paid off in a shorter time.

3. The author's impassioned narrative style is abandoned and a cautious treatment of theories of conspiracy is presented. But when the narrative line is picked up again, he invests his prose with the same vigor and force.

4. Many arguments were advanced against Darwinian evolution in the nineteenth century because basic assumptions about our place in the world were challenged by it. No longer were humans defined as privileged creatures but rather as a product of natural forces.

5. For many years, federal regulations concerning wiretapping have been ignored. Only recently have tighter restrictions been imposed on the circumstances that warrant it.

In these sentences, change passives to actives where appropriate and edit nominalizations into a more direct character-action style. Invent characters where necessary.

6. It is my belief that the social significance of smoking receives its clearest explication through an analysis of peer

interaction among adolescents. In particular, studies should be made of the manner in which interactive behavior is conditioned by social class.

7. These directives are written in a style of maximum simplicity as a result of an attempt at more effective communication with employees with limited reading skills.

8. The ability of the human brain to arrive at solutions to human problems has been undervalued because studies have not been done that would be considered to have scientific reliability.

Exercise 4.5

The excerpt below is from an actual letter from the chancellor of a state university to parents of students. Except for the second word, *you,* why is the first part so impersonal? Why is the last part more personal? Change the first part so that you name in subjects whoever performs an action. Then change the second part to eliminate all characters. How do the two parts now differ?

As you probably have heard, the U of X campus has been the scene of a number of incidents of racial and sexual harassment over the last several weeks. The fact that similar incidents have occurred on campuses around the country does not make them any less offensive when they take place here. Of the ten to twelve incidents that have been reported since early October, most have involved graffiti or spoken insults. In only two cases was any physical contact made, and in neither case was anyone injured.

U of X is committed to providing its students with an environment where they can live, work, and study without fear of being taunted or harassed because of their race, gender, religion, or ethnicity. I have made it clear that bigotry and intolerance will not be permitted and that U of X's commitment to diversity is unequivocal. We are also taking steps to improve security in campus housing. We at U of X are proud of this university's tradition of diversity . . .

This excerpt raises the question of misdirection, which we'll cover in Lesson Ten.

NOUN + NOUN + NOUN

One more stylistic choice does not directly involve characters and actions, but we discuss it here because it can distort the match that readers expect between the form of an idea and the grammar of its expression. It is the long COMPOUND NOUN phrase:

> Early *childhood thought disorder misdiagnosis* often results from unfamiliarity with recent *research literature* describing such conditions. This paper is a review of seven recent studies in which are findings of particular relevance to *pre-adolescent hyperactivity diagnosis* and to *treatment modalities* involving *medication maintenance level evaluation procedures.*

Some grammarians claim we should never modify one noun with another, but that would rule out common phrases such as *stone wall, student center, space shuttle,* and vast numbers of other useful terms.

But strings of nouns can feel lumpy, so avoid them. Especially avoid inventing your own. When you find a compound noun of your own invention, try revising, especially when the string includes nominalizations. To revise, just reverse the order of words and find prepositions to connect them:

1	2	3	4	5
early	childhood	thought	disorder	misdiagnosis
misdiagnose	disordered	thought	in early	childhood
5	4	3	1	2

Re-assembled, it looks like this:

Physicians misdiagnose[5] disordered[4] thought[3] in young[1] children[2] because they are unfamiliar with recent literature on the subject.

Exercise 4.6

Unpack the compound noun phrases in 1 through 4 by changing them into prepositional phrases or verbs.

1. The plant safety standards committee discussed recent air quality regulation announcements.
2. Diabetic patient blood pressure reduction may be brought about by renal depressor application.

3. The goal of this article is to describe text comprehension processes and recall protocol production.

4. On the basis of these principles, we may now attempt to formulate narrative information extraction rules.

In these, unpack compound nouns and revise nominalizations.

5. This paper is an investigation into information processing behavior involved in computer human cognition simulation.

6. Enforcement of guidelines for new automobile tire durability must be a Federal Trade Commission responsibility.

7. The Social Security program is a monthly income floor guarantee based on a lifelong contribution schedule.

8. Based on training needs assessment reviews and on office site visits, there was the identification of concepts and issues that can be used in our creation of an initial staff questionnaire instrument.

A LAST POINT: THE PROFESSIONAL VOICE

Every group expects its members to show that they accept its values by adopting its voice and vocabulary. The apprentice banker must learn not only to think and look like one, but to write and speak like one, as well. Too often, though, aspiring professionals think they sound like club members only when they write in the club's most complex technical language. It is an exclusionary style that erodes the trust a civil society depends on, especially in a world where information and expertise are increasingly the means to power and control.

It is true that some research can never be made clear to merely intelligent lay readers—but less often than many researchers think. Here is an excerpt from Talcott Parsons, a social scientist who was as influential in shaping his field as he was notorious for the opacity of his prose.

Apart from theoretical conceptualization there would appear to be no method of selecting among the indefinite number of varying kinds of factual observation which can be made about a concrete phenomenon or field so that the various descriptive statements about it articulate into a coherent whole, which constitutes an "adequate," a "determinate" description. Adequacy in description is secured insofar as determinate and verifiable answers can be given to all the scientifically important questions involved. What questions are important is largely determined by the logical structure of the generalized conceptual scheme which, implicitly or explicitly, is employed.

We can make that clearer to moderately well-educated readers:

When scientists lack a theory, they have no way to select from everything they could say about a subject only that which they can fit into a coherent whole that would be "adequate" or "determinate." Scientists describe something "adequately" only when they can verify answers to questions they think are important, and they decide what questions are important based on their implicit or explicit theories.

And we could make even that more concise:

Whatever you describe, you need a theory to fit its parts into a whole. You need a theory to decide even what questions to ask and to verify their answers.

My more concise versions lose the nuances of Parsons's style. But his own excruciating density numbs all but his most masochistically dedicated readers. Most readers would accept the tradeoff.

Here's the point: Whether you are a reader or a writer, you must understand three things about a style that seems complex:

- It may be necessary to express complex ideas precisely.
- It may needlessly complicate simple ideas.
- It may needlessly complicate already complex ideas.

Einstein said that everything should be made as simple as possible, but no simpler. But neither should it be made more complex. As a writer, your task is to recognize when you have committed that gratuitous complexity and, if you can, to revise it. When you do, you follow the Writer's Golden Rule: Write to others as you would have others write to you.

SUMMING UP

1. Readers judge prose to be clear when subjects of sentences name characters and verbs name actions.

Fixed	Subject	Verb	———
Variable	Character	Action	———

2. If you tell a story in which you make abstract nominalizations its main characters and subjects, use as few other nominalizations as you can:

> *A nominalization* IS a **replacement** of a verb by a noun, often resulting in **displacement** of characters from subjects by nouns.

> ✓ When *a nominalization* REPLACES a verb with a noun, *it* often DISPLACES characters from subjects.

3. Use a passive if the agent of an action is self-evident:

> *The voters* REELECTED the president with 54 percent of the vote.

> ✓ *The president* WAS REELECTED with 54 percent of the vote.

4. Use a passive if it lets you replace a long subject with a short one:

> Research demonstrating the soundness of our reasoning and the need for action SUPPORTED *this decision.*

> ✓ *This decision* WAS SUPPORTED BY research demonstrating the soundness of our reasoning and the need for action.

5. Use a passive if it gives your readers a coherent sequence of subjects:

> ✓ By early 1945, *the Axis nations* had BEEN essentially DEFEATED; all that remained was a bloody climax. *The German borders* had BEEN BREACHED, and both *Germany and Japan* were being bombed around the clock. *Neither country,* though, had BEEN so DEVASTATED that *it* could not RESIST.

6. Use an active verb if it is a metadiscourse verb:

> The terms of the analysis must BE DEFINED.

> ✓ We must DEFINE the terms of the analysis.

7. When convenient, rewrite long compound noun phrases:

> We discussed the **board**[1] **candidate**[2] **review**[3] **meeting**[4] **schedule**[5].
>
> ✓ We discussed the **schedule**[5] of **meetings**[4] to **review**[3] **candidates**[2] for the **board**[1].

Lesson

5

Cohesion and Coherence

in German, nouns are capitalized

If he would inform, he must advance regularly from Things known to things unknown, distinctly without Confusion, and the lower he begins the better. It is a common Fault in Writers, to allow their Readers too much knowledge: They begin with that which should be the Middle, and skipping backwards and forwards, 'tis impossible for any one but he who is perfect in the Subject before, to understand their Work, and such an one has no Occasion to read it.

—BENJAMIN FRANKLIN

The two capital secrets in the art of prose composition are these: first, the philosophy of transition and connection; or the art by which one step in an evolution of thought is made to arise out of another: all fluent and effective composition depends on the connections; secondly, the way in which sentences are made to modify each other; for the most powerful effects in written eloquence arise out of this reverberation, as it were, from each other in a rapid succession of sentences.

—THOMAS DE QUINCEY

mid 19th century

Understanding Coherence

So far, I've discussed clarity as if we could achieve it just by mapping CHARACTERS and ACTIONS onto SUBJECTS and VERBS. But readers need more than individually clear sentences for a whole passage to seem *coherent*. These two passages, for example, say much the same thing but feel very different:

> 1a. The basis of our American democracy—equal opportunity for all—is being threatened by college costs that have been rising fast for the last several years. Increases in family income have been significantly outpaced by increases in tuition at our colleges and universities during that period. Only the children of the wealthiest families in our society will be able to afford a college education if this trend continues. Knowledge and intellectual skills, in addition to wealth, will divide us as a people, when that happens. Equal opportunity and the egalitarian basis of our democratic society could be eroded by such a divide.

> ✓1b. In the last several years, college costs have been rising so fast that they are now threatening the basis of our American democracy—equal opportunity for all. During that period, tuition has significantly outpaced increases in family income. If this trend continues, a college education will soon be affordable only by the children of the wealthiest families in our society. When that happens, we will be divided as a people not only by wealth, but by knowledge and intellectual skills. Such a divide will erode equal opportunity and the egalitarian basis of our democratic society.

The first seems choppy, even disorganized; the second seems to "hang together" better.

But like the word *clarity,* the words *choppy* and *disorganized* refer not to what is on the page, but to how what is on the page makes us *feel.* What is it about the *arrangement* of words in (1a) that makes us feel that we are moving through it in fits and starts? Why does (1b) seem to flow so much more easily? We base those judgments on two aspects of word order:

- We judge sequences of sentences to be *cohesive* depending on how each sentence ends and the next begins.

- We judge a whole passage to be *coherent* depending on how all the sentences in a passage cumulatively begin.

I'll discuss both cohesion and coherence in this lesson, and say more about coherence in Epilogue One.

Cohesion: A Sense of Flow

In Lesson Four, we devoted a few pages (58–61) to that familiar advice, "Avoid PASSIVES." If we always did, we would choose the ACTIVE verb in sentence (2a) below over the passive in (2b):

> 2a. The collapse of a dead star into a point perhaps no larger than a marble CREATES$_{active}$ a black hole.

> 2b. A black hole IS CREATED$_{passive}$ by the collapse of a dead star into a point perhaps no larger than a marble.

But we might choose otherwise if we had to put one of those sentences between these two:

> [1]Some astonishing questions about the nature of the universe have been raised by scientists studying black holes in space. [2a/b][————]. [3]So much matter compressed into so little volume changes the fabric of space around it in puzzling ways.

Here's the active sentence there:

> 1a. [1]Some astonishing questions about the nature of the universe have been raised by scientists studying black holes in space. [2a]The collapse of a dead star into a point perhaps no larger than a marble creates a black hole. [3]So much matter compressed into so little volume changes the fabric of space around it in puzzling ways.

And here's the passive:

> 1b. [1]Some astonishing questions about the nature of the universe have been raised by scientists studying black holes in space. [2b]A black hole is created by the collapse of a dead star into a point perhaps no larger than a marble. [3]So much matter compressed into so little volume changes the fabric of space around it in puzzling ways.

Our sense of "flow" should call not for (2a), the sentence with the active verb, but for (2b), the one with the passive.

The reason is clear: the last four words of the first sentence introduce an important character—*black holes in space:*

> [1]Some astonishing questions about the nature of the universe have been raised by scientists studying **black holes in space.**

If we follow it with sentence (2a), the first concepts we hit are collapsed stars and marbles, information that seems to come out of nowhere:

> [1] . . . universe have been raised by scientists studying black holes in space. **[2a]The collapse of a dead star into a point perhaps no larger than a marble** creates . . .

But if we follow sentence (1) with (2b), the sentence with the passive verb, we connect them more smoothly, because now the first words we hit in (2b) pick up on what we just read at the end of (1):

> ¹ . . . studying **black holes in space. ²ᵇA black hole** is created by the collapse of . . .

Note too that the passive also lets us put at the *end* of sentence (2b) words that connect it to the *beginning* of sentence (3):

> ¹ . . . black holes in space. ²ᵇA black hole is created by the collapse of a dead star into **a point perhaps no larger than a marble. ³So much matter compressed into so little volume** changes the fabric of space around it in puzzling ways.

The passive sentence, (2b), is the better choice.

> *Here's the point:* Sentences are cohesive when the last few words of one set up information that appears in the first few words of the next one. That's what gives us our experience of "flow." And in fact, that's the biggest reason the passive is in the language: to arrange sentences so that they flow from one to the next easily. We can integrate that insight with our principles about subject and characters, and verbs and actions.

Fixed		
Variable	Familiar	
Fixed	Subject	Verb	———
Variable	Character	Action	———

DIAGNOSIS AND REVISION

That principle of reading suggests two principles of revision. They are mirror images of each other. The first is this:

1. **Begin sentences with information familiar to your readers.**
   Readers get that familiar information from two sources: first, they remember words from the sentence they just read. That's

why the beginning of sentence (2b) about black holes coheres with the end of (1) and why the beginning of (3) coheres with the end of (2b):

> [1] . . . questions about the nature of the universe have been raised by scientists studying **[black holes in space. [2b]A black hole]** is created by the collapse of a dead star into **[a point perhaps no larger than a marble. [3]So much matter compressed into so little volume]** changes the fabric of space . . .

Second, readers bring to a sentence a general knowledge of its subject. We would not have been surprised, for example, if a sentence (4) in that series about black holes had begun like this:

> . . . changes the fabric of space around it in puzzling ways. **[4]Astronomers have reported** that . . .

The word *Astronomers* did not appear in the preceding sentence, but since we are reading about space, we wouldn't be surprised by a reference to them.

The second principle is the flip side of the first.

2. **End sentences with information readers cannot anticipate.** Readers always prefer to read what's easy before what's hard, and what is familiar and simple is easier to understand than what is new and complex.

You can more easily see when others fail to observe those principles in their writing than you can in your own, because after you've worked on your own for a while, it all seems familiar—to you. But hard as it is to distinguish old from new in your own writing, you have to try, because readers want to begin sentences with information that is familiar to *them*, and only then move on to information that is new.

> *Here's the point:* In every *sequence* of sentences you write, you have to balance principles that make individual sentences in a passage clear and principles that make the whole passage cohesive. *But in that tradeoff, give priority to helping readers create a sense of cohesive flow.* That means starting sentences with information that readers are familiar with. Fortunately, this principle about old and new information

cooperates with the principle of characters as subjects. Once you mention your main characters, readers take them as familiar information. So when you regularly get characters up front, you also get up front familiar information.

Exercise 5.1

Revise these two passages to improve their old-new flow. In 1, I boldface the words that seem to me to be old information. Revise the sentences so that old information appears first.

1. Two aims—the recovery of the American economy and the modernization of America into a military power—were **in the president's mind when he assumed his office.** The drop in unemployment figures and inflation, and the increase in the GNP testifies to **his success in the first.** But our increased involvement in international conflict without any clear set of political goals indicates **less success with the second.** Nevertheless, increases in the military budget and a good deal of saber rattling **pleased the American voter.**

2. The components of Abco's profitability, particularly growth in Asian markets, will be highlighted in our report to demonstrate its advantages versus competitors. Revenue returns along several dimensions—product type, end-use, distribution channels, etc.—will provide a basis for this analysis. Likely growth prospects of Abco's newest product lines will depend most on its ability in regard to the development of distribution channels in China, according to our projections. A range of innovative strategies will be needed to support the introduction of new products.

Coherence: A Sense of the Whole

When you create cohesive flow, you take the first step toward helping readers think your prose hangs together. But they will judge you to be a good writer only when they feel that your writing is not just cohesive but *coherent,* a quality different from cohesion. It's easy to confuse the words *cohesion* and *coherence* because they sound so much alike.

- Think of *cohesion* as pairs of sentences fitting together the way two Lego® pieces do (recall the black hole sentences).
- Think of *coherence* as seeing what all the sentences in a piece of writing add up to, the way a hundred Lego® pieces create a building, bridge, or boat.

This next passage has great cohesive "flow" because we move from the end of each sentence to the next without a hitch:

> Sayner, Wisconsin, is the snowmobile capital of the world. The buzzing of snowmobile engines fills the air, and their tanklike tracks crisscross the snow. The snow reminds me of Mom's mashed potatoes, covered with furrows I would draw with my fork. Her mashed potatoes usually make me sick—that's why I play with them. I like to make a hole in the middle of the potatoes and fill it with melted butter. This behavior has been the subject of long chats between me and my analyst.

Though we can get from each of those sentences to the next easily, that passage as a whole is incoherent. (It was created by six different writers, one of whom wrote the first sentence, with the other five sequentially adding one sentence knowing only the immediately preceding one.) It is incoherent for three reasons:

1. The subjects of the sentences are entirely unrelated.
2. The sentences share no common "themes" or ideas.
3. Taken together, the sentences fail to focus on a single point. The paragraph has no one sentence that states what the whole passage supports or explains.

I will discuss that second point in the next lesson and the third one in Epilogue One. The rest of this lesson focuses on the first point, shared subjects.

Subjects, Topics, Grammar, and Coherence

For five hundred years, English teachers have defined *subject* in two ways:

1. the "doer" of the action
2. what a sentence is "about," its main topic

In Lessons Three and Four, we saw why that first definition doesn't work: the subjects of many sentences are actions.

But also flawed is that second schoolbook definition: "A subject is what a sentence is about." It is flawed because often, the subject of a sentence doesn't state its main topic, the idea that the rest of the sentence "comments" on; that function can be performed by other parts of a sentence. For example:

- The subject of this sentence (italicized) is *it*, but its topic (boldfaced) is *your claim*, the OBJECT of the PREPOSITION *for:*

  It is impossible for **your claim** to be proved.

- The subject of this sentence is *I*, but its topic is *this question*, the object of *to:*

  In regard to **this question**, *I* believe more research is needed.

- The subject of this sentence is *it*, but its topic is *our proposal*, the subject of a verb in a SUBORDINATE CLAUSE:

  It is likely that **our proposal** will be accepted.

- The subject of this sentence is *no one*, but its topic is *such results*, a DIRECT OBJECT shifted to the front for emphasis:

  Such results *no one* could have predicted.

> *Here's the point:* We use the term *topic* to mean what a sentence is "about," but that topic is not always its grammatical subject. *But readers expect it to be.* They judge writing to be clear and direct when they quickly see topics and subject/characters in the same words.

Diagnosing and Revising Topics

This passage feels choppy, out of focus, even disorganized:

> The particular ideas toward the beginning of sentences define what a passage is "about" for a reader. Moving through a paragraph from a coherent point of view is made possible by a sequence of topics that constitute a limited set of related ideas. A seeming absence of context for each sentence is one consequence of making random shifts in

topics. Feelings of dislocation, disorientation, and lack of focus in a passage occur when that happens.

Here's how to diagnose its problems and revise it.

1. **Diagnose:**

   a. Underline the first seven or eight words of every sentence in a passage.

   b. If you can, underline the first five or six words of every clause in those sentences, both subordinate and MAIN.

   > The particular ideas toward the beginning of sentences define what a passage is "about" for a reader. Moving through a paragraph from a coherent point of view is made possible by a sequence of topics that constitute a limited set of related ideas. A seeming absence of context for each sentence is one consequence of making random shifts in topics. Feelings of dislocation, disorientation, and lack of focus in a passage occur when that happens.

2. **Analyze:**

   a. Do the underlined words constitute a relatively small set of related ideas? Even if *you* see how they are related, will your readers? For that passage, the answer is no.

   b. Do those words name the most important characters, real or abstract? Again, the answer is no.

   c. What are the main topic/characters? Try giving the passage a title. Some of its words will identify what should be the topics of most of the sentences. In this case, the title would be something like "Readers' Responses to Consistent and Inconsistent Topics."

3. **Revise:**

   a. In most (not necessarily all) of the sentences, use subjects to name those topics.

   b. Put those subjects close to the beginning of the sentences.

Here is that passage revised.

> **Readers** look for consistent topics of sentences to tell them what a whole passage is "about." If **they** feel that its sequence of topics focuses on a limited set of related topics, then **they** will feel they are moving through that passage from a coherent point of view. But

if **topics** seem to shift randomly, then **readers** have to begin each sentence from no coherent point of view, and when that happens, **they** feel dislocated and disoriented, and the **passage** seems out of focus.

The Difficult Craft of Beginning a Sentence Well

It's hard to begin a sentence well. Readers want to get to topic/subjects quickly, but too often, writers begin sentences in ways that keep readers from getting there. It's called *throat-clearing*. Throat-clearing typically begins with METADISCOURSE that connects a sentence to the previous one, with transitions such as *and, but, therefore:*

> And therefore . . .

We then add a second kind of metadiscourse that expresses our attitude toward what is coming, words such as *fortunately, perhaps, allegedly, it is important to note, for the most part,* or *politically speaking:*

> And therefore, politically speaking . . .

Then we can indicate time, place, or manner:

> And therefore, politically speaking, in Eastern states since 1980 . . .

Only then do we get to the topic/subject:

> And, therefore, politically speaking, in Eastern states since 1980, **acid rain** has become a serious problem.

When you open several sentences like that, your readers have a hard time seeing not just what your individual sentences are "about," but the cumulative focus of a whole passage. When you find a sentence with lots of words before its subject/topic, revise:

> ✓ Since 1980, therefore, **acid rain** has become a serious political problem in Eastern states.

> *Here's the point:* In most of your sentences (not necessarily all), start with the subject and make that subject the topic of the sentence.

Integrating the Principles

We can bring together these principles about old and new and consistent topic strings with the principles about characters as subjects and actions as verbs (I'll fill in the empty boxes in Lesson Six):

Fixed	Topic	
Variable	Familiar	
Fixed	Subject	Verb	———
Variable	Character	Action	———

No unit of information is shorter and simpler than the name of a familiar character. So when you create a sequence of subjects out of a limited set of characters, real or abstract, you create a sequence of topics that your readers will think is clear and consistent, and that helps them create a sense of coherence.

Exercise 5.2

Revise these passages to give them consistent topic strings. First determine the characters, then their actions. Then start each sentence with a character, and let the sentence take you where it wants to go. In 1, words that could be consistent subject/topics are boldfaced.

1. **Vegetation** covers the earth, except for those areas continuously covered with ice or utterly scorched by continual heat. Richly fertilized plains and river valleys are places where **plants** grow most richly, but also at the edge of perpetual snow in high mountains. The ocean and its edges as well as in and around lakes and swamps are **densely vegetated.** The cracks of busy city sidewalks have **plants** in them as well as in seemingly barren cliffs. Before humans existed, the earth was covered with **vegetation,** and the earth will have **vegetation** long after evolutionary history swallows us up.

2. The power to create and communicate a new message to fit a new experience is not a competence animals have in their natural states. Their genetic code limits the number and kind of messages that they can communicate. Information about distance, direction, source, and richness of pollen in flowers constitutes the only information that can be communicated by bees, for example. A limited repertoire of messages delivered in the same way, for generation after generation, is characteristic of animals of the same species, in all significant respects.

3. The importance of language skills in children's problem-solving ability was stressed by Jones (1985) in his paper on children's thinking. Improvement in nonverbal problem solving was reported to have occurred as a result of improvements in language skills. The use of previously acquired language habits for problem articulation and activation of knowledge previously learned through language are thought to be the cause of better performance. Therefore, systematic practice in the verbal formulation of nonlinguistic problems prior to attempts at their solution might be an avenue for exploration in the enhancement of problem solving in general.

TWO QUALIFICATIONS

Alleged Monotony

At this point, you may be conflicted by that common advice "Vary how you begin your sentences." That's not a good idea, especially when you change how you start sentences just to make them different. True, you may think a passage is monotonous if you see the same topic in several of its sentences *in your own prose*. But your readers are less likely to notice, because they will be focusing on your ideas. On the other hand, you might revise if you find you have used exactly the same words for the same topics in the same positions. This passage goes over the top in that kind of consistency:

> **"Moral climate"** is created when an objectivized moral standard for treating people is accepted by others. **Moral climate** results from norms of behavior that are accepted by society whereby if people

conform they are socially approved of, or if they don't they are shunned. In this light, **moral climate** acts as a reason to refrain from saying or doing things that the community does not support. **A moral climate** encourages individuals to conform to a moral standard and apply that standard to their own circumstances.

Be cautious, though: most writers change topics too often.

Faked Coherence

Some writers try to fake coherence by lacing their prose with conjunctions like *thus, therefore, however,* and so on, regardless of whether they signal real logical connections. An example:

> Because the press is the major medium of interaction between the president and the people, how it portrays him influences his popularity. **Therefore,** it should report on the president objectively. Both reporters and the president are human, **however,** subject to error and favoritism. **Also,** people act differently in public than they do in private. **Hence,** to understand a person, it is important to know the whole person, his environment, upbringing, and education. **Indeed,** from the correspondence with his family, we can learn much about Harry S. Truman, our thirty-third president.

Experienced writers use explicit connecting devices, but depend more on the clear flow of their ideas. They are especially careful not to overuse words like *and, also, moreover, another,* and so on, words that say simply "Here's another thing." You need a *but* or *however* when you contradict or qualify what you just said, and you can use a *therefore* or *consequently* to wind up a line of reasoning. But avoid using words like those more than a few times a page. Your readers don't need them when your sentences are cohesive and the passage they constitute is coherent.

Exercise 5.3

Revise these passages to give them more consistent topic strings. First, decide who you think the main characters should be, then make them the subjects of verbs expressing important actions. In the first passage, I boldface topics so that you can see how inconsistent they are.

1. **Some potential threats** exist in the modern mass communications media, though there are many significant

advantages. If **a powerful minority** should happen to control it, **public opinion** could be manipulated through biased reporting. And while **a wide knowledge of public affairs** is a great advantage that results from national coverage, **divisiveness and factionalism** can be accentuated by connecting otherwise isolated, local conflicts into a single larger conflict as a result of showing that **conflicts about the same issues** are occurring in different places. It will always be true, of course, that **human nature** produces differences of opinion, but **the threat of faction and division** may be reinforced when **national coverage** publicizes uninformed opinions. According to some, **education** can suppress faction when **the true nature of conflicts** reaches the public through the media, but **history** has shown that as **much coverage** is given to people who encourage conflict as to people who try to remove conflict.

2. Some sort of palace revolt or popular revolution plagued seven out of eight reigns of the Romanov line after Peter the Great. In 1722, achievement by merit was made the basis of succession when the principle of heredity was terminated by Peter. This resulted in many tsars' not appointing a successor before dying, including Peter. Ivan VI was less than two months old when appointed by Czarina Anna, but Elizabeth, daughter of Peter the Great, defeated Anna and ascended to the throne in 1741. Succession not dependent upon authority resulted in the boyars' regularly disputing who was to become sovereign. Male primogeniture became the law in 1797 when Paul I codified the law of succession. But conspirators strangled him, one of whom was probably his son, Alexander I.

3. Many issues other than science, domestic politics in particular, faced Truman when he was considering the Oppenheimer committee's recommendation to stop the hydrogen bomb project. A Sino-Soviet bloc had been proclaimed by Russia and China, so the Cold War was becoming an issue. Support for Truman's foreign policy was shrinking among Republican leaders in Congress. And the first Russian atom bomb test made the public

demand a strong response from him. Truman's conclusion that he could not afford letting the public think that Russia had been allowed to be first in developing the most powerful weapon yet was an inevitable one. The risk in the Oppenheimer recommendation was worth taking according to some historians, but the political issues that Truman had to face were too powerful to ignore.

Exercise 5.4

The point of this exercise is to demonstrate that simply by changing subjects, you change the "feel" of a passage. In his essay, "Stranger in the Village," the eminent African-American writer James Baldwin reflects on his relationship to European Christianity. In the first sentence of that essay, he makes the cathedral at Chartres the topic and a metaphorical character:

> **The cathedral at Chartres,** I have said, says something to the people of this village which **it** cannot say to me, but it is important to understand that **this cathedral** says something to me which **it** cannot say to them.

But in the second sentence, he switches the topic/subjects to the villagers, then to himself:

> Perhaps **they** are struck by the power of the spires, the glory of the windows; but **they** have known God, after all, longer than **I** have known him, and in a different way, and **I** am terrified . . .

Nothing forced him to choose those topics. He could have written this:

> **I** have said that **I** hear something from the cathedral at Chartres that **the people** of this village do not hear, but it is important to understand that . . .

Experiment with Baldwin's passage by changing the topics. First, focus the passage on Baldwin (as above). Then revise a second time, focusing on the people of Chartres, then a third time focusing on the architecture. How does the feel of the passage change? Why did Baldwin make the choices he did, do you think? (No one can know the right answer.) Here is his passage. I boldface topics; you will not be able to change them all.

> **The cathedral at Chartres,** I have said, says something to the people of this village which **it** cannot say to me, but it is important to understand that **this cathedral** says something to me which **it** cannot say to them. Perhaps **they** are struck by the power of the spires, the glory of the windows; but **they** have known God, after all, longer than **I** have known him, and in a different way, and **I** am terrified by the slippery bottomless well to be found in the crypt, down which **heretics** were hurled to death, and by the obscene, inescapable gargoyles jutting out of the stone and seeming to say that **God and the devil** can never be divorced. **I** doubt that **the villagers** think of the devil when **they** face a cathedral because **they** have never been identified with the devil. But **I** must accept the status which **myth,** if nothing else, gives me in the West before **I** can hope to change the myth.

What does this exercise suggest about "natural" connections between characters and subjects? What does it imply about how we understand who's responsible for what actions? How much can a writer control how we decide who's responsible? We return to this matter in Epilogue One.

SUMMING UP

We can sum up this lesson in this model:

Fixed	Topic		
Variable	Familiar		
Fixed	Subject	Verb	———
Variable	Character	Action	———

It represents two principles:

1. Begin sentences with subjects that communicate information your readers are familiar with:

   > The number of dead in the Civil War exceeded all other wars in American history combined. A reason for the lingering animosity between North and South today is **the memory of this terrible carnage.**

   > ✓ Of all the wars in American history, none has exceeded the Civil War in the number of dead. **The memory of this terrible carnage** is one reason for the lingering animosity between North and South today.

2. Through a series of sentences, keep your topics short and reasonably consistent:

   > **Competition by Asian companies with American companies in the Pacific** is the first phase of this study. **Labor costs and the ability to introduce new products quickly in particular** are examined. **A plan that will show American industry how to restructure its facilities** will be developed from this study.

   > ✓ In the first phase of this study, **we** examine how **Asian companies** compete with American companies in the Pacific region. **We** examine in particular their labor costs and ability to introduce new products quickly. **We** develop from this study a **plan** that will show **American industry** how to restructure its facilities.

6

Emphasis

"Begin at the beginning," the King said, gravely,
"and go on till you come to the end; then stop."
—LEWIS CARROLL

Beginning and end shake hands with each other.
—GERMAN PROVERB

In the end is my beginning.
—T. S. ELIOT

All's well that ends well.
—WILLIAM SHAKESPEARE

UNDERSTANDING HOW SENTENCES END

If you consistently write sentences whose SUBJECT/TOPICS name a few central CHARACTERS and then join them to strong VERBS, you'll likely get the rest of the sentence right, and in the process create a passage that seems both cohesive and coherent. But if the first few words of a sentence are worth special attention, so are the last few, because how you end a sentence determines how readers judge both its clarity and its strength. In this lesson, we address clarity first, then strength, then how the right emphasis on the right words can contribute to a kind of coherence even more global than the coherence we get from consistent topics.

When readers get up speed in a sentence's first words, they more easily get through complicated material that follows. Compare:

> 1a. A sociometric and actuarial analysis of Social Security revenues and disbursements for the last six decades to determine changes in projecting deficits is the subject of this study.

> ✓1b. In this study, we analyze Social Security's revenues and disbursements for the last six decades, using sociometric and actuarial criteria to determine changes in projecting deficits.

As we start (1a), we struggle to understand its technical terms at the same time we are hacking through a twenty-two-word subject before we get to a verb. In (1b), we go through just five words to get past a subject and verb and twelve more before we hit a term that might slow us up. By that point we have enough momentum to carry us through the complexity to its end. In short, in (1a), we hit the complexity at the beginning; in (1b), we don't hit it until near the end, where we handle it better.

There are, however, two kinds of complexity: grammar and meaning.

Complex Grammar

Which of these two sentences do you prefer?

> 2a. Lincoln's claim that the Civil War was God's punishment of both North and South for slavery appears in the last part of the speech.

> ✓2b. In the last part of his speech, Lincoln claims that God gave the Civil War to both North and South as a punishment for slavery.

Most readers dislike (2a) because it begins with a long, complex grammatical subject. We prefer (2b) because it begins simply, then moves toward complexity.

Complex Terms

Readers have a problem with all kinds of unfamiliar technical terms, but especially when those new terms appear toward the beginning of a sentence. Compare these two passages:

3a. The role of calcium blocker drugs in the control of cardiac irregularity can be seen through an understanding of the role of calcium in the activation of muscle cells. The regulatory proteins actin, myosin, tropomyosin, and troponin make up the sarcomere, the basic unit of muscle contraction. ATPase, the energy-producing protein myosin, makes up its thick filament, while actin, tropomyosin, and troponin make up its thin filament. Interaction of myosin and actin triggers muscle contraction.

✓3b. When a muscle contracts, it uses calcium. We must therefore understand how calcium affects muscle cells to understand how cardiac irregularity is controlled by drugs called "calcium blockers." The basic unit of muscle contraction is the sarcomere. It has two filaments, one thin and one thick. Those filaments consist of four proteins that regulate contraction: actin, myosin, tropomyosin, and troponin. Muscles contract when the protein in the thin filament, actin, interacts with the protein myosin in the thick filament, an energy-producing or ATPase protein.

Both passages use the same technical terms, but (3b) is clearer to those who know nothing about the chemistry of muscles.

Those passages differ in two ways. First, information that is implicit in (3a) I stated explicitly in (3b):

3a. . . . and troponin make up the sarcomere, the basic unit of muscle contraction. ATPase, the energy-producing protein myosin, makes up . . .

✓3b. The basic unit of muscle contraction is the sarcomere. It has two filaments, one thin and one thick. . . .

More important, I moved the technical terms from the beginning of the sentences in (3a) to the end of the sentences in (3b). Note how almost all the technical terms in (3a) are at the beginning of their sentences:

3a. The role of **calcium blocker drugs** in the control of ·**cardiac irregularity** can be seen through an understanding of the role of calcium in the activation of muscle cells.

The regulatory proteins actin, myosin, tropomyosin, and troponin make up the **sarcomere,** the basic unit of muscle contraction.

> **ATPase, the energy-producing protein myosin,** makes up its thick filament, while **actin, tropomyosin, and troponin** make up its thin filament.
>
> **Interaction of myosin and actin** triggers muscle contraction.

In (3b), those technical terms appear at the ends of their sentences:

> . . . uses **calcium.**
>
> . . . controlled by drugs called **"calcium blockers."**
>
> . . . is the **sarcomere.**
>
> . . . four proteins that regulate contraction: **actin, myosin, tropomyosin, and troponin.**
>
> . . . in the thick filament, an **energy-producing or ATPase protein.**

These principles work for prose intended even for professional readers. In this next passage, from the *New England Journal of Medicine,* the writer deliberately uses METADISCOURSE to construct the second sentence just to get a new technical term at its end:

> The incubation of peripheral-blood lymphocytes with a lymphokine, interleukin-2, generates lymphoid cells that can lyse fresh, noncultured, natural-killer-cell-resistant tumor cells but not normal cells. *We term these cells* **lymphokine-activated killer (LAK) cells.**

Here's the point: Your readers want you to use the end of your sentences to help them manage two kinds of difficulty:

- long and complex PHRASES and CLAUSES, and
- new information, particularly unfamiliar technical terms.

We can integrate that principle with our others:

Fixed	Topic	
Variable	Short, simple, familiar	New, long, complex
Fixed	Subject	Verb	———
Variable	Character	Action	———

One More New Term: Stress

In the last lesson, we said that an important position in the *psychological* geography of a sentence is its first few words, because they name the topic of a sentence, its psychological subject (see pp. 79–80.) I've been discussing the end of a sentence in general, but the last few words are particularly important. You can sense that importance when you hear your voice rise and emphasize one syllable more strongly than you do the others:

> . . . more strongly than you do the ^{6}-thers.

We have the same experience even when reading silently.

We'll call this most emphatic part of a sentence its STRESS and add it to our last box. How you manage the emphasis in that stress position helps establish the voice readers hear in your prose.

Fixed	Topic		Stress
Variable	Short, simple, familiar	:	New, long, complex
Fixed	Subject	Verb	———
Variable	Character	Action	———

In Lesson Four, we saw how it was possible to manipulate subject/topics to create different points of view (pp. 62–63). To create different effects, you can manipulate the stress of a sentence as well.

Compare these passages. One was written to blame an American president for being weak with Iran on arms control. The other is my revision; it seems to blame Iran. You can tell which is which if you thump your finger as you read the boldface words at the ends of the sentences:

1a. The administration has blurred an issue central to arms control, **the issue of verification.** Irresponsible charges, innuendo, and leaks have submerged **serious problems with Iranian compliance.** The objective, instead, should be not to exploit these concerns in order to further poison our relations, repudiate existing agreements, or, worse still, terminate arms control altogether, but to **insist on compliance and clarify questionable behavior.**

1b. The issue of verification—so central to arms control—has been **blurred by the administration.** Serious problems with Iranian compliance have been submerged in **irresponsible charges, innuendo, and leaks.** The objective, instead, should be to clarify questionable behavior and insist on compliance—not to exploit these concerns in order to **further poison our relations, repudiate existing agreements, or, worse still, terminate arms control altogether.**

Here's the point: Just as you look at the first few words of your sentences for point of view, you can look at the last few words for special emphasis. You can manipulate a sentence to emphasize particular words that you want readers to hear stressed and thereby note as particularly significant.

DIAGNOSIS AND REVISION

If you have managed your subjects and topics well, you will almost by default emphasize the right words at the end of your sentences. But there are some ways to revise just for that purpose.

Three Tactical Revisions

1. **Trim the end.**

   Sociobiologists claim that our genes control our social behavior **in the way we act in situations we are in every day.**

   Since *social behavior* means *the way we act in situations . . . ,* we drop everything after *behavior:*

   ✓ Sociobiologists claim that our genes **control our social behavior.**

2. **Shift peripheral ideas to the left.**

   The data offered to prove ESP are too weak **for the most part.**

   ✓ **For the most part,** the data offered to prove ESP are **too weak.**

   Particularly avoid ending with anticlimactic metadiscourse:

   Job opportunities in computer programming are getting scarcer, **it must be remembered.**

✓ **It must be remembered** that job opportunities in computer programming are getting scarcer.

3. **Shift new information to the right.** A more common way to manage stress is by moving new information to the end of a sentence.

> **Questions about the ethics of withdrawing intravenous feeding** are *more difficult [than something just mentioned].*
>
> ✓ *More difficult* [than something just mentioned] are **questions about the ethics of withdrawing intravenous feeding.**

Six Syntactic Devices to Emphasize the Right Words

1. **Passives (for the last time)**   A passive verb lets you flip a subject and OBJECT. Compare these next two sentences. To stress the concept of genes influencing behavior, we revise the active verb into a passive to get that idea closer to the stress position:

> Some sociobiologists claim that **our genes** influence$_{active}$ aspects of behavior that we think are learned. **Our genes,** for example, seem to determine . . .
>
> ✓ Some sociobiologists claim that aspects of behavior that we think are learned are in fact influenced$_{passive}$ **by our genes. Our genes,** for example, seem to determine . . .

As we've seen, the passive is in the language so that we can get old and new information in the right order.

2. ***There***   Some editors discourage *there is/there are* constructions, but if you never used one, you'd lose a device that lets you shift a phrase toward the end of its sentence. Compare:

> Several syntactic devices let you manage where in a sentence you locate units of new information.
>
> ✓ **There are** several syntactic devices that let you manage where in a sentence you locate units of new information.

Experienced writers regularly use *there* at the beginning of a paragraph to introduce concepts that they develop in sentences that follow. Any delay adds emphasis to what follows, especially "there" constructions. They regularly appear at the beginnings of paragraphs and sections to announce a new topic—which emphasizes it (for more on introducing new concepts, see Epilogue One).

3. ***What*-shift**   This is another device that shifts a part of the sentence to the right:

> We need a monetary policy that would end fluctuations in money supply, unemployment, and inflation.
>
> ✓ **What** we need **is** a monetary policy that would end fluctuations in money supply, unemployment, and inflation.

4. ***It*-shift**   When you have a subject consisting of a long NOUN CLAUSE, you can move it to the end of the sentence and start with an *it:*

> **That oil prices would be set by OPEC** once seemed inevitable.
>
> ✓ *It* once seemed inevitable **that oil prices would be set by OPEC.**

5. ***Not only X, but Y (as well)***   In this next pair, note how the *but* emphasizes the last element of the pair:

> We must clarify these issues and **develop trust.**
>
> ✓ We must *not only* clarify these issues, *but* **develop trust.**

Unless you have reason to emphasize the negative, end with the positive:

> The point is to highlight our success, **not to emphasize our failures.**
>
> ✓ The point is not to emphasize our failures but **to highlight our success.**

The cost of these five devices is a few extra words, so use them sparingly.

6. **Repeated words and pronoun substitution**   This is a fine point: a sentence can end flatly if you repeat a word that you used just a few words before at the end of a sentence, because the voice we hear in our mind's ear drops off at the end of a sentence. If you read aloud the preceding sentence, this one, and the next, you can hear that drop at the end the sentence. To avoid that kind of flatness, rewrite or use a pronoun instead of repeating the word at the end of the sentence. For example:

> A sentence will seem to end flatly if you use a word at its end that you used just a few words before, because when you repeat that word, your voice **drops.** Instead of repeating the noun, use a **pronoun.** The reader will at least hear emphasis on the word just **before** *it.*

Exercise 6.1

Revise these sentences to emphasize the right words. In the first three, I boldfaced what I think should be stressed. Then eliminate wordiness, nominalizations, etc.

1. The judiciary's tendency **to rewrite the Constitution** is the biggest danger to the nation, in my opinion, at least.

2. A new political philosophy that could affect our society **well into the twenty-first century** may emerge from these studies.

3. There are **limited** opportunities for faculty to work with individual students in large American colleges and universities.

4. Building suburban housing developments in floodplains has led to the existence of extensive and widespread flooding and economic disaster in parts of our country in recent years, it is now clear.

5. The teacher who makes an assignment of a long final term paper at the end of the semester and who then gives only a grade and nothing else such as a critical comment is a common object of complaint among students at the college level.

6. Renting textbooks rather than buying them for basic required courses such as mathematics, foreign languages, and English, whose textbooks do not go through yearly changes, is feasible, however, economically speaking.

Exercise 6.2

Revise these passages so that their sentences begin with appropriate topics and end with appropriate emphasis.

1. The story of King Lear and his daughters was a popular one during the reign of Queen Elizabeth. At least a dozen available books offered the story to anyone wishing to read it, by the time Elizabeth died. The characters were undeveloped in most of these stories, however, making

the story a simple narrative that stated an obvious moral. When he began work on *Lear*, perhaps his greatest tragedy, Shakespeare must have had several versions of this story available to him. He turned the characters into credible human beings with complex motives, however, even though they were based on the stock figures of legend.

2. Whether the date an operation intends to close down might be part of management's "duty to disclose" during contract bargaining is the issue here, it would appear. The minimization of conflict is the central rationale for the duty that management has to bargain in good faith. In order to allow the union to put forth proposals on be-half of its members, companies are obligated to disclose major changes in an operation during bargaining, though the case law is scanty on this matter.

3. Athens' catastrophic Sicilian Invasion is the most impor-tant event in Thucydides' *History of the Peloponnesian War*. Three-quarters of the history is devoted to setting up the invasion because of this. Through the step-by-step decline in Athenian society that Thucydides describes, we can see how he chose to anticipate the Sicilian Inva-sion. The inevitability that we associate with the tragic drama is the basic reason for the need to anticipate the invasion.

This next passage will seem difficult because it deals with a strange subject. But even if you don't understand the words, you can still make it more readable.

4. Mucosal and vascular permeability altered by a toxin elaborated by the vibrio is a current hypothesis to ex-plain this kind of severe condition. Changes in small cap-illaries located near the basal surface of the epithelial cells, and the appearance of numerous microvesicles in the cytoplasm of the mucosal cells are evidence in favor of this hypothesis. Hydrodynamic transport of fluid into the interstitial tissue and then through the mucosa into the lumen of the gut is believed to depend on altered cap-illary permeability.

Revise this next passage so that the most important data are stressed.

5. Changes in revenues are as follows. An increase to $56,792 from $32,934, a net increase of approximately 73 percent, was realized July 1–August 31 in the Ohio and Kentucky areas. In the Indiana and Illinois areas there was in the same period a 10 percent increase of $15,370, from $153,281 to $168,651. However, a decrease to $190,580 from $200,102, or 5 percent, occurred in the Wisconsin and Minnesota regions in almost the same period of time.

Topics, Emphasis, Themes, and Coherence

There is one more function performed by the stress of certain sentences, one that is important in helping readers think a passage is coherent. As we saw in the last lesson, readers take the clearest topic to be a short noun phrase that comes early in a sentence, usually as its subject. That's why most of us judge this next paragraph to be unfocused: its sentences do not open from any consistent point of view. After you read this passage, skim its topics:

1a. Great strides in the early and accurate diagnosis of Alzheimer's disease have been made in recent years. Not too long ago, senility in an older patient who seemed to be losing touch with reality was often confused with Alzheimer's. Genetic clues have become the basis of newer and more reliable tests in the last few years, however. The risk of human tragedy of another kind, though, has resulted from the increasing accuracy of these tests: predictions about susceptibility to Alzheimer's have become possible, long before the appearance of any overt symptoms. At that point, an apparently healthy person could be devastated by such an early diagnosis.

If we revise that passage to make the topics more consistent, we make it more coherent:

✓1b. In recent years, **researchers** have made great strides in the early and accurate diagnosis of Alzheimer's disease. Not too long ago, when **a physician** examined an older patient who seemed out of touch with reality, **she** had to guess whether the **person** was senile or had Alzheimer's. In the past few years, however, **physicians** have been able to use new and more reliable tests focusing on genetic clues. But in **the accuracy of these new tests** lies the risk of another kind of human tragedy: **physicians** may be able to predict Alzheimer's long before its overt appearance, but **such an early diagnosis** could psychologically devastate an apparently healthy person.

The topics in that passage now focus on just two topics: researcher/physicians and testing/diagnosis.

But there is one more revision that would make that passage even more of a whole. This passage is not centrally about advances in diagnosis, as stated in the first sentence, but about their potential risks. That concept, however, does not appear in that paragraph until we are more than halfway through it.

Readers would understand that passage better if its key concepts appeared in the first sentence, and (here is where it gets tricky) *specifically toward the end of that opening sentence.* Readers read the opening sentence or two of a paragraph to find the key concepts that the paragraph will repeat and develop, *and they look for those concepts in the last few words of that opening.*

A new first sentence for the Alzheimer's paragraph would help readers pull the whole passage together around the key concepts not just of *Alzheimer's* and *new diagnoses,* but the concepts *new problem* and *informing those most at risk.*

> In recent years, though researchers have made great strides in the early and accurate diagnosis of Alzheimer's disease, those **diagnoses** have raised **a new problem** about **informing those most at risk before they show symptoms of it.**

We can call those key words that run through a passage its *themes.*

Look at the highlighted words in the passage below one more time:

- The boldfaced words are all about testing.
- The italicized words are all about mental states.
- The capitalized words are all about a new problem.

Each of those concepts is announced toward the end of a new opening sentence, especially the theme of the new problem.

> ✓1b. In recent years, though researchers have made great strides in the early and accurate **diagnosis** of *Alzheimer's disease,* those **diagnoses** have raised A NEW PROBLEM about INFORMING THOSE *MOST AT RISK* BEFORE THEY SHOW *SYMPTOMS OF IT*. Not too long ago, when a physician examined an older patient who seemed *out of touch with reality,* she had to **guess** whether that person had *Alzheimer's* or was

only senile. In the past few years, however, physicians have been able to use **new and more reliable tests** focusing on genetic clues. But in the accuracy of these **new tests** lies the RISK OF ANOTHER KIND OF HUMAN TRAGEDY: physicians may be able to **predict** *Alzheimer's* long before its overt appearance, but such an early **diagnosis** could PSYCHOLOGICALLY DEVASTATE AN APPARENTLY HEALTHY PERSON.

That passage now "hangs together" not for just one reason, but for three:

- Its topics consistently focus on physicians and diagnosis.
- Running through it are strings of words that focus on the themes of (1) tests, (2) mental conditions, and (3) a new problem.
- *And no less important, the opening sentence prepares us to notice those themes by emphasizing them at the end of its opening sentence.*

This principle applies not just to sentences that introduce individual paragraphs, but to sentences that introduce passages of any length: *locate at the end of an introductory sentence words that announce the key concepts that you intend to develop in the rest of the passage.* We will return to this question in Epilogue One.

Here's the point: We depend on concepts running through a passage to create a sense of coherence. You help readers identify those concepts in two ways:

- Repeat them as topics of sentences, usually as subjects.
- Repeat them as themes elsewhere in a passage in nouns, verbs, and adjectives.

Readers are more likely to notice those themes if you state them at the end of the sentence that introduces a passage, in its stress position.

Exercise 6.3

Here are three opening sentences and the rest of a paragraph that each of those sentences might introduce. Which introductory sentence best sets up the ideas that follow? Assume that the reader would be already familiar with the characters—Russian rulers. The best of the three sentences will in its last few words highlight the new concepts that we associate with those rulers.

1. The next century the situation changed, because disputes over succession to the throne caused some sort of palace revolt or popular revolution in **seven out of eight reigns of the Romanov line after Peter the Great.**

2. The next century the situation changed, because after Peter the Great seven out of eight reigns of the Romanov line were **plagued by turmoil over disputed succession to the throne.**

3. Because turmoil over disputed succession to the throne plagued seven out of eight reigns of the Romanov line after Peter the Great, **the situation changed in the next century.**

The problems began in 1722, when Tsar Peter the Great passed a law of succession that terminated the principle of succession by heredity and required the sovereign to appoint a successor when he died. But because many of the tsars, including Peter, died before they named successors, those who aspired to rule had no authority by appointment, and so their succession was often disputed by the boyars, lower-level aristocrats. There was turmoil even when successors were appointed. In 1740, Ivan VI was adopted by Czarina Anna Ivanovna and named as her successor at age two months, but his succession was challenged by Elizabeth, daughter of Peter the Great. In 1741, she defeated Anna and ascended to the throne herself. In 1797 Paul tried to eliminate these disputes by codifying a law: primogeniture in the male line. But turmoil continued. Paul was strangled by conspirators, one of whom was probably his son, Alexander I.

SUMMING UP

1. Use the end of a sentence to introduce long, complex, or otherwise difficult-to-process material, particularly unfamiliar technical terms and new information.

A determination of involvement of lipid-linked saccharides in the assembly of oligosaccharide chains of ovalbumin *in vivo* was the principal aim of this study. ***In vitro* and *in vivo* studies utilizing oviduct membrane preparations and oviduct slices and the antibiotic tunicamycin** were undertaken to accomplish this.

✓ The principal aim of this study was to determine how **lipid-linked saccharides are involved in the assembly of oligosaccharide chains of ovalbumin *in vivo*.** To accomplish this, studies were undertaken *in vitro* **and *in vivo*, utilizing the antibiotic tunicamycin on preparations of oviduct membrane and on oviduct slices.**

2. Use the stress position at the very end to emphasize words that you want your readers to hear emphasized in their minds' ear:

    The administration has blurred an issue central to arms control, **the issue of verification.** Irresponsible charges, innuendo, and leaks have submerged **serious problems with Iranian compliance.**

    The issue of verification—so central to arms control—has been **blurred by the administration.** Serious problems with Iranian compliance have been submerged in **irresponsible charges, innuendo, and leaks.**

3. Use the stress of a sentence that introduces a passage to announce the key concepts that the rest of the passage will develop:

    In recent years, though researchers have made great strides in the early and accurate diagnosis of *Alzheimer's disease*, those better **diagnoses** have raised A NEW PROBLEM in regard to INFORMING THOSE MOST AT *RISK* BEFORE THEY SHOW *SYMPTOMS* OF IT. Not too long ago, when a physician examined an older patient who seemed out of touch with reality, she had to **guess** whether that person was senile or had *Alzheimer's*. In the past few years, however, they have been able to use **new and more reliable tests** focusing on genetic clues. But in the accuracy of these **new tests** lies the RISK OF ANOTHER KIND OF HUMAN TRAGEDY: physicians may be able to **predict** *Alzheimer's* long before its overt appearance, but such an early **diagnosis** could PSYCHOLOGICALLY DEVASTATE AN APPARENTLY HEALTHY PERSON.

SUMMARY: PART 2

A simple English sentence is more than the sum of its words; it is a system of systems.

Fixed	Topic	Stress
Variable	Short, simple, familiar	New, long, complex
Fixed	Subject	Verb	———
Variable	Character	Action	———

Readers prefer sentences that reflect those principles.

1. They want to get to the subject of a main clause quickly, so avoid opening more than a few sentences with long, complex phrases and subordinate clauses.

2. They want to get past the subject of a main clause to a verb quickly.

   a. Keep subjects short and, if you can, concrete—ideally flesh-and-blood characters.

   b. Open sentences with familiar information.

3. Readers deal with complexity more easily at the end of a sentence, so put there information that they will find least familiar, most complex, most difficult to understand.

4. They are confused when in a series of sentences each opens with a different subject, so through a passage, focus on a few topics that define what that passage is centrally "about."

Underlying all that is this one simple principle: readers want sentences to open with subjects that are short, clear, simple, concrete, and familiar. Right after that short subject, they want to see a verb that expresses an important action. They want to see that pattern not just in the main clause of a sentence, but in every subordinate clause as well.

PART THREE

Grace

There are two sorts of eloquence; the one indeed scarce
deserves the name of it, which consists chiefly in
laboured and polished periods, an over-curious and
artificial arrangement of figures, tinseled over with a
gaudy embellishment of words. . . . The other sort of
eloquence is quite the reverse to this, and which may be
said to be the true characteristic of the holy Scriptures;
where the eloquence does not arise from a laboured
and farfetched elocution, but from a surprising mixture
of simplicity and majesty.
—LAURENCE STERNE

Concision

I write for those who judge of books, not by the quantity,
but by the quality of them: who ask not how long,
but how good they are? I spare both my reader's time
and my own, by couching my sense
in as few words as I can.
—JOHN WESLEY

Often I think writing is sheer paring away of oneself
leaving always something thinner, barer, more meager.
—F. SCOTT FITZGERALD

The ability to simplify means to eliminate the unnecessary
so that the necessary may speak.
—HANS HOFMANN

To a Snail: If "compression is the first grace of style," you have it.
—MARIANNE MOORE

UNDERSTANDING CONCISION

You are close to clarity when you match CHARACTERS and ACTIONS to SUBJECTS and VERBS, and closer yet when you get the right characters into TOPICS and the right words under STRESS. But readers may still think your prose is a long way from graceful if it's anything like this:

> In my personal opinion, it is necessary that we should not ignore the opportunity to think over each and every suggestion offered.

That writer matched characters with subjects, and actions with verbs, but in too many words: opinion is always personal, so we don't need *personal,* and since this whole statement is opinion, we don't even need *in my opinion. Think over* means *consider. Each and every* is redundant. A suggestion is by definition offered, and *not ignore* means *consider.* In fewer words,

✓ We should consider each suggestion.

Though not elegant, that sentence at least has style's first grace—that of compression, or as we'll call it, *concision.* Concision, though, is only a start. You must still make your sentences shapely. In this lesson, I focus on concision; in the next, on shape.

DIAGNOSIS AND REVISION

Five Principles of Concision

When I edited that sentence about suggestions, I applied five principles:

1. Delete words that mean little or nothing.
2. Delete words that repeat the meaning of other words.
3. Delete words implied by other words.
4. Replace a phrase with a word.
5. Change negatives to affirmatives.

Those principles are easy to state but hard to follow, because you have to inch your way through every word in every sentence you write, cutting here, compressing there, and that's labor-intensive. Those five principles, though, can guide you in that work.

1. Delete Meaningless Words   Some words are verbal tics that we use as unconsciously as we clear our throats:

| kind of | actually | particular | really | certain | various |
| virtually | individual | basically | generally | given | practically |

Productivity **actually** depends on **certain** factors that **basically** involve psychology more than **any particular** technology.

✓ Productivity depends on psychology more than on technology.

2. Delete Doubled Words   Early in the history of English, writers often paired a French or Latin word with a native English one, because foreign words sounded more learned. Now they are just redundant. Among the common pairs:

full and complete	hope and trust	any and all
true and accurate	each and every	basic and fundamental
hopes and desires	first and foremost	various and sundry

3. Delete What Readers Can Infer   This is a common redundancy but hard to identify, because it comes in so many forms.

Redundant Modifiers   Often, the meaning of a word implies its modifier:

Do not try to *predict* those **future** events that will **completely** *revolutionize* society, because **past** *history* shows that it is the **final** *outcome* of minor events that **unexpectedly** *surprises* us more.

✓ Do not try to predict revolutionary events, because history shows that the outcome of minor events surprises us more.

Some common redundancies:

terrible tragedy	various different	free gift
basic fundamentals	future plans	each individual
final outcome	true facts	consensus of opinion

Redundant Categories   Every word implies its general category, so you can usually cut a word that names it. Compare (the category is boldfaced):

During that *period* **of time,** the *membrane* **area** became *pink* **in color** and *shiny* **in appearance.**

✓ During that *period,* the *membrane* became *pink* and *shiny.*

When you do that, you may have to change an ADJECTIVE into an
ADVERB:

> The holes must be aligned in an *accurate* **manner.**
> ✓ The holes must be aligned *accurately.*

Sometimes you change an adjective into a NOUN:

> The county manages the *educational* **system** and *public recreational*
> **activities.**
> ✓ The county manages *education* and *public recreation.*

Here are some general nouns (boldfaced) often used redundantly:

large in **size**	round in **shape**	honest in **character**
unusual in **nature**	of a strange **type**	**area** of mathematics
of a bright **color**	at an early **time**	in a confused **state**

General Implications   This kind of wordiness is even harder
to spot because it can be so diffuse:

> Imagine someone trying to learn the rules for playing chess.

Learn implies *trying, playing a game* implies *rules.* More concisely,

> Imagine learning the rules of chess.

4. Replace a Phrase with a Word   This redundancy is especially
difficult to fix, because you need a big vocabulary and the wit to
use it. For example:

> As you carefully read what you have written to improve wording and
> catch errors of spelling and punctuation, the thing to do before any-
> thing else is to see whether you could use sequences of subjects and
> verbs instead of the same ideas expressed in nouns.

That is,

> ✓ As you edit, first replace nominalizations with clauses.

I compressed five phrases into five words:

carefully read what you have written	→	edit
the thing to do before anything else	→	first
use X instead of Y	→	replace
nouns instead of verbs	→	nominalizations
sequences of subjects and verbs	→	clauses

I can offer no principle to tell you when to replace a phrase with a word, much less give you the word. I can point out only that you often can, and that you should be alert for opportunities to do so—which is to say, try.

Here are some common phrases (boldfaced) to watch for. Note that some of these let you turn a nominalization into a verb (both italicized):

We must explain **the reason for** the *delay* in the meeting.

✓ We must explain **why** the meeting is *delayed.*

Despite the fact that the data were checked, errors occurred.

✓ **Even though** the data were checked, errors occurred.

In the event that you finish early, contact this office.

✓ **If** you finish early, contact this office.

In a situation where a class is closed, you may petition for admission.

✓ **When** a class is closed, you may petition for admission.

I want to say a few words **concerning the matter of** money.

✓ I want to say a few words **about** money.

There is a need for more careful *inspection* of all welds.

✓ You **must** *inspect* all welds more carefully.

We **are in a position** to make you an offer.

✓ We **can** make you an offer.

It is possible that nothing will come of this.

✓ Nothing **may** come of this.

Prior to the *end* of the training, apply for your license.

✓ **Before** training *ends,* apply for your license.

We have noted a **decrease/increase in** the number of errors.

✓ We have noted *fewer/more* errors.

5. Change Negatives to Affirmatives   When you express an idea in a negative form, not only must you use an extra word: *same* → *not different,* but you also force readers to do a kind of algebraic factoring. These two sentences, for example, mean much the same thing, but the affirmative is more direct:

> Do not write in the negative. → Write in the affirmative.

Do not translate a negative into an affirmative if you want to emphasize the negative. (Is that such a sentence? I could have written, *Keep a negative sentence when . . .*) But you can rewrite most negatives, some formulaically:

not different	→	similar	not many	→	few
not the same	→	different	not often	→	rarely
not allow	→	prevent	not stop	→	continue
not notice	→	overlook	not include	→	omit

Some verbs, prepositions, and conjunctions are implicitly negative:

Verbs	*preclude, prevent, lack, fail, doubt, reject, avoid, deny, refuse, exclude, contradict, prohibit, bar*
Prepositions	*without, against, lacking, but for, except*
Conjunctions	*unless, except when*

You can baffle readers if you combine *not* with these negative words. Compare these:

> **Except** when applicants have **failed** to submit applications **without** documentation, benefits will **not** be **denied.**

✓ You will receive benefits only if you submit your documents.

✓ To receive benefits, submit your documents.

And you baffle readers completely when you combine explicitly and implicitly negative words with passives and nominalizations:

> There should be **no** submission of payments **without** notification of this office, **unless** the payment does **not** exceed $100.

> Do not **submit** payments if you have not **notified** this office, unless you are **paying** less than $100.

Now revise the negatives into affirmatives:

✓ If you pay more than $100, notify this office first.

> ***Here's the point:***   Readers think you write clearly when you use only the words you need to say what you mean.

1. Delete words that mean little or nothing.
2. Delete words that repeat the meaning of other words.
3. Delete words implied by other words.
4. Replace a phrase with a word.
5. Change negatives to affirmatives.

Exercise 7.1

Prune the redundancy from these sentences.

1. Critics cannot avoid employing complex and abstract technical terms if they are to successfully analyze literary texts and discuss them in a meaningful way.

2. Scientific research generally depends on fully accurate data if it is to offer theories that will allow us to predict the future in a plausible way.

3. In regard to desirable employment in teaching jobs, prospects for those engaged in graduate-school-level studies are at best not certain.

4. Notwithstanding the fact that all legal restrictions on the use of firearms are the subject of heated debate and argument, it is necessary that the general public not stop carrying on discussions pro and con in regard to them.

5. Most likely, a majority of all patients who appear at a public medical clinical facility do not expect special medical attention or treatment, because their particular health problems and concerns are often not major and for the most part can usually be adequately treated without much time, effort, and attention.

Where appropriate, change the following negatives to affirmatives, and do any more editing you think useful.

6. Except when expenses do not exceed $250, the Insured may not refuse to provide the Insurer with receipts, checks, or other evidence of costs.

7. There is no possibility in regard to a reduction in the size of the federal deficit if reductions in federal spending are not introduced.

8. Do not discontinue medication unless symptoms of dizziness and nausea are not present for six hours.

9. No one should be prevented from participating in cost-sharing educational programs without a full hearing into the reasons for his or her not being accepted.

10. No agreement exists on the question of an open or closed universe, a dispute about which no resolution is likely as long as a computation of the total mass of the universe has not been done.

11. So long as taxpayers do not engage in widespread refusal to pay taxes, the government will have no difficulty in paying its debts.

12. No alternative exists in this country to the eventual development of tar sand, oil shale, and coal as sources of fuel, if we wish to stop being energy dependent on imported oil.

13. Not until a resolution between Catholics and Protestants in regard to the authority of papal supremacy is reached will there be a start to a reconciliation between these two Christian religions.

Exercise 7.2

Here are two actual sentences from two "free" offers.

> You will not be charged our first monthly fee unless you don't cancel within the first thirty days.

> To avoid being charged your first monthly fee, cancel your membership before your free trial ends.

Which is less clear? Why might it have been written like that? Revise it.

A Particular Kind of Redundancy: Metadiscourse

In Lesson Four, I described METADISCOURSE as language we use to refer to

- the writer's intentions: *to sum up, candidly, I believe*
- the writer's confidence: *may, perhaps, certainly, must*
- directions to the reader: *note that, consider now, as you see*
- the structure of the text: *first, second, finally, therefore, however*

Everything you write needs metadiscourse, but too much buries your ideas:

> The last point I would like to make is that in regard to men-women relationships, it is important to keep in mind that the greatest changes have occurred in how they work together.

Only nine words in that sentence address men-women relationships:

> men-women relationships . . . greatest changes . . . how they work together.

The rest is metadiscourse:

> The last point I would like to make is that in regard to . . . it is important to keep in mind that . . .

When we prune metadiscourse, we tighten the sentence:

> The greatest changes in men-women relationships have occurred in how they work together.

Now that we see what the sentence says, we can make it still more direct:

> ✓ Finally, men and women have changed their relationships most in how they work together.

Some teachers and editors urge us to cut all metadiscourse, but everything we write needs some. You have to read with an eye to how good writers in your field use it, then do likewise. There are, however, some types that you can usually cut.

Metadiscourse That Attributes Your Ideas to a Source   Don't announce that something has been anonymously *observed, noticed, noted,* and so on; just state the fact:

> High divorce rates **have been observed** to occur in areas that **have been determined to have** low population density.
> ✓ High divorce rates occur in areas with low population density.

Metadiscourse That Announces Your Topic   The boldface phrases tell your reader what your sentence is "about":

> **This section introduces another** problem, that of noise pollution.
> **The first thing to say about it is** that noise pollution exists not
> only . . .

You help readers catch a topic more easily if you reduce the
metadiscourse:

> ✓ **Another** problem is noise pollution. **First**, it exists not only . . .

You can use two other constructions to call attention to a word
or phrase, usually mentioned at least once before:

> **In regard to** a vigorous style, the most important feature is a short,
> concrete subject followed by a forceful verb.
>
> **So far as** China's industrial development **is concerned,** it will take
> only a few years to equal that of Japan.

But you can usually get those topics into a subject:

> ✓ The most important feature of a vigorous style is a short, concrete
> subject followed by a forceful verb.
>
> ✓ China will take only a few years to equal Japan's industrial devel-
> opment.

Look hard at a sentence opening with a metadiscourse subject
and verb that merely announce a topic:

> In this essay, **I will discuss** the role of metaphor in style.

I write that kind of sentence when I have no idea where I am going, saying in effect, "I have this topic and hope I eventually think
of something to say about it." On the other hand, that kind of sentence in a professional journal promises to develop what it names.

Excessive Hedging and Intensifying This kind of metadiscourse can not only be redundant, but influence how readers judge
your character, because it signals how well you balance caution
and confidence.

> *Hedges* These are common hedges:

Adverbs	*usually, often, sometimes, almost, virtually, possibly, perhaps, apparently, in some ways, to a certain extent, somewhat, in some/certain respects*
Adjectives	*most, many, some, a certain number of*
Verbs	*may, might, can, could, seem, tend, appear, suggest, indicate*

Some readers think all hedging is not just redundant, but mealy-mouthed:

> There **seems to be some** evidence to **suggest** that **certain** differences between Japanese and Western rhetoric **could** derive from historical influences **possibly** traceable to Japan's cultural isolation and Europe's history of cross-cultural contacts.

On the other hand, only a fool or someone with massive historical evidence would make an assertion as flatly confident as this:

> This evidence **proves** that Japanese and Western rhetorics differ because of Japan's cultural isolation and Europe's history of cross-cultural contacts.

In thoughtful academic writing, we more often state claims closer to this (and look at that for my own hedging; compare the more assertive, *In academic writing, we state claims like this*):

> ✓ This evidence **suggests** that **aspects** of Japanese and Western rhetoric differ because of Japan's cultural isolation and Europe's history of cross-cultural contacts.

This next paragraph introduced the article announcing the most significant breakthrough in the history of genetics, the discovery of the double helix of DNA. If anyone was entitled to be assertive, it was Crick and Watson. But they chose to be diffident, to hedge (note, too, the first person *we;* hedges are boldfaced):

> We **wish to suggest a** [note that they did not say *the*] structure for the salt of deoxyribose nucleic **acid** (D.N.A.) . . . A structure for nucleic acid has already been proposed by Pauling and Corey . . . **In our opinion,** this structure is unsatisfactory for two reasons: (1) **We believe** that the material which gives the X-ray diagrams is the salt, not the free acid . . . (2) **Some** of the van der Waals distances **appear** to be too small.
>
> —J. D. Watson and F. H. C. Crick,
> "Molecular Structure of Nucleic Acids"

Without the hedges, their claim would be more concise but more aggressive. Compare this (I boldface my stronger words, but most of the more aggressive tone comes from the absence of hedges):

> We ~~wish to suggest~~ **state the** structure for the salt of deoxyribose nucleic acid (D.N.A.) . . . A structure for nucleic acid has already been proposed by Pauling and Corey . . . ~~In our opinion,~~ this structure is unsatisfactory for two reasons: (1) ~~We believe that~~ the material which

gives the X-ray diagrams is the salt, not the free acid . . . (2) ~~Some of~~ the van der Waals distances ~~appear to be~~ **are** too small.

You can use the verbs *suggest* and *indicate* instead of *prove* or *show* to make a claim about which you are less than 100 percent certain, but confident enough to propose:

✓ The evidence **indicates** that some of these questions remain unresolved.

✓ These data **suggest** that further studies are necessary.

Intensifiers   These are common intensifiers:

Adverbs	*very, pretty, quite, rather, clearly, obviously, undoubtedly, certainly, of course, indeed, inevitably, invariably, always*
Adjectives	*key, central, crucial, basic, fundamental, major, principal, essential*
Verbs	*show, prove, establish, as you/we/everyone knows/can see, it is clear/obvious that*

Confident writers use intensifiers less often than they use hedges because they want to avoid sounding as assertive as this:

For a century now, **all** liberals have argued against **any** censorship of art, and **every** court has found their arguments so **completely** persuasive that **not a** person **any** longer remembers how they were countered. As a result, today, censorship is **totally** a thing of the past.

Some inexperienced writers think that an aggressive style is persuasive. Quite the opposite: If you state a claim moderately, readers are more likely to consider it thoughtfully:

For **about** a century now, **many** liberals have argued against censorship of art, and **most** courts have found their arguments persuasive **enough** that **few** people **may** remember **exactly** how they were countered. As a result, today, censorship is **virtually** a thing of the past.

Some claim that a passage hedged that much is wordy and weak. Perhaps. But it does not come on like a bulldozer. It leaves room for a reasoned and equally moderate response. In fact, in some academic areas, readers assume that if you begin with *It is obvious . . .* , what you then say is not.

The most common intensifier is the absence of a hedge. In this case, less is more. The first sentence below has no intensifiers at the blanks, but neither does it have any hedges, and so it seems like a strong claim:

> _____ Americans believe that the federal government is _____ intrusive and _____ authoritarian.

> **Many** Americans believe that the federal government is **often** intrusive and **increasingly** authoritarian.

Here's the point: You need some metadiscourse in everything you write, especially metadiscourse that guides readers through your text, words such as _first, second, therefore, on the other hand,_ and so on. You also need some metadiscourse that hedges your certainty, words such as _perhaps, seems, could,_ and so on. The risk is that you can easily use too many.

Exercise 7.3

Here are sentences that announce a topic rather than state a thesis. Delete the metadiscourse and rewrite what remains. Then decide whether the full statement makes a claim that readers would want to read about. For example:

> In this study, I examine the history of Congressional legislation regarding the protection of children in the workplace.

First, delete the metadiscourse:

> . . . the history of Congressional legislation regarding the protection of children in the workplace.

Then rewrite what is left into a full sentence:

> ✓ Congress has legislated the protection of children in the workplace.

That appears to be a self-evident, uninteresting claim.

1. This essay will survey research in schemata theory as applied to the pedagogy of mathematical problem solving.

2. I will analyze Frost's use of imagery of seasons in his longer poems published at the end of his career.

3. The methodological differences between English and American histories of the War of 1812 resulting in radically differing interpretations of the cause of the conflict are the topic of this study.

4. In this essay, I analyze the mistaken assumption underlying Freud's interpretation of dreams.

5. We will consider scientific thinking and its historical roots in connection with the influence of Egypt on Greek thought.

6. This article discusses needle sharing among drug users.

7. The relationship between birth order and academic success will be explored.

8. I intend to address the problem of the reasons for the failure and success of trade embargoes in this century.

Exercise 7.4

Edit these for both unnecessary metadiscourse and redundancy.

1. But on the other hand, we can perhaps point out that there may always be TV programming to appeal to our most prurient and, therefore, lowest interests.

2. In this particular section, I intend to discuss my position about the possible need to dispense with the standard approach to plea bargaining. I believe this for two reasons. The first reason is that there is the possibility of letting hardened criminals avoid receiving their just punishment. The second reason is the following: plea bargaining seems to encourage a growing lack of respect for the judicial system.

3. Turning now to the next question, there is in regard to wilderness area preservation activities one basic principle when attempting to formulate a way of approaching decisions about unspoiled areas to be set aside as not open to development for commercial exploitation.

4. It is my belief that in regard to terrestrial-type snakes, an assumption can be made that there are probably none in

unmapped areas of the world surpassing the size of those we already have knowledge of.

5. Depending on the particular position that one takes on this question, the educational system has taken on a degree of importance that may be equal to or perhaps even exceed the family as a major source of transmission of social values.

Productive Redundancy

Learning by Writing   Some teachers think any redundancy signals mental laziness. But we inevitably fall into some redundancy when we write about a subject that we are just learning. We signal membership in a community by what we say and how we say it, but a surer sign is what we know to leave unsaid—our community's common knowledge. Unfortunately, learning what not to say takes time.

Here, for example, is a paragraph by a student who was a good undergraduate writer (I checked). But he was writing his first paper in a new community, law school:

> It is my opinion that the ruling of the lower court concerning the case of *Haslem v. Lockwood* should be upheld, thereby denying the appeal of the plaintiff. The main point supporting my point of view on this case concerns the tenet of our court system which holds that in order to win his case, the plaintiff must prove that he was somehow wronged by the defendant. The burden of proof rests on the plaintiff. He must show enough evidence to convince the court that he is in the right.

To his legal writing teacher, everything after the first comma was redundant: *Obviously* if a court upholds a ruling, it denies the appeal; *obviously* the plaintiff can win only if he proves a defendant has wronged him; *obviously* the plaintiff has the burden of proof; *obviously* the plaintiff has to provide evidence. But at this early stage in his career, this writer was an outsider learning his community's common knowledge and so could not resist rehearsing it.

Metadiscourse about Thinking and Writing   Just as "belaboring the obvious" signals a writer new to a field, so does using metadiscourse to narrate one's thinking. When we are comfortable thinking through familiar problems, we don't have to narrate our mental life. But when we are inexperienced, we often feel compelled to give a running commentary about what we thought and did.

Look again at that paragraph by the first-year law student. Not only did he "belabor the obvious," he recorded some of his thinking. I boldface metadiscourse and italicize the self-evident:

> **It is my opinion that** *the ruling of the lower court concerning* the case of Haslem v. Lockwood should be upheld, *thereby denying the appeal of the plaintiff.* **The main point supporting my point of view on this case concerns** *the tenet of our court system which holds that in order to win his case, the plaintiff must prove that he was somehow wronged by the defendant. The burden of proof rests on the plaintiff. He must show enough evidence to convince the court that he is in the right.*

When we delete the mental narrative and commonplaces, we are left with something leaner:

> *Haslem* should be affirmed. Plaintiff failed his burden of proof.

Concise, Not Terse

Having stressed concision so strongly, I must now step back. Readers don't like flab, but neither do they like a style so terse that it's all gristle and bone. Here is some amiable advice from the most widely read book on style, Strunk and White's *The Elements of Style:*

> Revising is part of writing. Few writers are so expert that they can produce what they are after on the first try. Quite often you will discover, on examining the completed work, that there are serious flaws in the arrangement of the material, calling for transpositions. When that is the case, a word processor can save you time and labor as you rearrange the manuscript. You can select material on the screen and move it to a more appropriate spot, or, if you cannot find the right spot, move the material to the end of the manuscript until you decide whether to delete it. Some writers find that working with the printed copy of the manuscript helps them to visualize the process of changes; others prefer to revise entirely on screen. Above all, do not be afraid to experiment with what you have written. Save both the revised and the original versions; you can always use the computer to restore the manuscript to its original condition, should that course seem best. Remember, it is no sign of weakness or defeat

that your manuscript needs major surgery. This is a common occurrence in all writing, and among the best writers. (199 words)

We can shorten that paragraph just by erasing its redundancy:

Revising is part of writing. Few writers ~~are so expert that they can~~ produce what they are after on the first try. ~~Quite~~ Often you will discover, ~~on examining the completed work, that there are~~ serious flaws in ~~the~~ arrangement of the material, ~~calling for transpositions.~~ When that is the case, a word processor can save ~~you~~ time ~~and labor~~ as you rearrange the manuscript. You can select material on the screen and move it to a more appropriate spot, or, if you cannot find the right spot, ~~move the material~~ to the end of the manuscript until you decide whether to delete it. Some writers find that working with the printed ~~copy of the~~ manuscript helps them to visualize ~~the process of~~ changes; others prefer to revise ~~entirely~~ on screen. Above all, do not be afraid to experiment ~~with what you have written.~~ Save both the revised and the original versions; you can always ~~use the computer to~~ restore the manuscript to its original condition, ~~should that course seem best. Remember,~~ It is no sign of weakness ~~or defeat~~ that your manuscript needs ~~major~~ surgery. This is ~~a~~ common ~~occurrence~~ in all writing, and among the best writers. (148 words)

With some rewording, we can cut that version by another third:

Revising is part of writing, because few writers ~~produce what they are after on the first try~~ *write perfect first drafts. If you find* ~~Often you will discover serious~~ flaws in *the* arrangement *of yours,* ~~of the material. When that is the case~~ *use* a word processor ~~can~~ *to* save time ~~as you~~ *to* ~~rearrange the manuscript. You can select material on the screen and~~ move ~~it~~ *text* to a more appropriate spot, or if you cannot find *one* ~~the right spot,~~ to the end ~~of the manuscript~~ until you decide whether to delete it. Some writers find ~~that working with~~ the printed manuscript helps them ~~to~~ visualize changes; others prefer to revise on screen. Above all, do not be afraid to experiment. Save ~~both the revised and~~ the original version; you can always restore the manuscript to its original condition. ~~Remember,~~ it is no sign of weakness that your manuscript needs surgery. This is common in all writing, and among the best writers. (101 words)

And if we cut to the bone, we can shorten it more yet:

Most writers revise because few write a perfect first draft. To rearrange, move its parts around on a computer. You can always restore them. Even great writers revise, so if your manuscript needs surgery, it signals no weakness. (38 words)

But in boiling down Strunk and White's paragraph, I've bleached out its garrulous charm, a tradeoff that many readers would reject.

I can't tell you when you've written so concisely that your readers think you are not just concise but terse, even abrupt. That's why you should listen to what readers say about your writing. They know something you never can; they know how it feels to be your reader.

SUMMING UP

You need more than concision to guarantee grace, but when you clear away deadwood, you can see the shape of a sentence more clearly.

1. Redundant pairs

   If and when we can define our final aims and goals, each and every member of our group will be ready and willing to offer aid and assistance.

   ✓ If we define our goals, we will all be ready to help.

2. Redundant modifiers

   In the business world of today, official governmental red tape seriously destroys initiative among individual businesses.

   ✓ Government red tape destroys business initiative.

3. Redundant categories

   In the area of education, tight financial conditions are forcing school boards to cut nonessential expenses.

   ✓ Tight finances are forcing school boards to cut nonessentials.

4. Meaningless modifiers

   Most students generally find some kind of summer work.

   ✓ Most students find summer work.

5. Obvious implications

   Energy used to power industries and homes will in years to come cost more money.

   ✓ Energy will eventually cost more.

6. A phrase for a word

> A sail-powered craft that has turned on its side or completely over must remain buoyant enough so that it will bear the weight of those individuals who were aboard.

✓ A capsized sailboat must support those on it.

7. Indirect negatives

> There is no reason not to believe that engineering malfunctions in nuclear energy systems cannot be anticipated.

✓ Malfunctions in nuclear energy systems will surprise us.

8. Excessive metadiscourse

> It is almost certainly the case that totalitarian systems cannot allow a society to have what we would define as stable social relationships.

✓ Totalitarianism blocks stable social relationships.

9. Hedges and intensifiers

The only principle here is the Goldilocks rule: not too much, not too little, but just right. That's little help, but this is a matter where you have to develop and then trust your ear.

Too certain:	In my research, **I prove** that people with a gun in their home use it to kill themselves or a family member instead of to protect themselves from an intruder.
Too uncertain:	**Some** of my recent research **seems** to **imply** that there **may** be a **risk** that **certain** people with a gun in their homes **could** be **more prone** to use it to kill themselves or a family member than to protect themselves from **possible** intruders.
Just right?	My research **indicates** that people with a gun in their homes **are more likely** to use it to kill themselves or a family member than they are to protect themselves from an intruder.

8

Shape

The structure of every sentence is a lesson in logic.
—JOHN STUART MILL

Sentences in their variety run from simplicity to complexity,
a progression not necessarily reflected in length: a long sentence
may be extremely simple in construction—indeed must be simple
if it is to convey its sense easily.
—SIR HERBERT READ

A long complicated sentence should force itself upon you,
make you know yourself knowing it.
—GERTRUDE STEIN

You never know what is enough until you know
what is more than enough.
—WILLIAM BLAKE

UNDERSTANDING THE SHAPE OF SENTENCES

Clarity in Complexity

If you can write clear and concise sentences, you have achieved a lot, and much more if you can assemble them into coherent passages. But if you can't write a clear sentence longer than twenty words or so, you're like a composer who can write only jingles. Despite those who tell us not to write long sentences, you cannot communicate every complex idea in short ones, so you have to know how to write a sentence that is both long and clear.

Consider, for example, (1a):

> 1a. In addition to differences in ethnicity or religion that have for centuries plagued Bosnians, Serbs, and Croats, explanations seeking causes of their hatred must include all of the other social, economic, and cultural conflicts that have plagued them that are rooted in a troubled history that extends 1000 years into the past.

Even if that idea needs all those words (it doesn't), they could be arranged in a more shapely sentence.

We can start revising by editing the abstractions into CHARACTER/SUBJECTS and ACTION/VERBS and then break the sentence into shorter ones:

> 1b. Historians have tried to explain why Bosnians, Serbs, and Croats hate one another today. Many have claimed that the sources of conflict are age-old differences in ethnicity or religion. But they must study all the other social, economic, and cultural conflicts that have plagued them through their 1000 years of troubled history.

But if (1a) is shapeless, (1b) is choppy. We need something like this:

> ✓1c. To explain why Bosnians, Serbs, and Croats hate one another today, historians must study not only age-old differences of ethnicity and religion, but all the other social, economic, and cultural conflicts that have plagued them through their 1000 years of troubled history.

That sentence is long but doesn't sprawl. So it can't be length alone that makes a sentence ungainly. In this lesson, I focus on how to write sentences that are not only long and complex but clear and shapely.

DIAGNOSIS AND REVISION

It's easier to see sprawl in the writing of others than in your own because you know what you want your sentences to mean before you read them. So you have to diagnose your prose in ways that sidestep your intractable subjectivity.

Start by putting a slash mark after every period and question mark./Then pick out sentences longer than two lines and read them aloud./If in reading one of your long sentences you feel that you are about to run out of breath before you come to a place where you can pause to integrate all of its parts into a whole that communicates a single conceptual structure [breathe], you have found a sentence your readers would likely want you to revise, like this one./Or if your sentence, because of one interruption after another, seems to stop and start, your readers are, if they are typical, likely to judge that your sentence, as this one does, lurches from one part to the next.

Readers get a sense of shapeless length from three things:

- It takes them too long to get to the verb in the MAIN CLAUSE.
- After the verb, they have to slog through a shapeless sprawl of tacked on SUBORDINATE CLAUSES.
- They hesitate at one interruption after another.

Revising Long Openings

Some sentences seem to take forever to get to the point:

> Since most undergraduate students change their fields of study at least once during their college careers, many more than once, first-year students who are not certain about their program of studies should not load up their schedules to meet requirements for a particular program.

That sentence takes thirty-one words to get to its main verb, *should not load up*. The main claim of a sentence should usually be in the subject and verb of its main clause, so here are two rules of thumb about your sentence's beginning:

1. Get to the subject of the main clause quickly; avoid beginning more than a few sentences with long introductory PHRASES and clauses.

2. Get to the verb and OBJECT of the main clause quickly; avoid long, abstract subjects and interruptions between subjects and verbs and between verbs and their objects.

Rule of Thumb 1: Get to the Subject Quickly   We have a problem with sentences that open with long introductory phrases and clauses, because as we read them, we have to hold in mind that the subject and verb of the main clause are still to come, and that frustrates easy understanding.

Compare these. As we read the first seventeen words in (2a), we have to hold in mind that a subject of a main clause is coming. In (2b), we get past the subjects and verbs of the first two clauses in just a few words.

> 2a. **Since most undergraduate students change their major fields of study at least once during their college careers,** *first-year students* who are not certain about the program of studies they want to pursue SHOULD NOT LOAD UP their schedules to meet requirements for a particular program.

> ✓2b. **Most undergraduate students** CHANGE their major fields at least once during their college careers, so **first-year students** SHOULD NOT LOAD UP their schedules with requirements for a particular program if they are not certain about the program of studies they want to pursue.

If you open with a long introductory clause, try moving it to the end of its sentence or turning it into a sentence of its own.

Rule of Thumb 2: Get to the Verb and Object Quickly   Readers also want to get past the main subject to its verb and object. Therefore,

- keep subjects short,
- avoid interrupting the subject-verb connection,
- avoid interrupting the verb-object connection.

There are two ways to shorten subjects.

> ***Revise Long Subjects into Short Ones***   Start by underlining your WHOLE SUBJECTS. If you find a long subject (more than seven or eight words) including NOMINALIZATIONS, try turning the nominalization into a verb and finding a subject for it (review pp. 38–41):

Abco Inc.'s *understanding* **of the drivers of its profitability in the Asian market for small electronics** helped it pursue opportunities in Africa.

✓ **Abco Inc.** was able to pursue opportunities in Africa because it understood what drove profitability in the Asian market for small electronics.

A subject can also be long if it includes a long RELATIVE CLAUSE:

A company **that focuses on hiring the best personnel and then trains them not just for the work they are hired to do but for higher-level jobs** IS likely to earn the loyalty of its employees.

Try turning the relative clause into an introductory subordinate clause:

✓ **When a company focuses on hiring the best personnel and then trains them not just for the work they are hired to do but for higher-level jobs,** it is likely to earn the loyalty of its employees.

But if the introductory clause turns out to be as long as that one, move it to the end of its sentence, especially if the main clause is short and to the point and the moveable clause expresses newer and more complex information.

✓ A company is likely to earn the loyalty of its employees **when** it focuses on hiring the best personnel and then trains them not just for the work they are hired to do but for higher-level jobs.

Or turn it into a sentence of its own.

✓ Some companies focus on hiring the best personnel and then train them not just for the work they are hired to do but for higher-level jobs later. **Such companies are likely to earn the loyalty of their employees.**

Avoid Interrupting the Subject-Verb Connection   You also frustrate readers when you interrupt the connection between a subject and verb, like this:

Some scientists, **because they write in a style that is impersonal and objective,** do not easily communicate with laypeople.

That *because*-clause after the subject forces us to hold our mental breath until we reach the verb, *do not easily communicate.* Move the interruption to the beginning or end of its sentence, depending on whether it connects more closely to what came before or comes after. (Review pp. 75–76.):

✓ Because some scientists write in a style that is impersonal and objective, they do **not easily communicate with laypeople. This lack of communication** damages . . .

✓ Some scientists do not easily communicate with laypeople because they write in **a style that is impersonal and objective. It is a kind of style** filled with passives and . . .

We mind short interruptions less:

✓ Some scientists **deliberately** write in a style that is impersonal and objective.

Avoid Interrupting the Verb-Object Connection   We also like to get past the verb to its object quickly. This sentence doesn't let us do that:

We must develop, **if we are to become competitive with other companies in our region,** a core of knowledge regarding the state of the art in effective industrial organizations.

Move the interrupting element to the beginning or end of its sentence, depending on what comes next:

✓ **If we are to compete with other companies in our region,** we must develop a core of knowledge about the state of the art in **effective industrial organizations. Such organizations provide . . .**

✓ **We** must develop a core of knowledge about the state of the art in effective industrial organizations **if we are to compete with other companies in our region. Increasing competition . . .**

There is an exception to that advice. When a prepositional phrase you can move is shorter than a long object, try putting the phrase between the verb and object:

In a long sentence, put the newest and most important information that you want your reader to remember **at its end.**

✓ In a long sentence, put **at its end** the newest and most important information that you want your reader to remember.

This is an example of a very general principle that governs more than style: arrange elements in a sentence from short to long, from simple to complex. As we'll see in Epilogue One, it also covers paragraphs, sections, even whole documents.

Here's the point: Readers read most easily when you quickly get them

- to the subject of your main clause and
- past that subject to its verb and object.

Avoid long introductory phrases and clauses, long subjects, and interruptions between subjects and verbs, and between verbs and objects.

Exercise 8.1

These sentences have long introductory phrases and clauses. Revise.

1. Since workfare has not yet been shown to be a successful alternative to welfare because evidence showing its ability to provide meaningful employment for welfare recipients is not yet available, those who argue that all the states should make a full-scale commitment to workfare are premature in their recommendations.

2. While grade inflation has been a subject of debate by teachers and administrators and even in newspapers, employers looking for people with high levels of technical and analytical skills have not had difficulty identifying desirable candidates.

3. Although one way to prevent foreign piracy of videos and CDs is in the criminal justice systems of foreign countries and for cases to move faster through their systems and for stiffer penalties to be imposed, no improvement in the level of expertise of judges who hear these cases is expected any time in the immediate future.

4. Since school officials responsible for setting policy about school security have said that local principals may require students to pass through metal detectors before entering a school building, the need to educate parents and students about the seriousness of bringing onto school property anything that looks like a weapon must be made a part of the total package of school security.

5. If the music industry ignores the problem of how a rating system applied to offensive lyrics could be applied to music broadcast over FM and AM radio, then even if it were willing to discuss a system that could be used in the sale of music in retail stores, the likelihood of any significant improvement in its image with the public is nil.

These sentences have long subjects. Revise.

6. Explaining why Shakespeare decided to have Lady Macbeth die off stage rather than letting the audience see her die has to do with understanding the audience's reactions to Macbeth's death.

7. An agreement by the film industry and by television producers on limiting characters using cigarettes, even if carried out, would do little to discourage young people from smoking.

8. A student's right to have access to his or her own records, including medical records, academic reports, and confidential comments by advisers, will generally take precedence over an institution's desire to keep records private, except when limitations of those rights under specified circumstances are agreed to by students during registration.

These sentences are interrupted. First, eliminate wordiness, then correct the interruption.

9. The construction of the Interstate Highway System, owing to the fact that Congress, on the occasion when it originally voted funds for it, did not anticipate the rising cost of inflation, ran into serious financial problems.

10. Such prejudicial conduct or behavior, regardless of the reasons offered to justify it, is rarely not at least to some degree prejudicial to good order and discipline.

11. TV "reality" shows, because they have an appeal to our fascination with real-life conflict because of our voyeuristic impulses, are about the most popular shows that are regularly scheduled to appear on TV.

12. Insistence that there is no proof by scientific means of a causal link between tobacco consumption and various disease entities such as cardiac heart diseases and malignant growth, despite the fact that there is a strong statistical correlation between smoking behavior and such diseases, is no longer the officially stated position of cigarette companies.

13. The continued and unabated emission of carbon dioxide gas into the atmosphere, unless there is a marked reduction, will eventually result in serious changes in the climate of the world as we know it today.

Reshaping Sprawl

Once readers make the subject-verb-object connection, they can deal with longer, more complex chunks of information that follow. But they don't want to slog through sprawl like this:

Of the many areas of science important to our future, few are more promising than genetic engineering, which is a new way of manipulating the elemental structural units of life itself, which are the genes and chromosomes that tell our cells how to reproduce to become the parts that constitute our bodies.

A sentence sprawls when after the verb and object, it tacks on a series of subordinate clauses of the same kind. It looks like this:

Of the many areas of science important to our future,
[opening phrase]

few are more promising than genetic engineering,
[subject-verb core]

which is a new way of manipulating the elemental structural units of life itself, *[tacked-on relative clause]*

which are the genes and chromosomes
[tacked-on relative clause]

that tell our cells how to reproduce to become the parts
[tacked-on relative clause]

that constitute our bodies. *[tacked-on relative clause]*

Diagnose this problem by having someone read your prose aloud. If that reader gets confused or runs out of breath before getting to the end of a sentence, so will your silent reader. You can revise in three ways:

1. Cut

1. Try reducing some of the relative clauses to phrases by deleting *who/that/which* + *is/was*, etc.:

    ✓ Of the many areas of science important to our future, few are more promising than genetic engineering, ~~which is~~ a new way of manipulating the elemental structural units of life itself, ~~which are~~ the genes and chromosomes that tell our cells how to reproduce to become the parts that constitute our bodies.

    Occasionally, you have to rewrite the remaining verb into an *-ing* form:

    > The day is coming when we will all have numbers **that will identify** our financial transactions so that the IRS can monitor all activities **that involve** economic activity.

    ✓ The day is coming when we will all have numbers ~~that will~~ **identifying** our financial transactions so that the IRS can monitor all activities ~~that~~ **involving** economic activity.

2. Or break the subordinate clauses out into their own sentences.

    ✓ Many areas of science are important to our future, but few are more promising than genetic engineering. It is a new way of manipulating the elemental structural units of life itself, the genes and chromosomes that tell our cells how to reproduce to become the parts that constitute our bodies.

    If none of that works, you have to do some major restructuring.

2. Change Clauses to Modifying Phrases

You can write a long sentence but still avoid sprawl if you change relative clauses to one of three kinds of modifying phrases: resumptive, summative, or free. You have probably never read those terms before, but they refer to stylistic devices you should know how to use.

Resumptive Modifiers   These two examples contrast a relative clause and a resumptive modifier:

> Since mature writers often use resumptive modifiers to extend a sentence, we need a word to name what I have not done in this sentence, **which I could have ended after the word *sentence* but extended to show you a relative clause attached to a noun.**

✓ Since mature writers often use resumptive modifiers to extend a sentence, we need a word to name what I am about to do in this sentence, **a sentence that I could have ended at that comma, but extended to show you how resumptive modifiers work.**

The boldface resumptive modifier repeats a key word and starts again.

To create a resumptive modifier, find a key NOUN just before the tacked on clause, then pause after it with a comma:

> Since mature writers often use resumptive modifiers to extend a sentence, we need a word to name what I am about to do in this **sentence,**

Then repeat the noun:

> Since mature writers often use resumptive modifiers to extend a sentence, we need a word to name what I am about to do in this **sentence,**
>
> **a sentence . . .**

Then to that repeated word add a relative clause beginning with *that:*

> Since mature writers often use resumptive modifiers to extend a sentence, we need a word to name what I am about to do in this sentence,
>
> a sentence **that I could have ended at that comma, but extended to show you how resumptive modifiers work.**

You can also resume with an ADJECTIVE or verb. In that case, you don't add a relative clause; you just repeat the adjective or verb and continue.

✓ It was American writers who found a voice that was both **true** and **lyrical,**

> **true** to the rhythms of the working man's speech and **lyrical** in its celebration of his labor.

✓ All who value independence should **resist** the trivialization of government regulation,

> **resist** its obsession with administrative tidiness and compulsion to arrange things not for our convenience but for theirs.

Summative Modifiers   Here are two sentences that contrast relative clauses and summative modifiers. Notice how the *which* in the first one feels "tacked on":

> Economic changes have reduced Russian population growth to less than zero, **which will have serious social implications.**
>
> ✓ Economic changes have reduced Russian population growth to less than zero, **a demographic event that will have serious social implications.**

To create a summative modifier, end a grammatically complete segment of a sentence with a comma:

> Economic changes have reduced Russian population growth to less than zero,

Find a term that sums up the substance of the sentence:

> Economic changes have reduced Russian population growth to less than zero,
>
> **a demographic event . . .**

Then continue with a relative clause beginning with *that:*

> Economic changes have reduced Russian population growth to less than zero,
>
> a demographic event **that will have serious social implications.**

Free Modifiers   Like the other modifiers, a free modifier can appear at the end of a clause, but instead of repeating a key word or summing up what went before, it says something about the subject of the closest verb:

> ✓ Free modifiers resemble resumptive and summative modifiers, **letting you** [i.e., the free modifier lets you] **extend the line of a sentence while avoiding a train of ungainly phrases and clauses.**

Free modifiers usually begin with an *-ing* PRESENT PARTICIPLE, as those did, but they can also begin with a PAST PARTICIPLE verb, like this:

> ✓ Leonardo da Vinci was a man of powerful intellect,
>
> *driven* **by** [i.e., Leonardo was driven by] **an insatiable curiosity and** *haunted* **by a vision of artistic perfection.**

A free modifier can also begin with an adjective:

> ✓ In 1939, we began to assist the British against Germany,
>
> *aware* [i.e., we were aware] **that we faced another world war.**

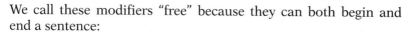
We call these modifiers "free" because they can both begin and end a sentence:

- ✓ **Driven by an insatiable curiosity,** Leonardo da Vinci was . . .
- ✓ **Aware that we faced another world war,** in 1939 we began . . .

Create a free modifier, however, and you risk dangling it. A modifier "dangles" when its implied subject differs from the explicit subject of the clause it attaches to:

> Hoping to find the flaw, the results of the tests were reviewed.

The modifier, *hoping to find,* dangles because its implicit subject (whoever hopes) differs from the explicit subject of the clause it attaches to (*the results of the tests*). To revise, make the implied and explicit subjects the same:

- ✓ **Hoping** to find the flaw, **we** reviewed the results of the tests.

Most readers ignore a dangling modifier when it is METADISCOURSE.

- ✓ **To summarize,** it is clear that . . .
- ✓ **Turning to our finances,** our first question is . . .

> *Here's the point:* When you have to write a long sentence, don't just add one phrase or clause after another, willy-nilly. Particularly avoid tacking one relative clause onto another onto another. Try extending the line of a sentence with resumptive, summative, and free modifiers. When you create a free modifier, however, be sure its implied subject matches the explicit subject of the verb closest to it.

3. Coordinate   It's harder to create good coordination than good modifiers, but when done well, it's more pleasing to the reader. Coordination is in fact the foundation of a gracefully shaped sentence. Compare these. My version is first; the original is second:

> The aspiring artist may find that even a minor, unfinished work which was botched may be an instructive model for how things should be done, while for the amateur spectator, such works are the daily fare which may provide good, honest nourishment, which can lead to an appreciation of deeper pleasures that are also more refined.

✓ For the aspiring artist, the minor, the unfinished, or even the botched work, may be an instructive model for how things should—and should not—be done. For the amateur spectator, such works are the daily fare which provide good, honest nourishment—and which can lead to appreciation of more refined, or deeper pleasures.

—Eva Hoffman, "Minor Art Offers Special Pleasures"

My revision sprawls through a string of tacked-on clauses:

> The aspiring artist may find that even a minor, unfinished work
> **which** was botched may be an instructive model for
> **how** things should be done,
> **while** for the amateur spectator, such works are the daily fare
> **which** may provide good, honest nourishment,
> **which** can lead to an appreciation of deeper pleasures
> **that** are also more refined.

Hoffman's original gets its shape from its multiple coordinations. Structurally, it looks like this:

For the aspiring artist,
$$
\left\{
\begin{array}{c}
\text{the minor,} \\
\text{the unfinished,} \\
\text{or} \\
\text{even the botched}
\end{array}
\right\}
\text{work may be}
$$

an instructive model for how things
$$
\left\{
\begin{array}{c}
\text{should} \\
\text{and} \\
\text{should not}
\end{array}
\right\}
\text{be done.}
$$

For the amateur spectator, such works are

the daily fare
$$
\left\{
\begin{array}{c}
\text{which provide} \left\{ \begin{array}{c} \text{good,} \\ \text{honest} \end{array} \right\} \text{nourishment—} \\
\text{and} \\
\text{which can lead to appreciation of} \left\{ \begin{array}{c} \text{more refined,} \\ \text{or} \\ \text{deeper} \end{array} \right\} \text{pleasures.}
\end{array}
\right\}
$$

That second sentence in particular shows how elaborate coordination can get.

A General Design Principle: Short to Long   We should note one feature that distinguishes well-formed coordination. You can hear it if you read this next passage aloud:

> We should devote a few final words to a matter that reaches beyond the techniques of research to the connections between those subjective values that reflect our deepest ethical choices and objective research.

That sentence seems to end too abruptly with *objective research*. Structurally, it looks like this:

$$\ldots \text{between} \begin{cases} \text{those subjective values that reflect our} \\ \text{deepest ethical choices} \\ \qquad\qquad \text{and} \\ \text{objective research.} \end{cases}$$

This next revision moves from shorter to longer by reversing the two coordinate elements and by adding a parallelism to the second one to make it longer. Read this one aloud:

> We should devote a few final words to a matter that reaches beyond the techniques of research to the connections between objective research and those subjective values that reflect our deepest ethical choices and strongest intellectual commitments.

Structurally, it looks like this:

$$\checkmark \ldots \text{between} \begin{cases} \text{objective research} \\ \qquad \text{and} \\ \text{those subjective} \\ \text{values that reflect our} \begin{cases} \text{deepest ethical choices} \\ \qquad \text{and} \\ \text{strongest intellectual} \\ \text{commitments.} \end{cases} \end{cases}$$

Here's the point: Coordination lets you extend the line of a sentence more gracefully than just by tacking on one element to another. When you can coordinate, try to order the elements so that they go from shorter to longer, from simpler to more complex.

Exercise 8.2

In these sentences, create resumptive, summative, and free modifiers. In the first five, start a resumptive modifier with the word in boldface. Then use the word in brackets to create another sentence with a summative modifier. For example:

✓ Within ten years, we could meet our energy **needs** with solar power. [a possibility]

Resumptive:

✓ Within ten years, we could meet our energy **needs** with solar power, **needs** that will soar as our population grows.

Summative:

✓ Within ten years, we could meet our energy needs with solar power, **a possibility** that few anticipated ten years ago.

Free:

✓ Within ten years, we could meet our energy needs with solar power, **freeing** ourselves of dependence on foreign oil.

But before you begin adding resumptive and summative modifiers, edit these sentences for redundancy, wordiness, nominalizations, and other problems.

1. Many different school systems are making a return back to traditional education in the **basics**. [a change]
2. Within the period of the last few years or so, automobile manufacturers have been trying to meet new and more stringent-type quality control **requirements**. [a challenge]
3. The reasons for the cause of aging are a **puzzle** that has perplexed humanity for millennia. [a mystery]
4. The majority of young people in the world of today cannot even begin to have an understanding of the **insecurity** that a large number of older people had experienced during the period of the Great Depression. [a failure]
5. The successful accomplishment of test-tube fertilization of embryos has raised many **issues** of an ethical nature

that continue to trouble both scientists and laypeople. [an event]

6. Many who lived during the period of the Victorian era were appalled when Darwin put forth the suggestion that their ancestry might have included creatures such as apes.

7. In the period known to scholars and historians as the Renaissance, increases in affluence and stability in the area of political affairs had the consequence of allowing streams of thought of different kinds to merge and flow together.

8. The field of journalism has to an increasing degree placed its focus on the kind of news stories and events that at one time in our history were considered to be only gossip of a salacious and sexual nature.

Exercise 8.3

The best way to learn coordination is by imitating it. Try imitating any of the passages laid out above. For example, imitating the Eva Hoffman passage (p. 142), you might write this:

> For the serious student, the library sometimes provides a chance to be alone and to think through problems that may be too complex or too painful to think about in a noisy and crowded dormitory.

You can find other examples in speeches and dictionaries of quotations.

Troubleshooting Long Sentences

Even when you manage their internal structures, though, long sentences can still go wrong.

Faulty Coordination   Ordinarily, we coordinate elements only of the same grammatical structure: clause and clause, PREPOSITIONAL PHRASE and prepositional phrase, and so on. When you coordinate different grammatical structures, readers may feel you have created an offensive lack of PARALLELISM. Careful writers avoid this:

The committee recommends

{
revising the curriculum to recognize trends in local employment
and
that the division be reorganized to reflect the new curriculum.
}

They would correct that to this:

✔ . . . recommends

{
that the curriculum be revised to recognize . . .
and
that the division be reorganized to reflect. . . .
}

Or to this:

✔ . . . recommends

{
revising the curriculum to recognize . . .
and
reorganizing the division to reflect. . . .
}

However, some nonparallel coordinations do occur in well-written prose. Careful writers coordinate a noun phrase with a *how*-clause:

✔ We will attempt to delineate

{
the problems of education in developing nations
and
how coordinated efforts can address them in economical ways.
}

Or they coordinate an ADVERB with a prepositional phrase:

✔ The proposal appears to have been written

{
quickly,
carefully,
and
with the help of many.
}

Careful readers do not blink at either.

We respond to coordination best when the elements are coordinate not only in grammar but in thought. Some inexperienced writers coordinate by just joining one element to another with *and:*

> Grade inflation is a problem at many universities, **and** it leads to a devaluation of good grades earned by hard work **and** will not be solved simply by grading harder.

Those *and*s obscure the relationships among those claims:

> ✓ Grade inflation is a problem at many universities, **because** it devalues good grades that were earned by hard work, **but** it will not be solved simply by grading harder.

Unfortunately, I can't tell you how to recognize when elements are not coordinate in thought.

Unclear Connections   Readers are also bothered by a coordination so long that they lose track of its internal connections and pronoun references:

> Teachers should remember that students are vulnerable and uncertain about those everyday ego-bruising moments that adults ignore and that they do not understand that one day they will become as confident and as secure as the adults that bruise them.

We sense a flicker of hesitation about where to connect:

> . . . and that they do not understand that one day they . . .

To revise a sentence like that, shorten the first half of the coordination so that you can start the second half closer to the point where the coordination began:

> ✓ Teachers should remember that students are vulnerable to ego-bruising moments that adults ignore and that they do not understand that one day . . .

If you can't do that, repeat a word that reminds the reader where the coordination began (thereby creating a resumptive modifier):

> ✓ Teachers should try to remember that students are vulnerable to ego-bruising moments that adults ignore, **to remember** that they do not understand that . . .

Misplaced Modifiers   Another problem with modifiers is that sometimes readers are unsure what they modify:

> Overtaxing oneself in physical activity too frequently results in injury.

What happens too frequently, overtaxing or injuries? We can make its meaning unambiguous by moving *too frequently:*

✓ Overtaxing oneself too frequently in physical activity results in injury.

✓ Overtaxing oneself in physical activity results too frequently in injury.

A modifier at the end of a clause can ambiguously modify either a neighboring or a more distant phrase:

> Scientists have learned that their observations are as subjective as those in any other field **in recent years.**

We can move the modifier to a less ambiguous position:

✓ **In recent years,** scientists have learned that . . .

✓ Scientists have learned that **in recent years** their . . .

> *Here's the point:* Even well-constructed long sentences can give readers a problem if they can't connect the second part of a coordination to its starting point or if they are unsure about what a phrase actually modifies.

Intrinsic Sense

You can use these devices to shape a long yet clear sentence, but not even the best syntax can salvage incoherent ideas. This next sentence appeared in a Sunday *New York Times* travel section. The sentence before it had introduced the professional women of Amsterdam's red-light district:

> They are so unself-conscious about their profession that by day they can be seen standing naked in doorways, chatting with their neighbors in the shadow of the Oudekerstoren Church, which offers Saturday carillon concerts at 4 P.M. and a panoramic view of the city from its tower in summer.

This syntactically well-formed sentence opens with a coherent clause:

> They are so unself-conscious about their profession that by day they can be seen standing naked in doorways . . .

It continues with a free modifier:

> . . . chatting with their neighbors in the shadow of the Oudekerstoren Church . . .

then concludes with a relative clause with a balanced pair of direct objects:

$$\ldots \text{which offers} \left\{ \begin{array}{c} \text{Saturday carillon concerts at 4 P.M.} \\ \text{and} \\ \text{a panoramic view of the city from} \\ \text{its tower in summer.} \end{array} \right\}$$

But the movement of ideas is goofy (or evidence of a sly sense of humor).

SUMMING UP

Here are the principles for giving sentences a coherent shape:

1. Get quickly to the subject, then to the verb and its object.

   a. Avoid long introductory phrases and clauses. Revise them into their own independent clauses:

      > Since most undergraduate students change their major fields of study at least once during their college careers, many more than once, **first-year students** who are not certain about the program of studies they want to pursue should not load up their schedules to meet requirements for a particular program.

      > ✓ **Most undergraduate students** change their major fields at least once during their college careers, so **first-year students** should not load up their schedules with requirements for a particular program if they are not certain about the program of studies they want to pursue.

   b. Avoid long subjects. Revise a long subject into an introductory subordinate clause:

      > **A company that focuses on hiring the best personnel and then trains them not just for the work they are hired to do but for higher-level jobs** is likely to earn the loyalty of its employees.

      > ✓ **When a company focuses on hiring the best personnel and then trains them not just for the work they are hired to do but for higher-level jobs later,** it is likely to earn the loyalty of its employees.

   If the new introductory clause is long, shift it to the end of its sentence:

✓ A company is likely to earn the loyalty of its employees **when it focuses on hiring the best personnel** . . .

Or just break it out in a sentence of its own:

✓ **Some companies focus on hiring the best personnel and then train them not just for the work they are hired to do but for higher-level jobs later.** Such companies are likely to earn the loyalty of their employees.

c. Avoid interrupting subjects and verbs, and verbs and objects. Move the interrupting element to either the beginning or end of the sentence, depending on what the next sentence is about:

Some scientists, **because they write in a style that is impersonal and objective,** do not easily communicate with laypeople.

✓ **Because some scientists write in a style that is impersonal and objective,** they do *not easily communicate with laypeople. This lack of communication* damages . . .

✓ Some scientists do not easily communicate with laypeople *because they write in a style that is impersonal and objective. It is a kind of style filled with passives* . . .

2. After the main clause, avoid adding one subordinate clause to another to another to another . . .

a. Trim relative clauses and break the sentences into two:

Of the many areas of science **that** are important to our future, few are more promising than genetic engineering, **which** is a new way of manipulating the elemental structural units of life itself, **which** are the genes and chromosomes **that** tell our cells how to reproduce to become the parts **that** constitute our bodies.

✓ Many areas of science are important to our future, but few are more promising than genetic engineering. It is a new way of manipulating the elemental structural units of life itself, **which** are the genes and chromosomes **that** tell our cells how to reproduce to become the parts that constitute our bodies.

✓ Of the many areas of science ~~that are~~ important to our future, few are more promising than genetic engineering, ~~which is~~ a new way of manipulating the elemental structural units of life itself, ~~which are~~ the genes and chromosomes that tell our cells how to reproduce to become the parts ~~that~~ constituting our bodies.

b. Extend a sentence with resumptive, summative, and free modifiers:

✓ **Resumptive:**   When we discovered the earth was not the center of the universe, it changed our understanding of who we are, **an understanding changed again by Darwin, again by Freud, and again by Einstein.**

✓ **Summative:**   American productivity has risen to new heights, **an achievement that only a decade ago was considered an impossible dream.**

✓ **Free:**   Global warming will become a central political issue of the twenty-first century, **raising questions whose answers will affect the standard of living in every Western nation.**

c. Coordinate elements that are parallel both in grammar and in sense:

Besides the fact that no civilization has experienced such rapid alterations in their spiritual and mental lives, the material conditions of their daily existence have changed greatly too.

✓ No civilization has experienced such rapid alterations in their spiritual and mental lives and in the material conditions of daily existence.

A last note: to write a long complex sentence that is also clear, you may need helpful punctuation. See the Appendix.

Elegance

Anything is better than not to write clearly. There is nothing to be said against lucidity, and against simplicity only the possibility of dryness. This is a risk well worth taking when you reflect how much better it is to be bald than to wear a curly wig.
—SOMERSET MAUGHAM

But clarity and brevity, though a good beginning, are only a beginning. By themselves, they may remain bare and bleak. When Calvin Coolidge, asked by his wife what the preacher had preached on, replied "Sin," and, asked what the preacher had said, replied "He was against it," he was brief enough. But one hardly envies Mrs. Coolidge.
—FRANK L. LUCAS

Read over your compositions, and wherever you meet with a passage which you think is particularly fine, strike it out.
—SAMUEL JOHNSON

In literature the ambition of the novice is to acquire the literary language; the struggle of the adept is to get rid of it.
—GEORGE BERNARD SHAW

UNDERSTANDING ELEGANCE

Anyone who can write clearly, concisely, and coherently should rejoice to achieve so much. But while most of us prefer bald clarity to the density of institutional prose, others feel that relentless simplicity can be dry, even arid. It has the spartan virtue of unsalted meat and potatoes, but such fare is rarely memorable. A flash of elegance can not only fix a thought in our minds, but give us a flicker of pleasure every time we recall it. This lesson is for those of you who aim at prose that is more than just clear and coherent, that offers a moment of pleasure not just for your reader but for yourself.

Unfortunately, I can't tell you how to do that. In fact, I incline toward those who think that the most elegant elegance is disarming simplicity—and so when you think you have written something fine, I second Samuel Johnson's advice: strike it out. Nevertheless, there are a few devices that can shape a thought in ways that are both elegant and clear.

Just knowing them, however, is about as useful as just knowing the ingredients in the bouillabaisse of a great cook, and then thinking you can make it. Knowing ingredients and knowing how to use them distinguish reading cookbooks and cooking. Maybe elegant clarity is a gift. But even a gift has to be educated and exercised.

Balance and Symmetry

What most makes a sentence graceful is a balance and symmetry among its parts, one echoing another in sound, rhythm, structure, and meaning. A skilled writer can balance almost any two parts of a sentence, but the most common balance is based on COORDINATION.

Balanced Coordination   Here is a balanced passage and my revision of it. A tin ear can distinguish which is which:

> 1a. The national unity of a free people depends upon a sufficiently even balance of political power to make it impracticable for the administration to be arbitrary and for the opposition to be revolutionary and irreconcilable. Where that balance no longer exists, democracy perishes. For unless all the citizens of a state are forced by circumstances to compromise, unless they feel that they can affect policy but that no one can wholly dominate it, unless by

habit and necessity they have to give and take, freedom cannot be maintained.

—Walter Lippmann

1b. The national unity of a free people depends upon a sufficiently even balance of political power to make it impracticable for an administration to be arbitrary against a revolutionary opposition that is irreconcilably opposed to it. Where that balance no longer exists, democracy perishes, because unless all the citizens of a state are habitually forced by necessary circumstances to compromise in a way that lets them affect policy with no one dominating it, freedom cannot be maintained.

My sentences lurch from one part to the next. In Lippmann's, we hear one CLAUSE and PHRASE echo another in word order, sound, and meaning, giving the whole passage an intricate architectural symmetry.

If we extend the idea of TOPIC and STRESS from a whole sentence to its parts, we can see how he balances even short segments. Note how each significant word in one phrase echoes another in its corresponding one (I boldface topics of phrases and italicize stresses):

The national unity of a free people depends upon a sufficiently even balance of political power to make it impracticable

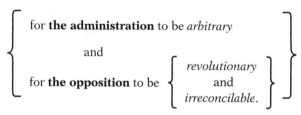

Lippmann balances the phrasal topics of *administration* and *opposition,* and closes by balancing the stressed sounds and meanings of *arbitrary, revolutionary,* and *irreconcilable.* He follows with a short concluding sentence whose stressed words are not coordinated, but are still balanced (I use square brackets to indicate non-coordinated balance):

Where [**that balance** *no longer exists,* **democracy** *perishes.*]

Then he creates an especially intricate design, balancing many sounds and meanings:

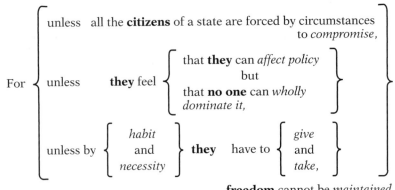

- He repeats *citizens* as the SUBJECT/topic of each clause: *all the citizens, they, they* (note the passive in the first one: *citizens* **are forced**).
- He balances the sound and sense of *force* against *feel*, and the meaning of *affect policy* against the meaning of *dominate it*.
- In the last *unless*-clause, he balances the meaning of *habit* against *necessity*, and the stressed *give* against *take*.
- He balances the meanings of *compromise, affect, dominate*, and *give and take*.
- Then to balance the clauses of that short preceding sentence, *balance no longer exists—democracy perishes*, he concludes with an equally short clause, *freedom cannot be maintained*, whose meaning and structure echo the corresponding pair in the preceding sentence:

balance	no longer exists
democracy	perishes
freedom	cannot be maintained

For those who care and notice, it is an impressive construction.

Uncoordinated Balance   We can also balance structures that are not grammatically coordinate. In this example, the subject balances the OBJECT:

> **Scientists** whose research   *creates revolutionary views of*
>   *the universe*
>
>   invariably upset
>
> **those of us** who   *construct our vision of reality*
>   *out of our common-sense experience*
>   *of it.*

Here, the PREDICATE of a RELATIVE CLAUSE in a subject balances the predicate of the sentence:

> A government   that is unwilling to *listen* to   the
>   *moderate hopes* of *its citizenry*
>
>   must eventually *answer* to   the *harsh*
>   *justice* of *its revolutionaries.*

Here a direct object balances the object of a PREPOSITION:

Those of us concerned with our school systems will not sacrifice

> the *intellectual growth* of   our *innocent children*
>   to
> the *social engineering* of   *incompetent bureaucrats.*

A more complicated balance:

> Were I trading[1a]   scholarly principles[2a]
>   for
>   financial security,[2b]
>
> I would not be writing[1b]   short books[3a]
>   on
>   minor subjects[3b]
>   for
>   small audiences.[3c]

In that sentence,

- a SUBORDINATE CLAUSE (1a), *Were I trading,* balances the MAIN CLAUSE (1b), *I would not be writing;*

- the object of that subordinate clause (2a), *scholarly principles,* balances the object in the prepositional phrase (2b), *financial security;*
- the object in the main clause (3a), *short books,* balances the objects in two prepositional phrases, (3b), *minor subjects,* and (3c), *small audiences* (and note the balance of *short, minor,* and *small*).

Keep in mind that you usually create the most rhythmical balance when the first element in a balance is shorter than the next ones (see p. 143).

Used to excess, these patterns can seem merely clever, but used prudently, they can emphasize an important point or conclude a line of reasoning with a flourish that careful readers notice.

These patterns even encourage you to think in ways that you might not have otherwise. In that sense, these patterns don't just frame thinking; they generate it. Suppose you begin a sentence like this:

> In his earliest years, Picasso was a master draftsman of the traditional human form.

Now try this:

> In his earliest years, Picasso was **not only** a master draftsman of the traditional human form, **but also** . . .

Now you have to wonder what else he might have been. Or not have been.

> ***Here's the point:*** The most striking feature of elegant prose is balanced sentence structures. You most easily balance one part of a sentence against another by coordinating them with *and, or, nor, but,* and *yet,* but you can also balance noncoordinated phrases and clauses.

Climactic Emphasis

How you begin a sentence determines its clarity; how you end it determines its rhythm and grace.

Light and Heavy Words   When we get close to the end of a sentence, we expect words that deserve stress (p. 95), so we may feel a sentence is anticlimactic if it ends on words of slight grammatical or semantic weight. At the end of a sentence, prepositions feel light—one reason we sometimes avoid leaving one there. The rhythm of a sentence should carry readers toward strength. Compare:

> Studies into intellectual differences among races is a project that only the most politically naive psychologist is willing to give support to.

> ✓ Studies into intellectual differences among races is a project that only the most politically naive scientist is willing to support.

ADJECTIVES and ADVERBS are heavier than prepositions, but lighter than NOUNS, the heaviest of which are NOMINALIZATIONS. Readers have problems with nominalizations in the subject of a sentence, but at the end they provide a satisfyingly climactic thump, particularly when two of them are in coordinate balance. Consider this excerpt from Winston Churchill's "Finest Hour" speech. Churchill ended it with a parallelism climaxed by a balanced pair of heavy nominalizations:

> . . . until in God's good time,
>
> the New World, with all its { power and might } steps forth to
>
> { the **rescue** and the **liberation** } of the old.

He could have written more simply, and more banally:

> . . . until the New World rescues us.

Elegant Stress: Three Devices   Here are three ways to end a sentence with special emphasis.

1. *of* + **Nominalization.** This seems unlikely, but it's true. Look at how Churchill ends his sentence: The light *of* (followed by a lighter *a* or *the*) quickens the rhythm of a sentence just before the stress of the climactic monosyllable, *old:*

   > . . . the rescue and the liberation of the **old.**

   We associate this pattern with self-conscious elegance, as in the first few sentences of Edward Gibbon's *History of the*

Decline and Fall of the Roman Empire (contrast that title with *The Roman Empire's Fall*):

> ✓ In the second century of the Christian era, the Empire of Rome comprehended **the fairest part** *of* **the earth,** AND **the most civilized portion** *of* **mankind.** The frontiers of that extensive monarchy were guarded **by ancient renown** AND **disciplined valour.** The gentle but powerful influence of laws and manners had gradually cemented **the union** *of* **the provinces.** Their peaceful inhabitants **enjoyed** AND **abused the advantages** *of* **wealth** AND **luxury.** The image of a free constitution was preserved with decent **reverence:** the Roman senate appeared to possess the sovereign authority, and devolved on the emperors all **the executive powers** *of* **government.**

In comparison, this is flat:

> In the second century AD, the Roman Empire comprehended **the earth's fairest, most civilized part.** Ancient renown and disciplined valour guarded **its extensive frontiers.** The gentle but powerful influence of laws and manners had gradually **unified the provinces.** Their peaceful inhabitants enjoyed and abused luxurious wealth while decently preserving what seemed to be **a free constitution.** Appearing to possess the sovereign authority, the Roman senate devolved on the emperors all **executive governmental powers.**

2. **Echoing Salience.** At the end of a sentence, readers hear special emphasis when a stressed word or phrase balances the sound or meaning of an earlier one. (These examples are all from Peter Gay's *Style in History.*)

> ✓ I have written these essays to anatomize this familiar yet really strange being, **style the centaur;** the book may be read as an extended critical commentary on Buffon's famous saying that **the style is the man.**

When we hear a stressed word echo an earlier one, these balances become even more emphatic:

> ✓ Apart from a few mechanical tricks of rhetoric, **manner** is indissolubly linked to **matter; style shapes,** and in turn is **shaped** by, **substance.**

> ✓ It seems frivolous, almost inappropriate, to be **stylish** about **style.**

Gay echoes both the sound and meaning of *manner* in *matter, style* in *substance, shapes* in *shaped by,* and *stylish* in *style.*

3. **Chiasmus.** This device (pronounced kye-azz-muss,) is interesting perhaps only to those fascinated with the most obscure figures of style. The word *chiasmus* is from the Greek word for "crossing." It balances elements in two parts of a sentence, but the second part reverses the order of the elements in the first part. For example, this would be both coordinate and parallel, but not a chiasmus, because the elements in the two parts are in the same order (AB : AB):

✔ A concise style can improve both { **our own**[1A] *thinking*[1B] and **our readers'**[2A] *understanding.*[2B] }

Were we seeking a special effect, we could reverse the order of elements in the second part to mirror those in the first. Now the pattern is not 1A1B : 2A2B, but rather 1A1B : 2B2A:

✔ A concise style can improve not only { **our own**[1A] *thinking*[1B] but the *understanding*[2B] **of our readers.**[2A] }

The next example is more complex. The first two elements are parallel, but the last three mirror one another: AB CDE : AB EDC:

You[A] reveal[B] **your own**[C] *highest rhetorical*[D] SKILL[E]
            by the way
you[A]   respect[B] THE BELIEFS[E] *most deeply held*[D] **by your reader.**[C]

Here's the point: An elegant sentence should end on strength. You can create that strength in four ways:

1. End with a strong word, typically a nominalization, or better, a pair of them.
2. End with a prepositional phrase introduced by *of.*
3. End with an echoing salience.
4. End with a chiasmus.

Extravagant Elegance

When writers combine all these elements in a single sentence, we know they are aiming at something special, as in this next passage by Joyce Carol Oates:

> Far from being locked inside our own skins, inside the "dungeons" of ourselves, we are now able to recognize that our minds belong, quite naturally, to a collective "mind," a mind in which we share everything that is mental, most obviously language itself, and that the old boundary of the skin is not boundary at all but a membrane connecting the inner and outer experience of existence. Our intelligence, our wit, our cleverness, our unique personalities—all are simultaneously "our own" possessions and the world's.

—Joyce Carol Oates, "New Heaven and New Earth"

Here is the anatomy of that passage:

Far from being locked **inside** our own skins,

        inside the "dungeons" of ourselves,

we are now able to recognize

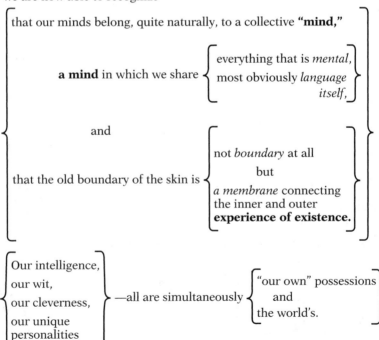

In addition to all the coordination, note the two resumptive modifiers:

> Far from being locked **inside** our own skins,
>   **inside** the "dungeons" of ourselves . . .
>
> our minds belong . . . to a collective **"mind,"**
>   **a mind** in which we share . . .

Note too the two nominalizations stressed at the end of the first sentence and the coordinate nominalizations at the end of the second:

> . . . the inner and outer experience of existence.
> . . . "our own" possessions and the world's.

But such patterns can be more elaborate yet. Here is the last sentence from Frederick Jackson Turner's *The Frontier in American History:*

> This then is the heritage of the pioneer experience—a passionate belief that a democracy was possible which should leave the individual a part to play in a free society and not make him a cog in a machine operated from above; which trusted in the common man, in his tolerance, his ability to adjust differences with good humor, and to work out an American type from the contributions of all nations—a type for which he would fight against those who challenged it in arms, and for which in time of war he would make sacrifices, even the temporary sacrifice of his individual freedom and his life, lest that freedom be lost forever.

Note the following:

- the summative modifier in the opening segment: *a passionate belief that* . . . ;
- the increased length and weight of the second element in each coordination, even the coordinations inside coordinations;
- the two resumptive modifiers beginning with *type* and *sacrifice.*

That may be over the top, especially the quadruple chiasmus in the last sixteen words:

> **the temporary**[1] sacrifice[2] of his individual FREEDOM[3] and *his life*[4],
>
> *lest*[4]   that FREEDOM[3] be   lost[2]   **forever**[1].

The meaning of *temporary* balances *forever; sacrifice* balances *lost; freedom* echoes *freedom;* and the sound of *life* balances *lest* (not to mention the near rhyme of *lest* in *lost*). You just don't see that kind of sentence any more.

Here is the anatomy of that sentence:

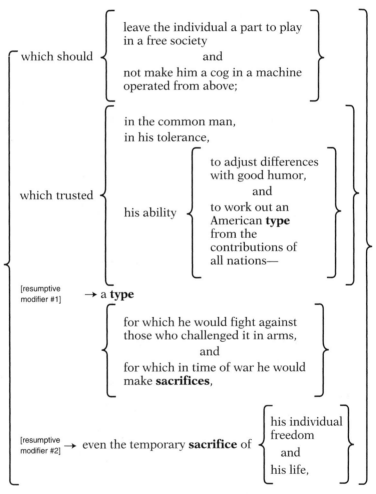

This then is the heritage of the pioneer experience—
[summative modifier]   a passionate belief that a democracy was possible

which should {
leave the individual a part to play in a free society
and
not make him a cog in a machine operated from above;
}

which trusted {
in the common man,
in his tolerance,
his ability {
to adjust differences with good humor,
and
to work out an American **type** from the contributions of all nations—
}
}

[resumptive modifier #1] → a **type**

{
for which he would fight against those who challenged it in arms,
and
for which in time of war he would make **sacrifices**,
}

[resumptive modifier #2] → even the temporary **sacrifice** of {
his individual freedom
and
his life,
}

lest that freedom be lost forever.

Exercise 9.1

You develop a knack for balance by imitating models, not word for word, just their general pattern:

> Survival in the wilderness requires the energy and wit to overcome the brute facts of an uncooperative Nature but rewards the person who acquires that power with the satisfaction of having done it once and with the confidence of being able to do it again.

Think of a subject close to that of the model to make your imitation easy—the academic life, then follow its outline:

> Life as a college student offers a few years of intellectual excitement but imposes a sense of anxiety on those who look ahead and know that its end is in sight.

Use models you find here or in sermons, political speeches, and dictionaries of quotations. Try imitating the long sentences on pages 142, 155, and 164.

Exercise 9.2

Here are some first halves of sentences to finish with balancing last halves. For example, given this:

> Those who keep silent over the loss of small freedoms . . .

finish with something like this:

> . . . will be silenced when they protest the loss of large ones.

1. Those who argue stridently over small matters . . .
2. While the strong are often afraid to admit weakness, the weak . . .
3. We should pay more attention to those politicians who tell us how to make what we have better than to those . . .
4. When parents raise children who do not value the importance of hard work, the adults those children become will . . .
5. Some teachers mistake neat papers that rehash old ideas for . . .

Exercise 9.3

These sentences end weakly. Edit them for clarity and concision, then revise them so that they end on more heavily stressed words, particularly with prepositional phrases beginning with *of*. For example:

> Our interest in paranormal phenomena testifies to the fact that we have **empty spirits and shallow minds.**
>
> ✓ Our interest in paranormal phenomena testifies to **the emptiness of our spirits and the shallowness of our minds.**

In the first three, I boldface words you might nominalize.

1. If we invest our sweat in these projects, we must avoid appearing to work only because we are **interested** in ourselves.
2. The blueprint for the political campaign was concocted by those who were not sensitive to what we **needed** most critically.
3. Throughout history, science has made progress because dedicated scientists have ignored a **hostile** public that is uninformed.
4. Not one tendency in our governmental system has brought about more changes in American daily life than federal governmental agencies that are very powerful.
5. The day is gone when school systems' boards of education have the expectation that local taxpayers will automatically go along with whatever extravagant things incompetent bureaucrats decide to do.

Nuances of Length and Rhythm

Most writers don't plan the length of their sentences, but that's not a problem, unless every sentence is shorter than fifteen or so words, or much longer. Artful writers, however, do use the length of a sentence for a purpose. Some write short sentences to strike a note of urgency:

> Toward noon Petrograd again became the field of military action; rifles and machine guns rang out everywhere. It was not easy to tell

who was shooting or where. One thing was clear; the past and the future were exchanging shots. There was much casual firing; young boys were shooting off revolvers unexpectedly acquired. The arsenal was wrecked. . . . Shots rang out on both sides. But the board fence stood in the way, dividing the soldiers from the revolution. The attackers decided to break down the fence. They broke down part of it and set fire to the rest. About twenty barracks came into view. The bicyclists were concentrated in two or three of them. The empty barracks were set fire to at once.

—Leon Trotsky, *The Russian Revolution,* trans. Max Eastman

Or terse certainty:

The teacher or lecturer is a danger. He very seldom recognizes his nature or his position. The lecturer is a man who must talk for an hour. France may possibly have acquired the intellectual leadership of Europe when their academic period was cut down to 40 minutes. I also have lectured. The lecturer's first problem is to have enough words to fill 40 or 60 minutes. The professor is paid for his time, his results are almost impossible to estimate . . . No teacher has ever failed from ignorance. That is empiric professional knowledge. Teachers fail because they cannot "handle the class." Real education must ultimately be limited to men who INSIST on knowing, the rest is mere sheep-herding.

—Ezra Pound, *ABC of Reading*

Or passion. Here, D. H. Lawrence breaks what could have been a long paragraph into urgent utterances.

Let us look at this American artist first. How did he ever get to America, to start with? Why isn't he a European still, like his father before him?

Now listen to me, don't listen to him. He'll tell you the lie you expect. Which is partly your fault for expecting it.

He didn't come in search of freedom of worship. England had more freedom of worship in the year 1700 than America had. Won by Englishmen who wanted freedom and so stopped at home and fought for it. And got it. Freedom of worship? Read the history of New England during the first century of its existence.

Freedom anyhow? The land of the free! This the land of the free! Why, if I say anything that displeases them, the free mob will lynch me, and that's my freedom. Free? Why I have never been in any country where the individual has such an abject fear of his fellow countrymen. Because, as I say, they are free to lynch him the moment he shows he is not one of them. . . .

All right then, what did they come for? For lots of reasons. Perhaps least of all in search of freedom of any sort: positive freedom, that is.

—D. H. Lawrence, *Studies in Classic American Literature*

Self-conscious stylists also write extravagantly long sentences. Here is just a piece of one whose sinuous length seems to mirror the confused progress of a protest march:

> In any event, up at the front of this March, in the first line, back of that hollow square of monitors, Mailer and Lowell walked in this barrage of cameras, helicopters, TV cars, monitors, loudspeakers, and wavering buckling twisting line of notables, arms linked (line twisting so much that at times the movement was in file, one arm locked ahead, one behind, then the line would undulate about and the other arm would be ahead) speeding up a few steps, slowing down while a great happiness came back into the day as if finally one stood under some mythical arch in the great vault of history, helicopters buzzing about, chop-chop, and the sense of America divided on this day now liberated some undiscovered patriotism in Mailer so that he felt a sharp searing love for his country in this moment and on this day, crossing some divide in his own mind wider than the Potomac, a love so lacerated he felt as if a marriage were being torn and children lost—never does one love so much as then, obviously, then—and an odor of wood smoke, from where you knew not, was also in the air, a smoke of dignity and some calm heroism, not unlike the sense of freedom which also comes when a marriage is burst— Mailer knew for the first time why men in the front line of battle are almost always ready to die; there is a promise of some swift transit . . . [it goes on]

—Norman Mailer, *The Armies of the Night*

We almost feel we are eavesdropping on Mailer's stream of thought. But of course, such a sentence is the product not of a spontaneous moment but of premeditated art.

- Mailer opens with short, staccato phrases to suggest confusion, but he controls them by coordination.
- He continues the sentence by coordinating free modifiers: *arms linked . . . (line twisting . . .) speeding up . . .*
- After several more free modifiers, he continues with a resumptive modifier: *a love so lacerated . . .*
- After another GRAMMATICAL SENTENCE, he adds another resumptive modifier: *a smoke of dignity and some calm heroism . . .*

Here's the point: Think about the length of your sentences only if they are all longer than thirty words or so or shorter than fifteen. Your sentences will vary naturally if you simply edit them in the ways you've seen here. But if the occasion allows, don't be reluctant to experiment.

Exercise 9.4

Combine Lawrence and Pound's sentences into longer ones, like Mailer's. Break up Mailer's sentence into shorter ones in the style of Lawrence and Pound. How do they differ? Imitate the style of Lawrence, Pound, and Mailer. Then transform your Lawrence imitation into a Mailer imitation, and vice versa. Only by expressing the same thought in different styles can you see how different styles can seem to change a thought (a self-conscious chiasmus there).

Metaphor

Clarity, vigor, symmetry, rhythm—prose so graced is a great achievement. But it does not excite admiration for the reach of its imagination. This next passage displays all the devices we've seen, but it reaches beyond its grammar to reveal a truth about pleasure. It embeds a figure of speech in a comparison that is itself metaphorical (I boldface the metaphors):

> The secret of the enjoyment of pleasure is to know when to stop. . . .
> We do this every time we listen to music. We do not **seize hold** of a
> particular chord or phrase and shout at the orchestra to go on play-
> ing it for the rest of the evening; on the contrary, however much we
> may like that particular moment of music, we know that its perpetu-
> ation would interrupt and **kill** the movement of the melody. We
> understand that the beauty of a symphony is less in these musical
> moments than in the whole movement from beginning to end. If the
> symphony tries to go on too long, if at a certain point the composer
> **exhausts** his creative ability and tries to carry on just for the sake of
> **filling** in the required **space** of time, then we begin to fidget in our
> chairs, feeling that he has denied the natural rhythm, has **broken the**

smooth curve from birth to death, and that though a **pretense of life** is being made, it is in fact a **living death**.

—Alan W. Watts, The Meaning of Happiness

Watts could have written this:

> . . . however much we like that moment, we know that its perpetuation would interrupt and spoil the movement of the melody. We begin to fidget, feeling he has denied the natural rhythm, has interrupted the regular movement from beginning to end, and that though he makes a pretense of wholeness, it is in fact a repeated end.

Those sentences are clear, but lack the startling metaphor of birth and its smooth curve into death.

Metaphor can vivify all kinds of prose. Social critics use it:

> The schoolmaster is the person who takes the children off the parents' hands for a consideration. That is to say, he establishes a child prison, engages a number of employee schoolmasters as turnkeys, and covers up the essential cruelty and unnaturalness of the situation by torturing the children if they do not learn, and calling this process, which is within the capacity of any fool or blackguard, by the sacred name of Teaching.

—George Bernard Shaw, Sham Education

So do historians:

> This is what may be called the common-sense view of history. History consists of a corpus of ascertained facts. The facts are available to the historian in documents, inscriptions, and so on, like fish on the fishmonger's slab. The historian collects them, takes them home, and cooks and serves them in whatever style appeals to him. Acton, whose culinary tastes were austere, wanted them served plain. . . . Sir George Clark, critical as he was of Acton's attitude, himself contrasts the "hard core of facts" in history with the "surrounding pulp of disputable interpretation"—forgetting perhaps that the pulpy part of the fruit is more rewarding than the hard core.

—E. H. Carr, What Is History?

So do biologists:

> Some of you may have been thinking that, instead of delivering a scientific address, I have been indulging in a flight of fancy. It is a flight, but not of mere fancy, nor is it just an individual indulgence. It is my small personal attempt to share in the flight of the mind into new realms of our cosmic environment. We have evolved wings for such flights, in shape of the disciplined scientific imagination. Support for

those wings is provided by the atmosphere of knowledge created by human science and learning: so far as this supporting atmosphere extends, so far can our wings take us in our exploration.

—Julian Huxley, "New Bottles for Old Wine,"
Journal of the Royal Anthropological Institute

And philosophers:

Quine has long professed his skepticism about the possibility of making any sense of the refractory idioms of intentionality, so he needs opacity only to provide a quarantine barrier protecting the healthy, extensional part of a sentence from the infected part.

—Daniel C. Dennett, "Beyond Belief"

And even physicists, when they lack terms for new ideas:

Whereas the lepton pair has a positive rest mass when it is regarded as a single particle moving with a velocity equal to the vector sum of the motions of its two components, a photon always has zero rest mass. This difference can be glossed over, however, by treating the lepton pair as the offspring of the decay of a short-lived photonlike parent called a virtual photon.

—Leon M. Lederman, "The Upsilon Particle,"
Scientific American

These metaphors serve different ends. Shaw and Carr use metaphor to make their language more intense. Dennett and Lederman use their comparisons simply to explain, and maybe to play a bit.

Of metaphor, Aristotle wrote,

By far the greatest thing is to be a master of metaphor. It is the one thing that cannot be learned from others. It is a sign of genius, for a good metaphor implies an intuitive perception of similarity among dissimilars.

But when that perception is not quite right, a metaphor can seem foolish—Huxley comes close with his wings of inquiry flapping in an atmosphere of knowledge.

We have to be especially careful that a metaphor does not distort the idea that we want to express, as do the metaphors in this passage:

Societies give birth to new values through the osmotic flow of daily social interaction. Conflicts evolve when old values collide with new, a process that frequently spawns a new set of values that synthesize the conflict into a reconciliation of opposites.

The metaphor of birth suggests a traumatic event, but new values, it is claimed, emerge from osmotic flow, a process of invisibly small events. Conflicts do not "evolve"; they more often occur in an instant, as implied by the metaphor of collision. The spawning image echoes the metaphor of birth, but by this point the image is just silly. The writer might have expressed himself in literal language more exactly:

> ✓ As we interact in small ways, we gradually create new social values. When we behave according to an old value and someone else according to a new one, our values may conflict, but may create a third value that reconciles the conflict.

Metaphors can also embarrass us when their buried literal meanings unexpectedly revive, as in this student example:

> The classic blitzkrieg relies on a tank-heavy offensive force, supported by ground-support aircraft, to destroy the defender's ability to fight by running amuck [sic] in his undefended rear, after penetrating his forward defenses.

Here's the point: The risk in striving for elegance is that you fail spectacularly and never risk it again. I can only encourage you to accept with good humor those first failures that we all survive.

SUMMING UP

The qualities of elegance are too varied and subtle to capture in a summary. Nevertheless, elegant passages typically have three characteristics that seem incompatible but are not:

- the simplicity of characters as subjects and actions as verbs;
- the complexity of balanced syntax, meaning, sound, and rhythm;
- the emphasis of artfully stressed endings.

Walter Lippmann's passage illustrates all three:

> The national unity of a free people depends upon a sufficiently even balance of political power to make it impracticable for the adminis-

tration to be arbitrary and for the opposition to be revolutionary and irreconcilable. Where that balance no longer exists, democracy perishes. For unless all the citizens of a state are forced by circumstances to compromise, unless they feel that they can affect policy but that no one can wholly dominate it, unless by habit and necessity they have to give and take, freedom cannot be maintained.

He uses only five nominalizations in eighty-eight words: *balance* twice, and *unity, necessity,* and *freedom* once each. Almost all subjects are short, naming his key characters, and most of his verbs express key actions. And he ends not just each sentence with the right stress, but every clause and even phrase.

You won't acquire an elegant style just by reading this book. You must also read enough writers who write elegantly until their style runs along your muscles and nerves. Only then can you look at your own prose and know when it is elegant or just inflated. To make that distinction, I think the only reliable rule is "Less is more." Of the many graces of style, the compression of a snail is still, I think, the first.

S U M M A R Y :   P A R T   3

In addition to the principles we laid out in Part Two, we add these four:

1. Prune redundancy.
2. Get to the verb in the main clause quickly.
   a. Keep introductory clauses and phrases short.
   b. Keep subjects short.
   c. Don't interrupt the subject-verb connection.
3. Avoid extending the line of a sentence by attaching more than one subordinate clause to one of the same kind. Instead,
   a. coordinate phrases and clauses, balanced ones if you seek a special effect,
   b. use resumptive, summative, and free modifiers.
4. Try balancing parts of sentences against one another, especially their last few words.

PART FOUR

Ethics

Ethics is in origin the art of recommending to others the sacrifices required for cooperation with oneself.
—BERTRAND RUSSELL

The Ethics of Style

There is no artifice as good and desirable as simplicity.
—St. Francis de Sales

Affected simplicity is refined imposture.
—La Rochefoucauld

Everything should be made as simple as possible,
but not simpler.
—Albert Einstein

Style is the ultimate morality of mind.
—Alfred North Whitehead

Beyond Polish

It is easy to think that style is just the polish that makes a sentence more appealing, but more than appeal is at stake in choosing SUBJECTS and VERBS in these two sentences:

    1a. **Serbs and Albanians** DISTRUST each other because **they** HAVE ENGAGED in generations of cultural conflict.

    1b. **Generations of cultural conflict** HAVE CREATED distrust between Serbs and Albanians.

Which sentence better reflects what really causes Serbs and Albanians to distrust each other—their deliberate actions, as in (1a), or, as in (1b), their history? Such a choice of subjects and verbs even implies a philosophy of human action: do we freely choose to act, or do circumstances cause us to? It is not a stretch to see in our choice of a subject and its verb a reflection of that age-old debate about free will and determinism.

So our choices of what character to tell a story about—people or their circumstances—involve more than ease of reading, even more than a philosophy of action, because such choices also have an ethical dimension.

The Ethical Responsibilities of Writers and Readers

In the last nine lessons, I have relentlessly emphasized the responsibility we owe our readers to be clear. But if we are responsible readers, we also have a responsibility toward writers to read hard enough to understand the genuine complexity of ideas that can't be expressed in Dick-and-Jane sentences. It would be impossible, for example, for an engineer to revise this into language clear to everyone:

> The drag force on a particle of diameter d moving with speed u relative to a fluid of density p and viscosity μ is usually modeled by $F = 0.5C_Du^2A$, where A is the cross-sectional area of the particle at right angles to the motion.

Most of us do work hard to understand—at least until we decide that a writer failed to work equally hard to help us reach that understanding, or, worse, has deliberately made our reading more difficult than it has to be. Once we decide that a writer was careless or thoughtless or lazy—well, our days are too few to spend them on those indifferent to our needs.

But that response to gratuitous complexity only reemphasizes our responsibility for our own writing, for it seems axiomatic that if we don't want others to impose carelessly complex writing on us, then we ought not impose it on others. If we are socially responsible writers, we should make our ideas no simpler than they deserve, but no more difficult than they have to be.

Responsible writers follow a rule whose more general theme you probably recognize:

> Write to others as you would have others write to you.

Few of us violate that principle deliberately. It's just that we are all so inclined to think that our own writing is clear that if our readers struggle to understand it, then the problem must be not our deep writing but their lazy reading.

But that's a mistake, because if you underestimate your readers' real needs, you risk losing more than their attention. You risk losing what writers since Aristotle have called a reliable *ethos*—the character that readers infer from your writing: does your writing make them think you are difficult or accessible? amiably candid or impersonally aloof? trustworthy or deceitful?

Over time, the ethos you project in individual pieces of writing settles into your reputation. So it's not just altruistically generous to go an extra step to help readers understand. It's pragmatically smart, because we tend to trust most a writer with a reputation for being thoughtful, reliable, and aware of her readers' needs.

But there is more at stake here than even reputation. What is at stake is the ethical foundations of a literate society.

An Ethic of Style

We write ethically when as a matter of principle, we would trade places with our intended readers and experience what they do as they read our writing. None of us wants to hack through gratuitously unclear writing, so it seems self-evidently unethical to impose that kind of writing on others. Unfortunately, it's not quite that simple. How, for example, do we think about those who write opaquely without knowing they do; or those who knowingly write that way but defend it?

Unintended Obscurity   Those who write in ways that seem dense and convoluted rarely think they do, much less intend to.

For example, I do not believe that the writers of this next passage *intended* to write it as unclearly as they did:

> A major condition affecting adult reliance on early communicative patterns is the extent to which the communication has been planned prior to its delivery. Adult speech behaviour takes on many of the characteristics of child language, where the communication is spontaneous and relatively unpredictable.
>
> —E. Ochs and B. Schieffelin,
> *Planned and Unplanned Discourse*

That means (I think),

> When adults speak spontaneously, they rely on patterns of child language.

The authors might object that I have oversimplified their meaning, but those eleven words express what I remember from their forty-four, and what really counts, after all, is not what we understand *as* we read, but how well we remember it the next day.

The ethical issue here is not those writers' willful indifference, but their innocent ignorance. In that case, when writers don't know better, readers who do (as you now do, I hope) have the duty to meet another term of the reader-writer contract: we must not just read carefully, but when given the opportunity, respond candidly and helpfully. I know many of you think that right now you do not have the standing to do that. But one day, you will.

Intended Misdirection

The ethics of writing are clearer when a writer knowingly uses language in self-interested ways.

Example #1: Who Made the Mistake?   For example, a few years ago, the Sears Company was accused of overcharging for automobile repairs. It responded with an ad saying:

> With over two million automotive customers serviced last year in California alone, mistakes may have occurred. However, Sears wants you to know that we would never intentionally violate the trust customers have shown in our company for 105 years.

In the first sentence, the writer avoided mentioning Sears as the party responsible for mistakes. He could have used a PASSIVE verb:

> . . . mistakes **may have been made.**

But that would have encouraged us to wonder "By whom?" Instead, the writer found a verb that moved Sears off stage by saying mistakes just "occurred," seemingly on their own.

In the second sentence of that ad, though, the writer focused on *Sears*, the specific responsible agent, because he wanted to emphasize its good intentions.

> **Sears** . . . would never intentionally violate . . .

If we revise the first sentence to focus on Sears and the second to hide it, we get a very different effect:

> When we serviced over two million automotive customers last year in California, we made mistakes. However, you should know that no intentional violation of 105 years of trust occurred.

That's a small point of stylistic manipulation, innocent of any malign motives. This next one is more significant.

Example #2: Who Pays the Bill?   Consider this letter from a natural gas utility telling me and hundreds of thousands of other customers that it was raising our rates. (The TOPIC/SUBJECT in every CLAUSE, MAIN or SUBORDINATE, is boldfaced.)

> **The Illinois Commerce Commission** has authorized a restructuring of our rates together with an increase in Service Charge revenues effective with service rendered on and after November 12, 1990. **This** is the first increase in rates for Peoples Gas in over six years. **The restructuring of rates** is consistent with the policy of the Public Utilities Act that **rates for service to various classes of utility customers** be based upon the cost of providing that service. **The new rates** move revenues from every class of customer closer to the cost actually incurred to provide gas service.

That notice is a model of misdirection: after the first sentence, the writer never begins a sentence with a human character, least of all the character whose interests are most at stake—me, the reader. He (or perhaps she) mentions me only twice, in the third person, never as a topic/agent/subject:

> . . . for service to various classes of utility **customers**
>
> . . . move revenues from every class of **customer**

The writer mentions the company only once, in the third person, and not as a responsible topic/agent/subject:

> . . . increase in rates for **Peoples Gas**

Had the company wanted to make clear who the real "doer" was and who was being done to, the notice would have read more like this:

> According to the Illinois Commerce Commission, **we** can now make you pay more for your gas service after November 12, 1990. **We** have not made you pay more in over six years, but under the Public Utilities Act, now **we** can.

If the writer *intended* to deflect responsibility, then we can reasonably charge him with breaching the First Rule of Ethical Writing, for surely, he would not want that same kind of writing directed to him, systematically hiding who is doing what in a matter close to his interests.

Example #3: Who Dies?   Finally, here is a passage that raises an even greater ethical issue, one involving life and death. Some time ago, the Government Accounting Office investigated why more than half the car owners who got recall letters did not comply with them. The GAO found that car owners could not understand the letters or were not sufficiently alarmed by them.

I received the following. It shows how writers can meet a legal obligation while evading an ethical one (I number the sentences):

> [1]A defect which involves the possible failure of a frame support plate may exist on your vehicle. [2]This plate (front suspension pivot bar support plate) connects a portion of the front suspension to the vehicle frame, and [3]its failure could affect vehicle directional control, particularly during heavy brake application. [4]In addition, your vehicle may require adjustment service to the hood secondary catch system. [5]The secondary catch may be misaligned so that the hood may not be adequately restrained to prevent hood fly-up in the event the primary latch is inadvertently left unengaged. [6]Sudden hood fly-up beyond the secondary catch while driving could impair driver visibility. [7]In certain circumstances, occurrence of either of the above conditions could result in vehicle crash without prior warning.

(When asked what make of car the letter refers to, I dodge the question.)

First, look at the subject/topics of the sentences.

[1]a defect	[2]this plate	[3]its failure
[4]your vehicle	[5]the secondary catch	
[6]sudden hood fly-up	[7]occurrence of either condition	

The main character/topic of that story is not me, the driver, but my car and its parts. In fact, the writers ignored me almost entirely (I am in *your vehicle* twice and *driver* once) and omitted all references to themselves. In sum, it says,

> There is a car that might have defective parts. Its plate could fail and its hood fly up. If they do, it could crash without warning.

The writers—probably a committee of lawyers—also nominalized verbs and made others passive when they referred to actions that might alarm me:

failure	vehicle directional control	heavy brake application
be misaligned	not restrained	hood fly-up
left unengaged	driver visibility	warning

If the writers intended to deflect my fear and maybe my anger, then they violated their ethical duty to write to me as they would have me write to them, for surely they would not swap places with a reader deliberately lulled into ignoring a condition that threatened his life.

Of course, being candid has its costs. I would be naive to claim that we are all free to write as we please, especially when a writer's job depends on protecting an employer's self-interest. Maybe the writers of that letter felt coerced into writing it as they did. But that doesn't mitigate the consequences. When we knowingly write in ways that we would not want others to write to us, we abrade the trust that sustains a civil society.

We should not, of course, confuse unethical indirectness with the human impulse to soften bad news. When a supervisor says "I'm afraid our new funding didn't come through" we know it means "You have no job." But that indirectness is motivated not by dishonesty, but by kindness.

It is important to note where these writers focused their attention. They chose the subject/topics of their sentences carefully to deflect attention from themselves and from their reader (me). Our choice of subjects is crucial not only when we want to be clear, but also when we want to be misleading.

Exercise 10.1

Revise the gas rate notice, using *you* as a topic/agent/subject. Then revise again, using *we*. For example:

> As the Illinois Commerce Commission has authorized, **you** will have to pay us higher service charges after November 12, 1990/**we** can charge you more after November 12 . . .

Would the company resist sending either revision? Why? Was the original "good" writing? What do you mean by "good"?

Exercise 10.2

Revise the recall letter, making *you* the subject of as many verbs and naming as many actions in verbs as you can. One of the sentences will read,

> If **you** BRAKE hard and the plate FAILS, **you** could . . .

Would the company be reluctant to send out that version? Is the original letter "good" writing? Which of the following, if either, is closer to the "truth"? Is that even the right question?

> If the plate fails, you could crash.
>
> If the plate fails, your car could crash.

Rationalizing Opacity

A more complicated ethical issue is how we should respond to those who know they write in a complex style, but claim they must, because they are breaking new intellectual ground. Are they right, or is that just self-serving rationalization? This is a vexing question, not just because we can settle it only case-by-case, but because we may not be able to settle it at all, at least not to everyone's satisfaction.

Here, for example, is a sentence from a leading figure in contemporary literary theory:

> If, for a while, the ruse of desire is calculable for the uses of discipline soon the repetition of guilt, justification, pseudo-scientific theories, superstition, spurious authorities and classifications can be seen as the desperate effort to "normalize" *formally* the disturbance of a discourse of splitting that violates the rational, enlightened claims of its enunciatory modality.
>
> —Homi K. Babba

Is that the expression of a thought so complex, so nuanced that what it says can be expressed only as written? Or is it babble? How do we decide whether in fact his nuances are, at least for ordinarily competent readers, just not accessible, given the time most of us have for finding them?

We owe readers an ethical duty to write precise and nuanced prose, but we ought not assume that they owe us an indefinite amount of their time to unpack it. If we choose to write in ways that we know will make readers struggle—well, it's a free country. In the marketplace of ideas, truth is the prime value, but not the only one. Another is the time it takes to extract it.

At the end of the day, I can suggest only that when writers claim their prose style must be difficult because their ideas are new, they are, as a matter of simple fact, more often wrong than right. The philosopher of language Ludwig Wittgenstein said,

> Whatever can be thought can be thought clearly; whatever can be written can be written clearly.

I'd add a nuance:

> Whatever can be written can usually be written *more* clearly, with just a bit more effort.

Salutary Complexity/Subversive Clarity

There are two more defenses of complexity: one claims that complexity is good for us, the other that clarity is actually bad.

As to the first claim, some argue that the harder we must work to understand what we read, the more deeply we must think and the better we will understand. Everyone should be happy to know that no evidence supports such a claim, and substantial evidence contradicts it.

As to the second claim, some argue that "clarity" is a device wielded by those in power to mislead us about who really controls our lives. By making things deceptively simple, they say, those who feed us information oversimplify it, rendering us unable to understand the full complexity of our political and social circumstances. Here is an example:

> The call to write curriculum in a language that is touted as clear and accessible is evidence of a moral and political vision that increasingly

collapses under the weight of its own anti-intellectualism. . . . [T]hose who make a call for clear writing synonymous with an attack on critical educators have missed the role that the "language of clarity" plays in a dominant culture that cleverly and powerfully uses "clear" and "simplistic" language to systematically undermine and prevent the conditions from arising for a public culture to engage in rudimentary forms of complex and critical thinking.

—Stanley Aronowitz,
Postmodern Education

He makes one good point: language is deeply implicated in politics, ideology, and control. In our earliest history, the educated elite used writing itself to exclude the illiterate, then Latin and French to exclude those who knew only English. More recently, those in authority have relied on a vocabulary thick with Latinate nominalizations and on a Standard English that requires those Outs aspiring to join the Ins to submit to a decade-long education, during which time they are expected to acquire not only the language of the Ins, but their values, as well.

Moreover, clarity is not a natural virtue, corrupted by fallen academics, bureaucrats, and others jealous to preserve their authority. Clarity is a value that is created by society and that society must work hard to maintain, for it is not just hard to write clearly. It is almost an unnatural act. It has to be learned, sometimes painfully (as this book demonstrates).

So is "clarity" an ideological value? Of course it is. How could it be otherwise? But those who attack clarity as part of an ideological conspiracy to oversimplify complicated social issues are as wrong as those who attack science because some use it for malign ends: neither science nor clarity is a threat; we are threatened by those who use clarity (or science) to deceive us. It is not clarity that subverts, but the unethical use of it. We must simply insist that, in principle, those who manage our affairs have a duty to tell us the truth as clearly as they can. They probably won't, but that just shifts the burden to us to call them on it.

With every sentence we write we have to choose, and the ethical quality of those choices depends on the motives behind them. Only by knowing motives can we know whether a writer of clear prose would willingly be the object of such writing, to be influenced (or manipulated) in the same way, with the same result.

That seems simple enough. But it's not.

An Extended Analysis

It's easy to abuse writers who manipulate us. It's more difficult to think about these matters when we are manipulated by those whom we would never charge with deceit. But it is just such cases that force us to think hard about matters of style and ethics.

The most celebrated texts in our history are the Declaration of Independence, the Constitution, and Abraham Lincoln's Gettysburg Address and Second Inaugural Address. In previous editions of this book, I discussed how Thomas Jefferson artfully manipulated the language of the Declaration and how Lincoln did the same in the Gettysburg Address. Here I examine his Second Inaugural Address.

Lincoln delivered it in March 1865, just before the end of the Civil War. He knew the North would win, but feared that it would punish the South for both slavery and the carnage of the war. As we have seen, he was right to worry. Anticipating that outcome, Lincoln tried to reconcile North and South in words engraved in our national memory:

> With malice toward none; with charity for all; with firmness in the right, as God gives us to see the right, let us strive on to finish the work we are in; to bind up the nation's wounds; to care for him who shall have borne the battle, and for his widow, and his orphan—to do all which may achieve and cherish a just, and a lasting peace, among ourselves, and with all nations.

We have, however, not committed to memory his opening sentences, because we are stirred by neither the elegance of their language nor the loftiness of their thought:

> Fellow-countrymen: At this second appearing to take the oath of the presidential office, there is less occasion for an extended address than there was at the first. Then a statement, somewhat in detail, of a course to be pursued, seemed fitting and proper. Now, at the expiration of four years, during which public declarations have been constantly called forth on every point and phase of the great contest which still absorbs the attention and engrosses the energies of the nation, little that is new could be presented. The progress of our arms, upon which all else chiefly depends, is as well known to the public as to myself; and it is, I trust, reasonably satisfactory and encouraging to all. With high hope for the future, no prediction in regard to it is ventured.

In fact, were that paragraph anonymous, we might judge it pedestrian, because it is as abstract and impersonal as the worst institutional prose. Lincoln could have written this:

> Fellow-countrymen: As **I appear** here for the second time to take the oath of the presidential office, **I** have less occasion to **address** you at length than **I** did at the first. Then **I** thought it fitting and proper that **I state** in detail the course to be pursued . . .

In fact, that is close to the style of his First Inaugural Address:

> Fellow-citizens of the United States: In compliance with a custom as old as the government itself, **I appear** before you to address you briefly, and to take before you the oath prescribed by the Constitution . . . **I** do not **consider** it necessary at present for me to discuss . . .

Or he could have written this:

> Fellow-countrymen: As **we** meet for this second taking of the oath of the presidential office, **we** have less need for an extended address than **we** had at the first. Then **we** felt a statement, describing in detail, the course **we** would pursue, would be fitting and proper . . .

And that is close to the style of the Gettysburg Address:

> Now **we** are engaged in a great Civil War, testing whether that nation, or any nation so conceived and so dedicated, can long endure. **We** are met on a great battlefield of that war. **We** have come to dedicate a portion of that field . . .

In fact, Lincoln seems so intent on impersonality that in his last sentence he dangled a modifier:

> **With high hope for the future,** no prediction in regard to it is ventured. [With high hope for the future, I do not venture to predict it.]

Either Lincoln dozed, or he had something else in mind.

In that first paragraph, the topics of his sentences deflect our attention from the participants and focus it on the event and his message (they are boldfaced):

> **this second appearing to take the oath of the presidential office,** there is . . .
>
> **a statement** . . . seemed fitting
>
> **public declarations** have been constantly called forth
>
> **little that is new** could be presented

The progress of our arms . . . is . . . well known

it [progress of arms] . . . is . . . encouraging to all.

no prediction . . . is ventured.

Why did he choose such an impersonal style (assuming he actually made a choice)? We might understand better if we looked at the rest of the speech. As you read, notice his subjects/topic (bold-faced):

On the occasion corresponding to this four years ago, **all thoughts** were anxiously directed to an impending civil war. **All** dreaded it—**all** sought to avert it. While **the inaugural address** was being delivered from this place, devoted altogether to saving the Union without war, **insurgent agents** were in the city seeking to destroy it without war— seeking to dissolve the Union, and divide effects, by negotiation. **Both parties** deprecated war, but **one of them** would make war rather than let **the nation** survive; and **the other** would accept war rather than let **it** perish. And **the war** came.

One eighth of the whole population** were colored slaves, not distributed generally over the Union, but localized in the southern part of it. **These slaves** constituted a peculiar and powerful interest. **All** knew that **this interest** was, somehow, the cause of the war. **To strengthen, perpetuate, and extend this interest** was the object for which **the insurgents** would rend the Union, even by war; while **the government** claimed no right to do more than to restrict the territorial enlargement of it. **Neither party** expected for the war the magnitude or the duration which **it** has already attained. **Neither** anticipated that **the cause of the conflict** might cease with, or even before, **the conflict** itself should cease. **Each** looked for an easier triumph and a result less fundamental and astounding. **Both** read the same Bible, and pray to the same God; and **each** invokes His aid against the other. It may seem strange that **any men** should dare to ask a just God's assistance in wringing their bread from the sweat of other men's faces; but let **us** judge not, that **we** be not judged. **The prayers of both** could not be answered; **that of neither** has been answered fully. **The Almighty** has His own purposes. "Woe unto the world because of offences! for it must needs be that offences come; but woe to that man by whom the offence cometh." If we shall suppose that **American slavery** is one of **those offences which** in the providence of God, must needs come, but which, having continued through His appointed time, **He** now wills to remove, and that **He** gives to both North and South, this terrible war as the woe due to those by whom **the offence** came, shall **we** discern therein any departure from those divine attributes which **the believers in a Living**

God always ascribe to Him? Fondly do **we** hope—fervently do **we** pray—that **this mighty scourge of war** may speedily pass away. Yet, if **God** wills that **it** continue until **all the wealth piled by the bondman's two hundred and fifty years of unrequited toil** shall be sunk, and until **every drop of blood drawn with the lash** shall be paid by another drawn with the sword, as was said three thousand years ago, so still **it** must be said, "**the judgments of the Lord**, are true and righteous altogether."

With malice toward none; with charity for all; with firmness in the right, as **God** gives us to see the right, let **us** strive on to finish the work **we** are in; to bind up the nation's wounds; to care for **him who** shall have borne the battle, and for his widow, and his orphan—to do all which may achieve and cherish a just, and a lasting peace, among ourselves, and with all nations.

In the first sentence of the second paragraph, Lincoln continues the impersonal style of his introduction, both nominalized and passive:

On the occasion corresponding to this four years ago, **all thoughts** were . . . directed to an impending civil war.

He could have written *everyone was thinking of an impending civil war.*

Then for two short clauses, he switches to the simplicity we expect:

All dreaded it—**all** sought to avert it.

But in the next sentence, he adopts the impersonal passive again:

While **the inaugural address** was being delivered . . .

But then he returns to the direct, subject/agent–verb/action style for several sentences (note, however, that the subjects are general, not specific):

insurgent agents were in the city seeking to destroy it

Both parties deprecated war

one of them would make war

the other would accept war

And **the war** came.

(How can war just "come"? How else could he have expressed that idea?)

He then writes an oddly awkward passive sentence about slavery:

One eighth of the whole population were colored slaves, not distributed generally over the Union, but localized in the southern part of it.

This would have been more direct:

Slaves were one eighth of the population, most of them in the South.

In the indirectness of his sentence, Lincoln seems to hold slavery at a distance. He does the same in the next two sentences. They begin clearly, but toward their ends, they slip into impersonality:

These slaves constituted a peculiar and powerful interest.

All knew that **this interest** was, somehow, the cause of the war.

(Why didn't he write, *All knew that slavery caused the war,* or even, *The South caused the war?*)

Most of the subjects and verbs in the rest of the sentences reflect the direct style that we associate with Lincoln, but note how indirectly he keeps referring to slavery (I italicize references to it and boldface subject/topics):

To strengthen, perpetuate, and extend *this interest* was the object . . .

the insurgents would rend the Union

the government claimed no right to do more than to restrict *the territorial enlargement of it*

Neither party expected for the war the magnitude or the duration

it has already attained.

Neither anticipated

the cause **of the conflict** might cease

the conflict itself should cease

(How can slavery and war just "cease"? How else could he have written that?)

At this point, Lincoln's style quickens through a series of short clauses that introduce God as a character, not yet as an active agent, but as a passive OBJECT of prayers and requests (references to God are italicized):

Each looked for an easier triumph

Both read the same Bible, and pray to the same *God*

each invokes *His* aid against the other.

any men should dare to ask a *just God's assistance* in wringing their bread from the sweat of other men's faces

let **us** judge not

Then in three short passive clauses, Lincoln implies that God can act, but has not yet acted as either side has prayed:

> that **we** be not judged [by God?]
>
> **The prayers of both** could not be answered [by God];
>
> **that of neither** has been answered fully.

Lincoln then returns to his direct active style, naming God in the subject of four of the next eleven clauses as an acting, purposeful agent:

> *The Almighty* has His own purposes.
>
> If **we** shall suppose that
>
> **American slavery** . . . must needs come
>
> *He* now wills to remove
>
> *He* gives to both North and South this terrible war
>
> shall **we** discern therein any departure from those divine attributes
>
> **the believers in** *a living God* always ascribe to *Him?*
>
> Fondly do **we** hope—fervently do **we** pray
>
> **this mighty scourge of war** may speedily pass away.
>
> Yet, if *God* wills that
>
> **it** continue until
>
> **all the wealth piled . . . toil** shall be sunk,
>
> **every drop of blood . . .** shall be paid by another
>
> **the judgments of** *the Lord*, are true

Then the majestic climax we all remember:

> With malice toward none . . . let **us** strive on to finish the work we are in . . .

In other words, once Lincoln gets past that first abstract and indirect paragraph and a half, he demonstrates what we take to be his classic American prose style: clear, candid, simple, and direct.

With one striking and powerful exception.

Of all the sentences crafted by American writers, none, I think, is craftier than this one, the longest in the speech, by far the most complex, and certainly the most important:

> If we shall suppose that American slavery is one of those offences which in the providence of God, must needs come, but which, having continued through His appointed time, He now wills to remove, and

that He gives to both North and South this terrible war as the woe due to those by whom the offence came, shall we discern therein any departure from those divine attributes which the believers in a living God always ascribe to Him?

In that seventy-eight-word sentence Lincoln implies that the North has no right to punish the South for the war, because the war was given by God:

> **He** gives to both North and South this terrible war . . .

Nor can the North take credit for ending slavery. God did that, too:

> **He** now wills to remove [this offence of American slavery]

And (as Lincoln implies a few sentences later) it will not be a triumphant North that ends the war, but God, at a time of His own choosing:

> If **God** wills [to] continue [the war]

In other words, the North has no right to punish the South for the war or to take credit for ending it or slavery: it's all God's doing. That's the whole point of the speech. It justifies its great last sentence.

But before he made God responsible for the war and for ending both it and slavery, he wrote this oddly indirect passage about slavery's origin:

> **American slavery** is one of those **offences which** in the providence of God, must needs come

Offences . . . must needs come echoes the clauses *the war came, the cause of the conflict might cease,* and, *the conflict itself should cease.* It all seems to happen on its own.

That clause about slavery is ambiguous in two ways. First, how are we to parse the phrase *American slavery?* Is *American* the agent of slavery as in *Americans enslave Africans,* or its victim, as in *Americans are enslaved?* Or both?

Second, how should we parse the verb *continued?*

> . . . one of those offencee . . . which, having continued through His appointed time, He now wills to remove

It could mean *the offence of slavery continued through His appointed time,* or it could mean *God continued the offense of slavery through His appointed time.* Which is it? Or is it both?

But what really distinguishes this passage is its nominalizations. There are only five in these seventy-eight words, a strikingly low proportion for a dramatic speech. But three of them occur in just the first sixteen words: *slavery offence,* and *providence.* We could revise them into verbs and assign them subject/agents:

American **slavery**	→	Americans ENSLAVE Africans
is one of those **offences**	→	Americans OFFENDED God
which in the **providence** of God	→	God PROVIDES [something]

If we reassemble those clauses into a sentence, we get a startling claim:

> God provided that Americans enslave Africans, and that offended God.

Might we reasonably suppose that Lincoln thought a statement so direct would raise a theological issue so thorny that, at least on this occasion, he would just as soon avoid it?

To be sure, Lincoln believed that God had ordained every terrible thing that happened to both North and South. And he had no problem saying clearly that God *gave* the war to both sides, that God *willed* the end of slavery (as opposed to its just "ceasing," as he had written earlier), and though he prays the war will "pass away," he also knows that God might *will* it to continue.

But Lincoln seems unwilling to assign the origin of slavery to God. He uses direct verbs to express God's agency in bringing the war and ending both it and slavery, but he nominalizes verbs that would make God responsible for slavery, then buries that agency and action in the middle of the sentence (*in the providence of God*). Lincoln seemed to want it both ways: God is responsible for everything, including slavery, but he doesn't want to say so.

That seventy-eight-word sentence is, I think, the stylistic *tour de force* of American literature.

But what does that have to do with his impersonal opening paragraph? Perhaps this: Lincoln believed that the enormity of the war was God's doing and that both North and South had earned God's punishment. In fact, the only time he refers to North or South by name, he makes them the object of God's wrath:

> He gives to both North and South this terrible war . . .

He made all the other subject/topic/agents nonspecific, even vague: *agents, parties, one, the other, both, all, each, neither, any man.* In fact, Lincoln seems deliberately to avoid assigning any action to any specific agent, until he introduces God as the Ultimate Agent.

And perhaps that explains the impersonality of that opening paragraph. Knowing he would later focus on God as the only specific agent in the story of the Civil War, Lincoln wanted to create an indefinite, impersonal blue/gray–gray/blue background of minor players to subordinate their—and his—role in American history to God's direct agency.

It is a great speech, especially that last sentence whose words are part of our national conscience. Even the parts that feel uninspired now seem at least explicable.

But now recall the question that motivated this discussion. What are we to make of these stylistic sleights-of-hand, of the hypercomplexity of that key sentence? How do we judge the way Lincoln (what word do we use here—manipulates? handles? manages?) shapes the responses of his audience? In so doing, was he unethical? The easy answer is no, and I think that's right, at least if we judge by his intentions. But the question forces us to think hard about the ethic of clarity as an unqualified, foundational value. At the crucial moment in his speech, Lincoln was not clear, and, I think, deliberately and rightly so.

Exercise 10.3

There are 702 words in the Second Inaugural. In most prose, the proportion of nominalizations to other words is roughly 1:10, with 1:6 high and 1:20 very low. Count the nominalizations in this speech. What do you make of their proportion to all words? Nine nominalizations appear in the first 134 words, or about 1:15. What is the proportion in the rest of the speech? Where are the other nominalizations concentrated? Why? Do you think that proportion affects how we respond to this speech?

Exercise 10.4

Find every mention of the word *war* or references to it. (There are sixteen.) Does Lincoln use the word systematically as a subject or object? Compare it to how he uses the word *slavery* and words for it, such as *interest* and *cause*. What do you make of how he uses those terms?

Exercise 10.5

Lincoln distanced God from slavery as deliberately as the writer of the automobile recall letter distanced the manufacturer from its defective product. What kinds of ethical distinctions, if any, would you make between them? Does the First Rule of Ethical Writing apply here (*Write to others as . . .*)?

Exercise 10.6

Break up the "If we shall suppose" sentence into shorter sentences. What is the effect? You could begin

Suppose that American slavery . . .

Exercise 10.7

For this exercise, you will need a copy of the Declaration of Independence. The Declaration of Independence has three parts:

- An explanation of when one form of government may be replaced with another. Most of the subjects in this part are abstractions.

- Beginning at *To prove this,* a list of charges against King George. Most of the subjects in this section are *he.*

- Beginning at *In every stage of these Oppressions,* an account of attempts to avoid separation, followed by the last sentence declaring independence. Most subjects in this section are *we.*

Why does Jefferson shift his subject/agent/topics so systematically?

Exercise 10.8

Here is the first sentence of the first section of the Declaration of Independence:

> When in the Course of human events, **it becomes necessary** for one people to dissolve the political bands which have connected them with another . . .

He could have written,

> In the course of human events, **we** have decided that **we** have to dissolve . . .

He wrote the first charge against King George like this:

> **He** has refused his Assent to Laws.

He could have written it like either of these two:

> There have been **repeated refusals** of Assent to Laws.
> **We** have been refused his Assent to Laws.

And he wrote the first sentence of the last part like this:

> Nor have **We** been wanting in attention to our British brethren.

He could have written it like either of these two:

> Nor have **our British brethren** been wanting for our attention.
> **Attention** has been directed to our British brethern as well.

Revise more sentences in the first part so that they are like sentences in the last part, more sentences in the last part so that they are like those in the first part, then some in the middle part so that they are like those in either the first or last parts. What effect do those changes have? In particular, what do you make of these next constructions? (Review p. 193.) Subjects are boldfaced, verbs capitalized.

> **a decent respect to the opinions of mankind** REQUIRES
> **Prudence,** indeed, will DICTATE
> **all experience** hath SHEWN
> **the necessity** . . . CONSTRAINS them to alter their . . . Government
> **the necessity** . . . DENOUNCES [proclaims] our Separation

SUMMING UP

How, finally, do we decide what counts as "good" writing? Is it clear, graceful, and candid, even if it fails to achieve its end? Or is it writing that does a job, regardless of its integrity and means? We have a problem so long as *good* can mean either ethically sound or pragmatically successful. We resolve that dilemma by our First Principle of Ethical Writing: we write well when we would willingly experience what our readers do when they read what we've written. That puts the burden on us to imagine our readers and their feelings.

If you are even moderately advanced in your academic or professional career, you've experienced the consequences of unclear writing, especially when it is your own. If you are in your early years of college, though, you may wonder whether all this talk about clarity, ethics, and ethos is just so much finger wagging. At the moment, you may be happy to find enough words to fill three pages, much less worry how clear they are. And you may be reading textbooks that have been heavily edited to make them clear to first-year students. So you may not yet have experienced much carelessly dense writing. But it's only a matter of time before you will.

Some wonder why they should struggle to learn to write clearly when bad writing seems so common and has no cost. What experienced readers know, and you eventually will, is that clear and graceful writers are so few that when we find them, we are desperately grateful for them. They do not go unrewarded.

I also know that for many writers the pleasure of crafting a good sentence or paragraph is often just in the achievement of it, for its own sake. It is an ethical satisfaction some of us find not just in writing, but in everything we do: we take pleasure in doing good work, no matter the job. It is a view expressed by the philosopher Alfred North Whitehead, with both clarity and grace:

> Finally, there should grow the most austere of all mental qualities; I mean the sense for style. It is an aesthetic sense, based on admiration for the direct attainment of a foreseen end, simply and without waste. Style in art, style in literature, style in science, style in logic, style in practical execution have fundamentally the same aesthetic qualities, namely, attainment and restraint. The love of a subject in itself and for itself, where it is not the sleepy pleasure of pacing a mental quarter-deck, is the love of style as manifested in that study. Here we are

brought back to the position from which we started, the utility of education. Style, in its finest sense, is the last acquirement of the educated mind; it is also the most useful. It pervades the whole being. The administrator with a sense for style hates waste; the engineer with a sense for style economizes his material; the artisan with a sense for style prefers good work. Style is the ultimate morality of mind.

—Alfred North Whitehead, *The Aims
of Education and Other Essays*

EPILOGUE 1

From Clarity
to Coherence

The beginning is half of the whole.
—PLATO

One of the most difficult things [to write] is the first paragraph.
I have spent many months on a first paragraph,
and once I get it, the rest just comes out very easily.
In the first paragraph you solve most of the problems
with your book. The theme is defined,
the style, the tone.
—GABRIEL GARCIA MARQUEZ

UNDERSTANDING COHERENCE

We can struggle through clotted sentences if we must, but incoherence just defeats us. Like the terms *clotted* and *unclear*, though, the terms *coherent* and *incoherent* don't refer to anything on the page. Coherence is an experience we create for ourselves as we make sense of what we read. That experience depends most on knowledge we bring to our reading. We can make sense of almost anything if we already know a lot about its subject matter. But when we lack perfect knowledge, we depend quite a bit on signals and cues we see on the page to help us integrate what we read there with the knowledge we already have. You help your readers do that by building those signals and cues into your writing. In this first Epilogue, I explain how to do that.

But no matter how clear and coherent your document might be, your readers will value it only if they read it. We all know that some readers will, inevitably, read what we write and say *I don't agree*. We accept that. What we can't accept is that many will say *I don't care* and not read at all. In Epilogue Two, I discuss how to help readers not only understand what you write, but *want* to.

Local Coherence

In Lessons Five and Six, we looked at three features that help readers create "local" coherence in short passages:

- A sentence introducing the passage states at its end the key concepts that run through the rest of the passage (pp. 101–103).
- All the sentences follow the old-new principle (pp. 75–78).
- Collectively, their TOPICS focus on a few related characters (pp. 101–103).

But readers need more than locally coherent passages to grasp the larger coherence of a whole document. To help them do that, you can use a principle we've already looked at for writing clear sentences: begin each unit of a document—each paragraph, section, and whole—with a short, easily grasped segment that introduces a longer, more complex part.

The ideas in this epilogue have been developed and refined together with Greg Colomb, Department of English, University of Virginia.

We've seen how that principle works in a sentence:

1a. Greater knowledge of pre-Columbian civilizations and the effect of European colonization on them has led to a historical reassessment of Columbus's role in world history.

✓1b. Historians are reassessing Columbus's role in world history, because they know more about pre-Columbian civilizations and how European colonization affected them.

Sentence (1a) opens with a long, complex, hard-to-grasp subject, *Greater knowledge of pre-Columbian civilizations and the effect of European colonization on them.* We read sentence (1b) more easily because each of its two CLAUSES begins with a short, easily grasped segment—a short SUBJECT connected to a specific VERB:

✓1b. **Historians** ARE REASSESSING . . . , because **they** KNOW . . .

But sentence (1b) seems clearer for two more reasons. First, the sentence opens with a short, easily grasped MAIN CLAUSE that introduces a longer, more complex SUBORDINATE CLAUSE.

[Historians are reassessing Columbus's role in world history], *short and simple* [because they know more about pre-Columbian civilizations and how European colonization affected them]. *longer and more complex*

That is just another example of the short-before-long principle.

A second principle that makes (1b) clearer is one not yet discussed, but is crucial to the reader's sense of coherence. That short opening clause states the *main point* of the sentence, its most important claim: *Historians are reassessing Columbus's role . . .* That claim is then supported by the longer and more complex clause that follows. Those two principles are crucial to helping readers understand not just a complex sentence, but the global coherence of every paragraph, every section, and the whole.

Global Coherence

To grasp the coherence of a unit *of any length,* readers must see three things:

1. a short, easily grasped segment that introduces each unit, whether that unit is a paragraph, a section, or the whole;

2. at the end of that introductory segment, a sentence that states the *point* of that unit, a statement that the rest of the unit develops, explains, or supports;

3. toward the end of that point sentence, the key concepts that the rest of that unit develops.

The point of a paragraph is often called its *topic sentence;* the point of a whole document is sometimes called its *thesis*. We have no special term for the point of a section. I will use the term *point* to name the key statement in units of all sizes, from a paragraph to the whole. When readers see that point sentence in a short, easily grasped opening segment, they read and understand the longer and more complex following segment more easily.

For example, read this paragraph:

> 1a. Thirty sixth-grade students wrote essays that were analyzed to determine the effectiveness of eight weeks of training to distinguish fact from opinion. That ability is an important aspect of making sound arguments of any kind. In an essay written before instruction began, the writers failed almost completely to distinguish fact from opinion. In an essay written after four weeks of instruction, the students visibly attempted to distinguish fact from opinion, but did so inconsistently. In three more essays, they distinguished fact from opinion more consistently, but never achieved the predicted level. In a final essay written six months after instruction ended, they did no better than they did in their preinstruction essay. Their training had some effect on their writing during the instruction period, but it was inconsistent and six months after instruction it had no measurable effect.

The first few sentences introduce us to what follows, but we do not see in them the key concepts that follow: *inconsistently, never achieved, no better, no measurable effect,* terms crucial to the *point* of the passage. Worse, we don't read that point sentence until the end of the paragraph. As a consequence, it seems to ramble.

Compare this version:

> 1b. In this study, thirty sixth-grade students were taught to distinguish fact from opinion. They did so during the instruction period, but the effect was inconsistent, less than predicted, and six months after instruction ended, the instruction had no measurable effect. In an essay written before instruction began, the writers failed almost completely to distinguish fact from opinion. In an essay written after four weeks of instruction, the students visibly attempted to distinguish fact from opinion, but did so inconsistently. In three more essays, they distinguished fact from opinion more consistently, but never achieved the predicted level. In a final essay written six months after instruction ended, they did no better than

they did in their preinstruction essay. We thus conclude that short-term training to distinguish fact from opinion has no consistent or long-term effect.

In that paragraph, we quickly grasp that the first two sentences introduce the paragraph. And in the second sentence, we see two things: the point of the paragraph and its key terms. As a consequence, we feel the paragraph hangs together better and we read it with more understanding.

In this brief Epilogue, we can look at only short passages to illustrate these principles, but we can imagine how they apply to longer stretches of prose. Imagine two documents: in one, the point of each paragraph, each section, and the whole appears at its *end* (as in [1a]); in the other, each point appears in an *introductory* segment to every paragraph, section, and of the whole (as in [1b]). Which would be easier to read and understand? The second, of course.

Keep in mind this principle about where to put the point sentence in its opening segment: put it at its *end;* make it the *last* sentence that your reader reads before starting the longer, more complex segment that follows.

- In a paragraph, the introductory segment is usually just a single sentence, so by default, it will be the last sentence readers read before they read the rest of the paragraph.

- Some paragraphs, however, have a *two*-sentence introduction (as did [1b]). In that case, be sure the point of the paragraph is the *second* sentence, making it the last thing readers read before they start the rest of the paragraph.

- For longer sections, your introduction may be a paragraph or more. For a whole document, you might need several paragraphs. Even in those cases, put your point sentence at the end of that introductory segment, no matter how long it is (shorter is usually better). Make your point sentence the last thing readers read before they begin reading the longer, more complex segments that follow.

Some inexperienced writers think that if they tip off their main point early, readers will be bored and not read on. That fear is baseless. If you ask an interesting question, readers will want to see how you support your answer (for more on that issue, see Epilogue Two).

Here's the point: To write a document that readers will think is coherent, open every paragraph, section, and the whole with a short, easily grasped introductory segment. Put at the end of that opening segment a sentence that states both the point of the unit and the key concepts that follow. Point sentences constitute the outline of your document, its logical structure. If readers miss them, they may judge your writing to be incoherent.

Two More Requirements for Coherence

We can make sense of almost anything we read if we know its points. But readers read most easily when they see two more things.

1. **Readers must see how everything is *relevant* to a point.** Consider this paragraph:

   > We analyzed essays written by sixth-grade students to determine the effectiveness of training in distinguishing fact from opinion. In an essay written before training, the students failed almost completely to distinguish fact and opinion. These essays were also badly organized in several ways. In the first two essays after training began, the students attempted to distinguish fact from opinion, but did so inconsistently. They also produced fewer spelling and punctuation errors. In the essays four through seven, they distinguished fact from opinion more consistently, but in their final essay, written six months after completion of instruction, they did no better than they did in their first essay. Their last essay was significantly longer than their first one, however. Their training thus had some effect on their writing during the training period, but it was inconsistent and transient.

   What are those sentences about spelling, organization, and length doing there? When readers can't see the relevance of lots of sentences to a point, they judge what they read to be incoherent.

   I'm sorry to say that I can't give you a simple way to judge relevance, because it's so abstract a quality. I can list only its most important kinds. Sentences are relevant to a point when they offer this:

   - background or context,
   - points of paragraphs, sections, and the whole,

- reasons supporting a point,
- evidence, facts, or data supporting a reason,
- an explanation of reasoning or methods,
- consideration of other points of view.

If your readers can't put most of what they read into one of those categories, they may judge your writing to be incoherent.

2. **Readers must see how the parts of your document are ordered.** Readers want to see not just the relevance of everything they read to a point, but the principle behind the order of its parts. We look for three kinds of order: chronological, coordinate, and logical.

- **Chronological** This is the simplest order, from earlier to later (or vice versa), either as a narrative or as cause and effect. Signal time with *first, then, finally;* signal cause and effect with *as a result, because of that,* and so on. The paragraph about the essay research was chronologically organized.

- **Coordinate** Two or more sections are coordinate when they are like pillars equally supporting a common roof. *There are three reasons why* . . . Order those sections so that their sequence makes sense to your reader—by importance, complexity, and so on—then signal that order with words and phrases such as *first, second,* . . . or *also, another, more important, in addition,* and so on. That's how this section on order is organized.

- **Logical** This is the most complex order, by example and generalization (or vice versa), premise and conclusion (or vice versa), or by assertion and contradiction. Signal logic with *for example, on the other hand, it follows that* . . .

DIAGNOSIS AND REVISION

To diagnose how well your readers will see your points and the coherence of your document, do this:

1. Draw a line after the introduction to your whole document.
2. Divide the body of the document into sections and subsections. (You might even introduce them with headings.)
3. Circle the introductory segment of each section. (If you are ambitious, do the same for every paragraph.)

4. Highlight the point of the whole document (it should be at the end of your introduction and again toward the beginning of your conclusion.)

5. Circle the point of every section.

Now look for the following:

1. Introductory segments for the whole document and for each of its sections should be separate paragraphs.

2. The point sentence for each unit should be close to or at the end of each introductory segment.

3. Each point sentence should state at its end the key concepts that run through what follows.

4. When read in sequence, those point sentences should coherently summarize your whole document.

If your readers might not see those features quickly, revise so that they will.

The Costs and Benefits of Cookie-Cutter Writing

Some writers fear that this kind of writing inhibits their creativity or that readers will be bored by the predictability of their sentences and paragraphs. That's a reasonable concern, but *only* if you are writing an essay in which you are exploring your ideas, even discovering them, *and* you are writing for yourself, or for readers who not only expect but want to follow twists and turns that lead to an unexpected insight. If you are writing that kind of essay for that kind of willing reader, go to it. Don't tie yourself to what I've said here. (Having said that, I cannot resist adding that all these principles are far less restrictive than the conventions of a sonnet, a form that did not crimp the creativity of generations of English poets, including Shakespeare.)

On most occasions, however, most of us read and write not for pleasure, but for a more practical end—we write to communicate easily with readers who want to understand what they read quickly. You help them do that when you locate point sentences where they look for them and when your sentences follow the principles we've looked at over the course of ten lessons.

Such writing may seem cut-and-dried—to you, because you will be so conscious of it. But it earns the gratitude of readers who have too little time to read, understand, and remember everything they must and who will, in any event, focus more on understanding the substance of your writing than on critiquing its form.

A last word on creativity: far from hindering it, this kind of careful, systematic writing (and planning) encourages you to think about your thinking more carefully than you might have otherwise. The more easily you can *see* the logic of your essay or report in its points, the more critically you can think about what you have written.

SUMMING UP

Plan your paragraphs, sections, and the whole on this model:

<u>Researchers</u> have made strides in the **early and accurate diagnosis** of *Alzheimer's*, [But <u>those **diagnoses**</u> have raised A NEW HUMAN PROBLEM about **informing** *those at risk* before they show any *symptoms of it*.] _{point}

Open each unit, with a relatively short segment introducing it.

End that segment with a sentence stating the point of that unit.

Toward the end of that point sentence, use key terms that the rest of the unit develops.

Not too long ago, when <u>physicians</u> examined an older patient who seemed *out of touch with reality,* <u>they</u> had to **guess** whether that person had *Alzheimer's* or was *only senile.* In the past few years, however, <u>they</u> have been able to use **new and more reliable tests** focusing on genetic clues. But in <u>**the accuracy of these new tests**</u> lies the RISK OF ANOTHER KIND OF HUMAN TRAGEDY: <u>Physicians</u> may be able to **predict** *Alzheimer's* long before its overt appearance, but such an <u>**early diagnosis**</u> could PSYCHOLOGICALLY DEVASTATE AN APPARENTLY HEALTHY PERSON.

In the longer segment that follows, use consistent topics (underlined).

Make every sentence follow the old-new principle.

Repeat key terms introduced toward the end of the opening segment (boldfaced, italicized, and capitalized).

Order sentences, paragraphs, and sections in a way that readers understand.

Make all sentences relevant to the point of the unit that they constitute.

EPILOGUE 2
Motivating Readers

A problem well-put is half solved.
—JOHN DEWEY

Looking back, I think it was more difficult
to see what the problems were
than to solve them.
—CHARLES DARWIN

The uncreative mind can spot wrong answers,
but it takes a creative mind to spot wrong questions.
—ANTONY JAY

Readers must see the elements I described in Epilogue One to think what they read is coherent, but they might not find them if they don't feel like looking. If we are deeply interested in a topic, we'll read anything about it we can get our hands on. We read even more carefully, however, when we read not just about a topic, but about a problem that is important to us—from finding a good job to eradicating AIDS. When we are motivated by a problem, we don't need persuading to read something that tells us its solution. So even before you begin drafting, don't imagine your task as just writing about a topic that happens to interest *you*. See yourself as posing and solving a problem that is (or should be) important to *your readers*.

Often, however, the problem you'll have to write about is one that your readers might not care about, or even know. If so, you face a challenge not just because you must overcome your readers' natural inclination to say *So what?*, but because you get only one shot at capturing their attention, in the introduction to your document. That's where you must not only state your main point and establish your key concepts, but motivate readers to care about them. For example, read this introduction (all these examples are much shorter than typical introductions).

> When college students go out to relax on the weekend, many now "binge," downing several alcoholic drinks quickly until they are drunk or even pass out. It is a behavior that has been spreading through colleges and universities across the country, especially at large state universities. It once was done mostly by men, but now even women binge. It has drawn the attention of parents, college administrators, and researchers.

That introduction offers only a topic; it does not motivate us to care about it: unless a reader is already interested in the issue, she may shrug and ask *So what? Who cares?*

Contrast that introduction with this one: it tells us why bingeing is an issue worth our attention:

> Alcohol has been a big part of college life for hundreds of years. From football weekends to fraternity parties, college students drink and often drink hard. But a kind of drinking known as "binge" drinking is spreading through our colleges and universities. It is drinking quickly just to get drunk or even to pass out. Bingeing is far from the harmless fun long associated with college life. In the last six months, it has been cited in at least six deaths, many injuries, and considerable destruc-

tion of property. It is behavior that crosses the line from fun to reck-lessness that kills and injures not just drinkers but those around them. We may not be able to stop bingeing entirely, but we must try to con-trol its worst costs by educating students in how to manage its risks.

As short as that introduction is, it has three parts that appear in many, if not most of the introductions that we read in print. Each part has a role in motivating a reader to read on. The parts are

Shared Context – Problem – Solution.

Part 1: Establishing a Shared Context

Not all pieces of writing open with a shared context, but so many do that you may not even be aware of it. We see a shared context in the second introduction above:

> **Alcohol has been a big part of college life for hundreds of years. From football weekends to fraternity parties, college students drink and often drink hard.** *shared context* But a kind of . . .

That particular shared context offers historical background, but it has a special role in motivating you to read on: I wanted you to agree with that context *just so that I could then qualify it, to say, in effect, that while you think you know the whole story, you don't.* That *but* signals the coming qualification:

> . . . drink and often drink hard *shared context* **But a kind of drinking known as "binge" drinking is spreading . . .**

In other words, college drinking seems unproblematic, *but it turns out not to be.* And I hoped that small surprise would motivate you to read on, to see that what you believed is in fact at least incom-plete, maybe even wrong.

No opening move is more common among experienced writers: open with a seeming truth, then qualify it. You can find countless examples of it in articles in newspapers, magazines, and profes-sional journals. It can be a single sentence, as in that example, or, in a professional journal, pages long, where it is called a "literature review" that lays out what other researchers have said and that the writer will qualify or even contradict.

Not every piece of writing opens with this move; some open with the second element of an introduction: a statement of a problem.

Part 2: Stating the Problem

If the writer opens with the shared context, she will typically introduce the problem with a *but* or *however:*

> Alcohol has been a big part of college life for hundreds of years. From football weekends to fraternity parties, college students drink and often drink hard. *shared context* **[But a kind of drinking known as "binge" drinking is spreading through our colleges and universities. It is drinking quickly just to get drunk or even to pass out. Bingeing is far from the harmless fun long associated with college life. In the last six months, it has been cited in at least six deaths, many injuries, and considerable destruction of property. It is behavior that crosses the line from fun to recklessness that kills and injures not just drinkers but those around them.]** *problem* We may not be able to . . .

Problems, however, are more complicated than they seem. For readers to think that something is a problem, it must have two parts:

- The first is some condition, situation, or recurring event: terrorism, rising tuition, HIV, binge drinking.
- The second part of a problem is the *consequence* of that condition, a *cost* that readers don't want to pay, that they want to eliminate or at least ameliorate, because it makes them unhappy: the cost of terrorism is injury and death; the cost of rising tuition is less money for other things or even a lost education; for HIV, sickness and death.

You can identify the cost of a problem if you imagine someone asking *So what?* after you state the condition. What follows should answer it.

> But a kind of drinking known as "binge" drinking is spreading through our colleges and universities. It is drinking quickly just to get drunk or even to pass out. *condition* [So what?] Bingeing is far from the harmless fun long associated with college life. In the last six months, it has been cited in at least six deaths, many injuries, and considerable destruction of property. It is behavior that crosses the line from fun to recklessness that kills and injures not just drinkers but those around them.] *cost of the condition*

The condition part of the problem is binge drinking; the cost is death and injury. If bingeing had no cost, it would be no problem. The condition and cost *together* constitute the problem.

Two Kinds of Problems: Pragmatic and Conceptual

But now it gets complicated, because there are two kinds of problems. They motivate readers in different ways, and so have to be written about differently. One kind of problem is common in the world of practical affairs; we'll call it *pragmatic*. The other is more commonly written about in the academic world; we'll call it *conceptual*.

Pragmatic Problems   Binge drinking is an example of a pragmatic problem because its costs make (or at least should make) readers unhappy. If we can't avoid a pragmatic problem, we must *do* something in the world at least to ameliorate its costs, at best to eliminate their cause.

We can usually name a pragmatic problem in a word or two: *cancer, unemployment, binge drinking.* But that term names only the *condition* of the problem, the cause of its costs. You may think that the costs of a problem like bingeing are too obvious to state, but a callous reader might think, *So what if college students injure or kill themselves? What's that to me?* If so, you have to figure out how to make that reader see how those costs affect them. If you can't describe those costs, your readers have no reason to care about what you've written (unless they are already interested in the problem).

Writers outside the academic world address mostly pragmatic problems, but most writers inside the academic world address conceptual ones.

Conceptual Problems   A conceptual problem has the same two parts as a pragmatic one, a condition and its costs. But beyond that, the two problems are very different.

- The condition of a pragmatic problem is *anything* that makes a reader unhappy. The condition of a conceptual problem, however, is always the same: it is something we do not know or understand.

We can express the condition part of a conceptual problem, what we don't know, as a question: *How much does the universe weigh? Why does the hair on your head keep growing but the hair on your legs doesn't?*

- The cost of a pragmatic problem is always unhappiness. The cost of a conceptual problem is *something more important* we do not understand as a result of not understanding the first thing.

I know that sounds baffling. It's why students new to academic writing find it so hard to grasp. Think of it like this:

- Cosmologists do not know how much the universe weighs. *So what?* Well, if they knew, they might figure out something more important: what is the fate of existence? Will time and space go on forever, or end, and if they do, when and how?

- Biologists don't know why some hair keeps growing and other hair stops. *So what?* If they could figure it out, they might understand something more important: what turns growth on and off?

Here is another difference between pragmatic and conceptual problems:

- We solve pragmatic problems by getting readers (or someone) to *do* something to eliminate or at least ameliorate the costs. We solve a conceptual problem when we answer a question that readers accept and that helps them answer the second question: *How much does the universe weigh? Well, it weighs _____. And now that we know that, we can answer that second question, What is the fate of existence? The answer is that in 50 billion years or so, the universe will (or will not) exist.*

Framing a Conceptual Problem in Writing   There are countless ways to frame a conceptual problem. The best way to learn how is to read lots of introductions carefully. But however you frame your conceptual problem, focus on what your readers don't know but should want to. Then imagine them asking *So what?* To complete the problem, answer that question. (What follows is abbreviated; each sentence could be expanded to several):

> Colleges are reporting that binge drinking is increasing. Its effects are well understood—death, injury, property damage, *shared context* **[but its causes are not: Is it a consequence of a personality attracted to risk taking, of specific social situations, or some combination of those causes?]** *condition/first thing not known* *[So what?]* **[A better understanding of the causes of bingeing will provide clues to understanding risk-taking behavior in general.]** *cost/second thing not known* [In this study, we analyzed the risk-taking behavior of 300 first- and second-year college students to determine whether those who binged

were also more likely to engage in other risky behavior. We found that . . .] *solution*

That introduction is a fraction as long as a real one, but its structure reflects most introductions in academic writing.

All this is hard to grasp if you're new to the academic world. We all understand pragmatic problems because they make us pay a palpable cost. But those new to academic research don't know what gaps in understanding make good conceptual problems, because they don't yet know what others in their field don't know, but should want to. That's a pragmatic problem that only time and experience solve.

Part 3: Stating the Solution

Some writers aim only at making readers aware that a pragmatic problem exists. They end their introduction with the condition of a problem, then develop the body of their document around its costs. They may gesture toward a solution, but they don't try to explain it in any detail. In most academic writing, however, readers expect that a writer who poses a problem will offer a solution and then support it. We covered solutions when we discussed points (pp. 203–206), because the point of a paper posing a problem is its solution. If the solution solves a pragmatic problem, it proposes that the reader (or someone) *do* something to change a condition in the world:

> . . . It is behavior that crosses the line from fun to recklessness that kills and injures not just drinkers but those around them.] *cost*
> **[We may not be able to stop bingeing entirely, but we must try to control its worst costs by educating students in how to manage its risks.]** *solution/point*

If the solution solves a conceptual problem, it will be a statement of something the writer wants readers to *understand* or *believe:*

> . . . behavior or at least to mitigate its consequences.] *cost/second thing not known* [This study reports on our analysis of the risk-taking behavior of 300 first- and second-year college students . . . **We found that students most highly attracted to risky behavior were more likely to binge than students who were least attracted to risky behavior.]** *solution/point*

Nothing is more difficult for academic writers than finding a good question to ask and answer.

SUMMING UP

You motivate purposeful reading with this plan for introductions: the key is to state the costs of a pragmatic problem so clearly that readers will not ask *So what?* but think *What do we do?* That's easy with a pragmatic problem, because costs are always some kind of unhappiness. Here is a plan for introducing a pragmatic problem:

Alcohol has been a part of college life for hundreds of years. From football weekends to fraternity parties, college students drink and often drink hard. _{shared context}	Open the introduction with *shared context*, a brief statement of what you will go on to qualify or even contradict.
But a kind of drinking known as "binge" drinking is spreading through our colleges and universities. It is drinking quickly just to get drunk or even to pass out. [*So what?*] _{condition of the problem}	Follow that with a statement of the condition of the problem. Introduce it with a *but, however, on the other hand,* etc. Imagine a *So what?* after it.
Bingeing is far from harmless. In the last six months, it has been cited in six deaths, many injuries, and considerable destruction of property. It is behavior that crosses the line from fun to recklessness that kills and injures not just drinkers but those around them. _{costs of the problem}	Answer that imagined *So what?* with a statement of the consequences of that condition, its costs *to your readers,* costs that they do not want to pay.
We may not be able to stop bingeing entirely, but we must try to control its worst costs by educating students in how to manage its risks. _{solution of the problem}	Conclude with a statement of the solution to the problem, an *action* that will eliminate or at least ameliorate the costs.

Conceptual problems are harder to frame because you need a question worth answering. *What color were Lincoln's socks when he delivered the Gettysburg Address?* The answer to that question is unlikely to help us understand anything important. *How did Lincoln plan the Address?* If we knew that, we might learn about something much more important: the nature of the creative process. Here is a plan for introducing conceptual problems:

Colleges are reporting that binge drinking is increasing. Its effects are well understood—death, injury, property damage, shared context

Open the introduction with *shared context*, a brief statement of what you will go on to qualify or even contradict.

but its causes are not: is it a consequence of a personality attracted to risk taking or of particular social situations?] [*So what?*] condition of the problem/first thing not known

Follow that with a statement of the condition of the problem. Introduce it with a *but, however, on the other hand,* etc. State something that is not known or well understood. Imagine a *So what?* after it.

[A better understanding of the causes of bingeing will provide clues to understanding risk-taking behavior in general.] cost/second thing not known

Answer that imagined *So what?* with the cost of the condition, a larger and more important issue that is not known or understood as a consequence of not understanding the first thing.

In this study, we analyzed the risk-taking behavior of 300 first- and second-year college students to determine . . . We found that . . .]
solution of the problem

Conclude your introduction with a statement of the solution to the problem, an answer to the first question that helps answer the second one, as well.

AFTERWORD
A Reliable Generalization

I said in the preface I would offer a generalization about style and structure that related sentences to paragraphs to sections and subsections to a whole document. It is this:

Readers are more likely to judge as clear any unit of writing, from a single sentence to a whole discourse, when that unit opens with a short, specific, easily grasped segment that informatively frames a longer and more complex segment that follows.

- In a simple sentence, that short, easily grasped segment is a subject/topic. Compare these two:

  1a. <u>Resistance in Nevada against its use as an atomic waste disposal site</u> has been heated.

  1b. <u>Nevada</u> has heatedly resisted its use as an atomic waste disposal site.

- In a complex sentence, that short, easily grasped segment is a main clause that expresses the *point* of a sentence. Compare these two:

  2a. <u>The senator's claim</u> first half of point that there will be an economic recovery because of improvements in the job picture in the high-tech industry <u>is lacking factual support</u> second half of point·

  2b. <u>The senator has no facts to support his claim</u> whole point that the economy will recover because the job picture in the high-tech industry has improved.

- In a paragraph, that short, easily grasped unit is an introductory sentence or two that both expresses the point of the paragraph and introduces its key concepts. Compare these two paragraphs:

   3a. Thirty sixth-grade students wrote essays that were analyzed to determine the effectiveness of eight weeks of training to distinguish fact from opinion. That ability is an important aspect of making sound arguments of any kind. In an essay written before instruction began, the writers failed almost completely to distinguish fact from opinion. In an essay written after four weeks of instruction, the students visibly attempted to distinguish fact from opinion, but did so inconsistently. In three more essays, they distinguished fact from opinion more consistently, but never achieved the predicted level. In a final essay written six months after instruction ended, they did no better than they did in their pre-instruction essay. Their training had some effect on their writing during the instruction period, but it was inconsistent, and six months after instruction it had no measurable effect.

   3b. <u>In this study, thirty sixth-grade students were taught to distinguish fact from opinion. They did so during the instruction period, but the effect was **inconsistent, less than predicted**, and six months after instruction ended, the instruction had **no measurable effect**</u> _{opening segment/point}. In an essay written before instruction began, the writers failed almost completely to distinguish fact from opinion. In an essay written after four weeks of instruction, the students visibly attempted to distinguish fact from opinion, but did so inconsistently. In three more essays, they distinguished fact from opinion more consistently, but never achieved the predicted level. In a final essay written six months after instruction ended, they did no better than they did in their pre-instruction essay. We thus conclude that short-term training to distinguish fact from opinion has no consistent or long term effect.

   Paragraph (3a) has no clearly demarcated opening unit, and it does not announce the key themes of the paragraph. Paragraph (3b) has a clearly demarcated opening unit that states the point and clearly announces the key themes of the paragraph.

- In a subsection, section, or the whole, that short, easily grasped unit may be just a paragraph, though in much longer units, it might be proportionally longer. Even so, it expresses the point of the relevant unit and introduces the larger key concepts that follow. Space does not allow me to illustrate how that principle applies to a passage several paragraphs long, but it is easy to imagine.

Here's the point: From a sentence to a paragraph to a whole document, readers have the same need: to grasp a short, specific segment of meaning that frames a following segment that is longer and more complex. Fix that image firmly in mind: short, simple, and informative before longer and more complex. It is a principle that works perhaps not every time, but it works often enough to serve as a reliable guide to both writing and revision.

APPENDIX
Punctuation

I know there are some Persons who affect to despise it, and treat
this whole Subject with the utmost Contempt, as a Trifle far
below their Notice, and a Formality unworthy of their Regard:
They do not hold it difficult, but despicable; and neglect it, as being
above it. Yet many learned Men have been highly sensible to its Use;
and some ingenious and elegant Writers have condescended to point
their Works with Care; and very eminent Scholars have not
disdained to teach the Method of doing it with Propriety.
—JAMES BURROW

In music, the punctuation is absolutely strict; the bars and rests
are absolutely defined. But our prose cannot be quite strict,
because we have to relate it to the audience. In other words
we are continually changing the score.
—SIR RALPH RICHARDSON

There are some punctuations that are interesting
and there are some that are not.
—GERTRUDE STEIN

Most writers think that punctuation is governed by the same kind of rules that govern grammar, and so managing commas and semicolons must be about as interesting as sorting socks. In fact, you have more choices in how to punctuate sentences than you might think, and if you make those choices thoughtfully, you can help readers not only understand a complex sentence but create nuances of emphasis that readers will notice. It takes more than a few commas to turn a monotone into the Hallelujah Chorus, but a little care can produce gratifying results.

SOME BASIC CONCEPTS

I'll address punctuation as a functional problem: how do we punctuate the end of a sentence, its beginning, and its middle? But first, I have to distinguish two kinds of sentences.

Punctuated and Grammatical Sentences

I'll call whatever begins with a capital letter and ends with a period or question/exclamation mark a *punctuated sentence*. We have to distinguish two kinds of punctuated sentences, however, because readers do; the one you are now reading, for example, is one long punctuated sentence, but it is not as hard to read as a shorter one that you will read in a moment; I have chosen to punctuate as one sentence what I might have punctuated as a series of shorter ones; those semicolons and the comma before *but* could have been periods, for example—and that dash could have been a period too.

Here is the sentence you just read repunctuated with virtually no change in its grammar:

> We have to distinguish two kinds of punctuated sentences, however, because readers do. The one you are now reading, for example, is a short punctuated sentence. But this paragraph is not as hard to read as a shorter one that you will read in a moment. I have chosen to punctuate as separate sentences what I could have punctuated as one long one. The period before *but,* for example, could have been a comma. The last two periods could have been semicolons. And that period could have been a dash.

On the other hand, I can write a different kind of long punctuated sentence, one that I cannot break into shorter punctuated sentences just by replacing commas and semicolons with periods, because it is a sentence consisting of several SUBORDINATE CLAUSES, all depending on one MAIN or INDEPENDENT CLAUSE—a complex construction that you have almost finished but that probably feels longer and certainly more complex than did that first long sentence, even though it is actually shorter.

The difference between those two long punctuated sentences is this: as you read the first one, it didn't force you to hold in mind a lot of grammatical relations, because it consists of a lot of little independent grammatical sentences that we call *independent clauses*. At the comma, semicolons, and dash, your mind dumped the grammatical structure from your memory and treated what followed as a new sentence, at which point, grammatically speaking, you started over figuring out the grammar.

On the other hand, that second long sentence forced you to keep figuring out its grammar, right to the end. Just as that first long sentence does, the second one starts with an independent clause:

I can write a different kind of long punctuated sentence . . .

But instead of continuing with a series of independent grammatical sentences that you process individually, it continues with a series of subordinate clauses that you have to keep integrating into a single grammatical structure (the brackets enclose subordinate clauses):

. . . punctuated sentence,

[1][that I cannot break into shorter punctuated sentences just by replacing commas and semicolons with periods],

[2][because it is a sentence consisting of several subordinate clauses, all depending on one main or independent clause

[3]—a complex construction]

[4][that you have almost finished]

[5][but that probably feels longer and certainly more complex]

[6][than did that first long sentence,]

[7][even though it is actually shorter].

In this second sentence, you have to keep figuring out to the end how its parts fit together, and that requires more mental work.

You have to distinguish the different styles of those two kinds of punctuated sentences, because readers respond to them differently: it is easier for them to read a long punctuated sentence consisting of short grammatical sentences than it is for them to read a long punctuated sentence that is one long grammatical sentence.

Exercise A.1

Revise that second long sentence beginning with *I can write a different kind of long punctuated sentence* making some of the subordinate clauses independent clauses. Then set off those independent clauses first with commas, semicolons, and colons. Then punctuate that revised sentence a second time, this time with periods. How have you changed the style of the sentence? Which revision changes the style of the original sentence more radically: periods, or commas and semicolons?

Exercise A.2

You will find long sentences on pp. 142, 156, and 164. Re-punctuate them into shorter ones. How do the changes affect the way you respond to them?

Simple, Compound, and Complex Sentences

At this point, you may be thinking about sentences called *simple, compound,* and *complex.* Most of us learned that if a sentence is one independent clause, it is *simple:*

> SIMPLE: The greatest English dictionary is the *Oxford English Dictionary.*

If it has two or more independent clauses, it is *compound:*

> COMPOUND: [There are many good dictionaries][1],
> [but the greatest is the *Oxford English Dictionary*][2].

If it has an independent clause and one or more subordinate clauses, it is *complex.*

> COMPLEX: [While there are many good dictionaries] subordinate clause
> [the greatest is the *Oxford English Dictionary*] independent clause.

But those terms can mislead us, because they suggest that a grammatically simple sentence should *seem* simpler than one that is grammatically complex, and that's not always true. For example, most readers think that of the next two sentences, the grammatically simple one *feels* more complex than the grammatically complex one:

GRAMMATICALLY SIMPLE: Our review of the test led to our modification
of it as a result of complaints by teachers.

GRAMMATICALLY COMPLEX: After we reviewed the test, we modified
it because teachers complained about it.

Like the words *active* and *passive*, the terms *simple* and *complex* can refer both to our impressions and to grammatical structure.

To avoid that confusion in what follows, I use terms that are a bit different from those you might recall. I will refer only to *grammatical* and *punctuated* sentences.

By *grammatical sentence*, I mean one independent clause plus all of its attached subordinate clauses, if any. The term therefore covers both simple and complex sentences:

I left.

I left because I was tired.

What we call a *compound* sentence includes at least two grammatical sentences.

[I left], grammatical sentence 1 [but I returned] grammatical sentence 2.

A *punctuated* sentence begins with a capital letter and ends with a period or question/exclamation mark. It may consist of one or more grammatical sentences. The hallmark of a literate writer is knowing how to punctuate the end of a grammatical sentence.

PUNCTUATING THE ENDS OF SENTENCES

Beyond all other considerations, you have to let readers know where one grammatical sentence stops and the next begins, unlike this sentence:

In 1967, Congress passed civil rights laws that remedied problems of registration and voting this had political consequences throughout the South.

You can separate that pair of grammatical sentences in ten ways. Three are common:

Three Common Forms of End Punctuation

1. Period (or Question/Exclamation Mark) Alone   The simplest way to signal the end of a grammatical sentence is with a period:

✓ In 1967, Congress passed civil rights laws that remedied problems of registration and **voting. This** had political consequences throughout the South.

But if you create too many short punctuated sentences, your readers may feel your prose is choppy or simplistic. Experienced writers revise a series of short grammatical sentences into subordinate clauses or phrases, turning two or more grammatical sentences into one:

✓ **When Congress passed civil rights laws to remedy problems of registration and voting in 1967, they** had political consequences throughout the South.

✓ The civil rights laws **that Congress passed in 1967 to remedy problems of registration and voting** had political consequences throughout the South.

Be cautious, though: combine too many short grammatical sentences into one long one, and you create a sentence that sprawls.

2. Semicolon Alone   A semicolon is like a soft period; whatever is on either side of it should be a grammatical sentence (with an exception we'll discuss on p. 244). Use a semicolon instead of a period only when the first grammatical sentence is not long and the second grammatical sentence is closely linked to the first:

✓ In 1967, Congress passed civil rights laws that remedied problems of registration and **voting; those** laws had political consequences throughout the South.

If readers can't see a link between them, they experience a small twinge of confusion:

In 1967, Congress passed civil rights laws to remedy problems of registration and **voting; by 1995** Southern states had thousands of sheriffs, mayors, and other officials from their African-American communities.

A few shared concepts would make the connections clearer:

✓ In 1967, Congress passed civil rights laws to remedy racial problems of registration and voting, particularly in the South; by 1995 Southern states had elected thousands of sheriffs, mayors, and other officials from their African-American communities.

A SPECIAL PROBLEM WITH SEMICOLONS AND *HOWEVER:* In one context, even well-educated writers often incorrectly use a comma to end one grammatical sentence when they begin the next sentence with *however.* They should use a semicolon. The punctuation in this next example is confusing because we don't know whether the *however* goes with the first grammatical sentence or with the second:

> Taxpayers have supported public education, **however,** they now object because taxes have risen so steeply.

If the *however* introduces the second grammatical sentence, then the writer must use a semicolon to signal where the first grammatical sentence ends.

> ✓ Taxpayers have supported public education**; however,** they now object because taxes have risen so steeply.

A fairly reliable rule of thumb: If you see more than ten or so words before a *however* and as many after, you probably need to change the comma *before* the *however* to a semicolon or period, because that *however* probably begins a new grammatical sentence.

3. Comma + Coordinating Conjunction   Readers also recognize the end of a grammatical sentence when they see a comma followed by

- a coordinating conjunction: *and, but, yet, for, so, or, nor,* ~~FANBOYS~~ *or but*
- and that conjunction is followed by another Subject and Verb.

> ✓ In the 1950s religion was viewed as a bulwark against **communism, so it was** not long after that that atheism was felt to threaten national security.
> ✓ American intellectuals have often followed **Europeans, but our culture** has proven inhospitable to their brand of socialism.

But choose a period if the two grammatical sentences are long and have their own internal punctuation.

When readers begin a coordinated series of three or more grammatical sentences, they accept just a comma between them, but only if they are short and have no internal punctuation:

> ✓ Baseball satisfies our admiration for **precision, basketball** speaks to our love of speed and **grace, and** football appeals to our lust for violence.

If either of the first two clauses has internal punctuation, separate them with a semicolon:

✓ Baseball, the oldest indigenous American sport and essentially a rural one, satisfies our admiration for **precision; basketball,** our newest sport and now more urban than rural, speaks to our love of speed and **grace; and** football, a sport both rural and urban, appeals to our lust for violence.

An exception: Omit the comma between a coordinated pair of short grammatical sentences if you introduce them with a modifier that applies to both of them:

✓ By 1995, the economies of the Soviet Union's former satellites had begun to **rebound but** Russia's had yet to hit bottom.

Four Less Common Forms of End Punctuation

Some readers have reservations about these next four ways of signaling the end of a grammatical sentence, but careful writers everywhere use them.

4. Period + Coordinating Conjunction   Some readers think it's wrong to begin a punctuated sentence with a coordinating conjunction such as *and* or *but*. But they are wrong; this is entirely correct:

✓ Education cannot guarantee a **democracy. But** without it, democracy cannot survive.

Use this pattern no more than once or twice a page, especially with *and*.

5. Semicolon + Coordinating Conjunction   Writers occasionally end one grammatical sentence with a semicolon and begin the next with a coordinating conjunction:

In the 1950s religion was viewed as a bulwark against **communism; so** soon thereafter atheism was felt to threaten national security.

Use a comma there if the two grammatical sentences are short. But readers are grateful for a semicolon if the two grammatical sentences are long with their own internal commas:

✓ Problem solving, one of the most active areas of psychology, has made great strides in the last decade, particularly in understanding the problem-solving strategies of experts; **so** it is no surprise that educators have followed that research with interest.

But then they would probably appreciate a period there even more.

6. Comma Alone   Though readers do not expect to see just a comma separate two grammatical sentences, they can manage if the sentences are short and closely linked in meaning, such as cause-effect, first-second, *if-then*, etc.

> Act in haste, repent at leisure.

Be sure, though, that neither has internal commas; this would be confusing:

> Women, who have always been underpaid, no longer accept that discriminatory treatment**,** they are now doing something about it.

A semicolon would be clearer:

> ✓ Women, who have always been underpaid, no longer accept that discriminatory treatment; they are now doing something about it.

But a warning: writers of the best prose do this, but many teachers disapprove, so be sure of your readers before you experiment.

7. Conjunction Alone   Some writers signal a close link between short grammatical sentences with a coordinating conjunction alone, omitting the comma:

> ✓ Oscar Wilde violated a fundamental law of British **society and** we all know what happened to him.

But the same warning: though writers of the best prose do this, many teachers consider it an error.

Three Special Cases: Colon, Dash, Parentheses

These last three ways of signaling the end of a grammatical sentence are a bit self-conscious, but might be interesting to those writers who like going beyond the ordinary.

8. Colon   Discerning readers think you are a more than common writer if you end a sentence with an appropriate colon: they take it as shorthand for *to illustrate, for example, that is, let me expand on, therefore.*

> ✓ Dance is not widely **supported: no** company operates at a profit, and there are few outside major cities.

A colon signals more obviously than a comma or semicolon that you are balancing the structure, sound, and meaning of one clause against another:

✓ Civil disobedience is the public conscience of a democracy: mass enthusiasm is the public consensus of a tyranny.

If you follow the colon with a grammatical sentence, capitalize the first word or not, depending on how much you want to emphasize what follows.

A rule of thumb: Avoid a colon if it breaks a clause into two pieces, neither of which is a grammatically complete sentence. Avoid this:

Genetic counseling requires: a knowledge of statistical genetics, an awareness of choices open to parents, and the psychological competence to deal with emotional trauma.

Neither chunk before or after that colon could be a grammatical sentence. Instead, put the colon after a whole SUBJECT-VERB-OBJECT structure:

✓ **Genetic counseling requires the following: a** knowledge of statistical genetics, an awareness of choices open to parents, and the psychological competence to deal with emotional trauma.

9. Dash   You can also signal balance more informally with a dash—it suggests a casual afterthought:

✓ Stonehenge is a **wonder—only** a genius could have conceived it.

Try that with a colon: it makes a difference.

10. Parentheses   You can attach a short grammatical sentence to another one with parentheses, if what is in the parentheses is like a short afterthought. Omit the period before the last parenthesis; put it outside:

✓ Stonehenge is a **wonder (only** a genius could have conceived it**).**

Here's the point: You can end a grammatical sentence in ten ways. Three are conventional and common:

1. Period	I win. You lose.
2. Semicolon	I win; you lose.
3. Comma + coordinating conjunction	I win, and you lose.

Four are a bit debatable, but good writers use them, especially the first:

4. Period + coordinating conjunction	I win. And you lose.
5. Semicolon + coordinating conjunction	I win; and you lose.
6. Comma alone	I win, you lose.
7. Coordinating conjunction alone	I win and you lose.

Three are for writers who want to be a bit stylish in their punctuation:

8. Colon	I win: you lose.
9. Dash	I win—you lose.
10. Parentheses	I win (you lose).

Though some ways of punctuating the end of a sentence are flat-out wrong, you can choose from among many that are right. If you look again at the short sentences on pp. 166–168 and Mailer's long sentence on p. 168, you can see those choices in contrast. But all those writers could have chosen otherwise and thereby created a different stylistic effect.

PUNCTUATING BEGINNINGS

You have no problem punctuating the beginning of a sentence when you begin a sentence directly with its subject, as I did this one. However, as with this one, when a sentence forces a reader to plow through several introductory words, phrases, and clauses, especially when they have their own internal punctuation, and readers might be confused by it all (as you probably are right now), forget trying to punctuate it right: rewrite it.

There are a few rules that your readers expect you to follow, but more often you have to rely on judgment.

Five Reliable Rules

1. Always separate an introductory element from the subject of a sentence with a comma if a reader might misunderstand the structure of the sentence. Do not do this:

   > When a lawyer concludes her argument has to be easily remembered by a jury.

   Do this:

   > ✓ When a lawyer **concludes, her** argument has to be easily remembered by a jury.

2. Never end an introductory clause or phrase with a semicolon, no matter how it long is. Readers take semicolons to signal the end of a grammatical sentence (but see p. 244). Not this:

   > Although the Administration knew that Iraq's invasion of Kuwait threatened American interests in Saudi **Arabia; it** did not immediately prepare a military response.

   Always use a comma there:

   > ✓ Although the Administration knew that Iraq's invasion of Kuwait threatened American interests in Saudi **Arabia,** it did not immediately prepare a military response.

   But if that introductory element is long and complicated, consider breaking it out as a grammatical sentence.

   > ✓ The Administration knew that Iraq's invasion of Kuwait threatened American interests in Saudi **Arabia, but** it did not immediately prepare a military response.

3. Never put a comma right after a subordinating conjunction if the next element of the clause is its subject. Never this:

   > **Although, the** art of punctuation is simple, it is rarely mastered.

4. Do not put a comma after the coordinating conjunctions *and, but, yet, for, so, or,* and *nor* if the next element is the subject. Do not do this:

   > **But, we** cannot know whether life on other planets exists.

   Some writers who punctuate heavily put a comma after a coordinating conjunction if an introductory word or phrase follows:

   > ✓ **Yet, during this period, prices** continued to rise.

Heavy punctuation retards a reader a bit, but it's your choice. These are also correct and for the reader, perhaps a bit swifter:

✓ Yet during this **period, prices** continued to rise.

✓ Yet during this **period prices** continued to rise.

5. Put a comma after an introductory word or phrase if it comments on the whole of the following sentence or if it connects one sentence to another.

   These include elements such as *fortunately, allegedly,* etc. and conjunctions like *however, nevertheless, regardless,* etc. Since readers hear sentences in their mind's ear, they expect a pause after such words.

   ✓ **Fortunately, we** proved our point.

   But avoid starting many sentences with an introductory element and a comma. When we read a series of such sentences, the whole passage feels hesitant.

   Three Common Exceptions: We typically omit a comma after *now, thus,* and *hence:*

   ✓ **Now it** is clear that many will not support this position.

   ✓ **Thus the** only alternative is to choose some other action.

Three Reliable Principles

1. Readers need no punctuation between a short introductory phrase and the subject:

   ✓ **Once again we** find similar responses to such stimuli.

   ✓ **In 1945 few** realized how the war had transformed us.

   It is not wrong to put a comma there, but it slows readers just as you may want them to be picking up speed.

2. Readers need a comma after a long introductory phrase or clause:

   ✓ When a lawyer begins her opening statement with a dry recital of the law and how it must be applied to the case before the **court, the** jury is likely to nod off.

   But there are other considerations: how long is too long and how closely do you want to connect the meanings of the two clauses? Readers don't need a comma when the introductory clause is shorter than, say, ten or so words, its subject is the same as the subject of the main clause, and its meaning closely depends on the meaning of the main clause:

✓ When **Hitler** realized that he had lost the **war he** ordered his army to raze every city through which it retreated.

But if the subjects of the clauses differ and the ideas contrast, a comma helps the reader sense the opposition. Compare:

✓ Since **we** accepted the IRS's **data we** dropped further appeals.

✓ Although the **IRS** overruled **us, we** still follow our procedures.

3. Readers do not expect a comma to separate a subject from its verb. Do not do this:

> A sentence that consists of many complex subordinate clauses and long phrases that all precede a **verb, may** seem to some students to demand a comma somewhere.

Readers generally dislike long subjects. If you keep them short, you won't feel the need of a comma. Readers do, however, need a comma between a subject and a verb when a phrase or clause clearly interrupts that expected connection. (See the next section on interruptions.)

Occasionally, you cannot avoid a long subject, especially if it consists of a list of items with internal punctuation, like this:

> **The president, the vice president, the secretaries of the departments, senators, members of the House of Representatives, and Supreme Court justices take** an oath that pledges them to uphold the Constitution.

That is complicated. You can help readers sort it out like this:

- Insert a colon or a dash at the end of that long subject:

> The president, the vice president, the secretaries of the departments, senators, members of the House of Representatives, and Supreme Court justices:

- Then insert a word that summarizes the preceding list:

> ✓ The president, the vice president, the secretaries of the departments, senators, members of the House of Representatives, and Supreme Court justices: **all** take an oath that pledges them to uphold the Constitution.

Choose a dash or a colon depending on how formal you want to seem.

Here's the point: These are strong rules of punctuation. Observe them.

1. Always separate an introductory element from the subject if a reader might misunderstand the structure of the sentence.

2. Never end an introductory clause or phrase with a semicolon.

3. Never put a comma after a subordinating conjunction if the next element of the clause is its subject.

4. Avoid putting a comma after a coordinating conjunction if the next element is the subject.

5. Put a comma after a short introductory word or phrase if it comments on the whole of the following sentence or if it connects one sentence to another.

These are reliable principles:

6. Put a comma after a short introductory phrase or not, as you choose.

7. Readers usually need a comma after a long introductory phrase or clause.

8. Readers do not need a comma to separate a subject from its verb.

PUNCTUATING MIDDLES

This is where explanations get messy, because to punctuate inside a grammatical sentence—more specifically, inside a clause—you have to consider not only the grammar of that clause, but the nuances of its rhythm, its meaning, and the emphasis that you want your readers to hear in their mind's ear.

Interruptions

When you insert an interrupting phrase or clause between a subject and verb or verb and object, readers have a harder time making the grammatical connections that hold those basic elements of a sentence together. So in general, avoid interruptions, except for reasons of emphasis or nuance (see pp. 133–134). In that case, you have to help your reader recognize the interruption by setting it off with *paired* commas or dashes:

> A sentence, **if it consists of many complex subordinate clauses and long phrases and all precede a verb,** may seem to need commas.

But that sentence needs more than commas to make it clear. That *if*-clause should be moved to the end:

> A sentence may seem to need commas **if it consists of many complex subordinate clauses and long phrases and all precede a verb.**

Generally speaking, do not use a comma when you tack a subordinate clause at the end of an independent clause, if that clause is necessary to understand the meaning of the sentence (this is analogous to a RESTRICTIVE RELATIVE CLAUSE):

> No one should violate the law just because it seems unjust.

If the clause is not necessary, separate it from the main clause with a comma.

> No one should violate the law, because in the long run, it will do more harm than good.

This distinction can be very tricky at times.

You can use commas before and after short interrupting ADVERBIAL PHRASES, depending on the emphasis you want readers to hear. The general principle is that readers feel emphasis on what immediately precedes and follows a pause. Compare the different emphases in these:

- ✓ Modern poetry has become more relevant to the average reader **in recent years.**
- ✓ Modern poetry **has, in recent years, become** more relevant to the average reader.
- ✓ Modern poetry has **become, in recent years, more** relevant to the average reader.

- ✓ The antagonism between Congress and the president has created utter distrust **among every group of voters.**
- ✓ The antagonism between Congress and the president has created, **among every group of voters,** utter distrust.

Loose Commentary

"Loose commentary" differs from an interruption, because you can usually move an interruption elsewhere in a sentence. But loose commentary modifies what it is next to, so it usually cannot be moved. It still needs to be set off with commas, parentheses, or dashes.

It is difficult to explain exactly what counts as loose commentary because it depends on both grammar and meaning. One familiar distinction is between RESTRICTIVE and NONRESTRICTIVE CLAUSES (see pp. 17–19) and APPOSITIVES.

We use no commas with restrictive modifiers, modifiers that uniquely identify the noun they modify:

✓ The **house that I live in** is 100 years old.

But we always set off nonrestrictive modifiers with *paired* commas (unless the modifier ends the sentence):

✓ We had to reconstruct the **larynx, which is the source of voice,** with cartilage from the shoulder.

An appositive is actually just a truncated nonrestrictive clause:

✓ We had to rebuild the **larynx, the source of voice,** with cartilage from the shoulder.

You can achieve a more casual effect with a dash:

✓ We had to rebuild the **larynx—the source of voice—with** cartilage from the shoulder.

A dash is useful when the loose commentary has internal commas. Readers are confused by the long subject in this sentence:

The nations of Central Europe, Poland, Hungary, Romania, Bulgaria, the Czech Republic, Slovakia, Bosnia, Serbia have for centuries been in the middle of an East-West tug-of-war.

They can understand that kind of structure more easily when they can see that loose modifier set off with dashes or parentheses:

✓ The nations of Central **Europe—Poland, Hungary, Romania, Bulgaria, the Czech Republic, Slovakia, Bosnia, Serbia—have** for centuries been in the middle of an East-West tug-of-war.

Use parentheses when you want readers to hear your comment as a *sotto voce* aside:

✓ The brain **(at least that part that controls nonprimitive functions)** may comprise several little brains operating simultaneously.

Or use it as an explanatory footnote inside a sentence:

✓ Lamarck **(1744–1829)** was a pre-Darwinian evolutionist.

✓ The poetry of the *fin de siècle* **(end of the century)** was characterized by a world-weariness and fashionable despair.

When loose commentary is at the end of a sentence, use a comma to separate it from the first part of the sentence. Be certain, however, that the meaning of the commentary is not crucial to the meaning of the sentence. If it is, do not use a comma. Contrast these:

✓ I wandered through **Europe, seeking a place** where I could write undisturbed.

✓ I spent my **time seeking a place** where I could write undisturbed.

✓ Offices will be closed July **2–6, as announced in the daily bulletin.**

✓ When closing offices, secure all safes **as prescribed in the manual.**

✓ Historians have studied social changes**, at least in this country.**

✓ These records must be kept **at least until the IRS reviews them.**

Here's the point: These are reliable rules of internal punctuation. Observe them.

1. Do not interrupt a subject and verb or verb and object with any punctuation, unless absolutely necessary for clarity.

2. Inside a clause, always set off long interruptions with *paired* marks of punctuation—commas, parentheses, or dashes. Never use semicolons.

3. Put a comma at the end of an independent clause before a tacked-on subordinate clause when that clause is not essential to the meaning of the sentence.

PUNCTUATING COORDINATED ELEMENTS

Punctuating Two Coordinate Elements

Generally speaking, do not put a comma between just two coordinated elements. Compare these:

As computers have become **sophisticated, and** powerful they have taken over more **clerical, and** bookkeeping tasks.

✓ As computers have become **sophisticated and** powerful they have taken over more **clerical and** bookkeeping tasks.

Three Exceptions

1. For a dramatic contrast, put a comma after the first coordinate element to emphasize the second (keep the second short):

   ✓ The ocean is nature's most glorious **creation, and** its most destructive.

   To emphasize a contrast, use a comma before a *but* (keep the second part short):

   ✓ Organ transplants are becoming more **common, but** not less expensive.

2. If you want your readers to feel the cumulative power of a co-ordinated pair (or more), drop the *and* and leave just a comma. Compare these:

   ✓ Lincoln never had a formal **education and** never owned a large library.

   ✓ Lincoln never had a formal **education, never** owned a large library.

   ✓ The lesson of the pioneers was to ignore conditions that seemed difficult or even **overwhelming and** to get on with the business of subduing a hostile environment.

   ✓ The lesson of the pioneers was to ignore conditions that seemed difficult or even **overwhelming, to** get on with the business of subduing a hostile environment.

3. Put a comma between long coordinate pairs only if you think your readers need a chance to breathe or to sort out the grammar. Compare:

   It is in the graveyard that Hamlet finally realizes that the inevitable end of life is the **grave and clay and that the** end of all pretentiousness and all plotting and counter-plotting, regardless of one's station in life, must be dust.

   A comma after *clay* and *life* signals a natural pause:

   ✓ It is in the graveyard that Hamlet finally realizes that the inevitable end of all life is the **grave and clay, and that the** end of all pretentiousness and all plotting and counter-plotting, regardless of one's station in life, must be dust.

More important, the comma after *clay* sorts out the structure of a potentially confusing *grave and clay and that regardless*.

In this next sentence, the first half of a coordination is long, so a reader might have a problem connecting the second half to its origin:

> Conrad's *Heart of Darkness* brilliantly dramatizes those primitive impulses that lie deep in each of us and stir only in our darkest **dreams but asserts** the need for the values that control those impulses.

A comma after *dreams* would clearly mark the end of one coordinate member and the beginning of the next:

> ✓ Conrad's *Heart of Darkness* brilliantly dramatizes those primitive impulses that lie deep in each of us and stir only in our darkest **dreams, but asserts** the need for the values that control those impulses.

On the other hand, if you can make sense out of a complicated sentence like that only with punctuation, you need to revise the sentence.

Punctuating Three or More Coordinated Elements

Finally, there is the matter of punctuating a series of three or more coordinated elements. Writers disagree on this one, but you can put a comma before the last element or not, depending on your taste (some insist a comma must always precede the last one):

> ✓ His wit, his **charm and his loyalty** made him our friend.

> ✓ His wit, his **charm, and his loyalty** made him our friend.

Both are correct, but be consistent.

If any of the items in the series has its own internal commas, then use semicolons to show how readers should group the coordinated items:

> ✓ In mystery novels, the principal action ought to be economical, organic, and **logical; fascinating**, yet not **exotic; clear,** but complicated enough to hold the reader's interest.

Here's the point: Use commas to separate items in a series if the items have no internal punctuation. Use semicolons to set off items in a series only if they do.

SUMMING UP

Rather than summarize this detailed material, I offer just three bits of advice:

- Always signal the end of a grammatical sentence.
- Always observe the five reliable rules on pages 236–237.
- Always set off long interrupting elements with commas.

Beyond that, use your judgment: punctuate in ways that help your readers see the connections and separations that they have to see to make sense of your sentences. That means you must put yourself in the place of your reader, not easy to do, but something you must learn. On the other hand, write a clearly structured sentence in the first place, and your punctuation will take care of itself.

Exercise A.3

These passages lack their original punctuation. Slash marks indicate grammatical sentences. Punctuate them three times, once using the least punctuation possible, a second time using as much varied punctuation as you can, and then a third time as you think best. You might also analyze these passages for features of elegance, especially how their sentences begin and end. You can even improve them some.

1. Scientists and philosophers of science tend to speak as if "scientific language" were intrinsically precise as if those who use it must understand one another's meaning even if they disagree / but in fact scientific language is not as different from ordinary language as is commonly believed / it too is subject to imprecision and ambiguity and hence to imperfect understanding / moreover new theories or arguments are rarely if ever constructed by way of

clear-cut steps of induction deduction and verification or falsification / neither are they defended rejected or accepted in so straightforward a manner / in practice scientists combine the rules of scientific methodology with a generous admixture of intuition aesthetics and philosophical commitment / the importance of what are sometimes called extra-rational or extra-logical components of thought in the *discovery* of a new principle or law is generally acknowledged / . . . but the role of these extra-logical components in persuasion and acceptance in making an argument convincing is less frequently discussed partly because they are less visible / the ways in which the credibility or effectiveness of an argument depends on the realm of common experiences or extensive practice in communicating those experiences in a common language are hard to see precisely because such commonalities are taken for granted / only when we step out of such a "consensual domain" when we can stand out on the periphery of a community with a common language do we begin to become aware of the unarticulated premises mutual understandings and assumed practices of the group / even in those subjects that lend themselves most readily to quantification discourse depends heavily on conventions and interpretation, conventions that are acquired over years of practice and participation in a community.

—Evelyn Fox Keller, *A Feeling for the Organism:*
The Life and Work of Barbara McClintock

2. In fact of course the notion of universal knowledge has always been an illusion / but it is an illusion fostered by the monistic view of the world in which a few great central truths determine in all its wonderful and amazing proliferation everything else that is true / we are not today tempted to search for these keys that unlock the whole of human knowledge and of man's experience / we know that we are ignorant / we are well taught it / and the more surely and deeply we know our own job the better able we are to appreciate the full measure of our per-

vasive ignorance / we know that these are inherent limits compounded no doubt and exaggerated by that sloth and that complacency without which we would not be men at all / but knowledge rests on knowledge / what is new is meaningful because it departs slightly from what was known before / this is a world of frontiers where even the liveliest of actors or observers will be absent most of the time from most of them / perhaps this sense was not so sharp in the village that village which we have learned a little about but probably do not understand too well the village of slow change and isolation and fixed culture which evokes our nostalgia even if not our full comprehension / perhaps in the villages men were not so lonely / perhaps they found in each other a fixed community a fixed and only slowly growing store of knowledge of a single world / even that we may doubt / for there seem to be always in the culture of such times and places vast domains of mystery if not unknowable then imperfectly known endless and open.

—J. Robert Oppenheimer, "The Sciences and Man's Community,"
from *Science and the Common Understanding*

GLOSSARY

Grammar is the ground of all.
—WILLIAM LANGLAND

Most of the grounds of the world's troubles
are matters of grammar.
—MONTAIGNE

There is a satisfactory boniness about grammar which the
flesh of sheer vocabulary requires before it can become
vertebrate and walk the earth. But to study it for its own sake,
without relating it to function, is utter madness.
—ANTHONY BURGESS

Thou hast most traitorously corrupted the youth of the realm
in erecting a grammar school. . . . It will be proved to thy face,
that thou hast men about thee that usually talk of a noun
and a verb, and such abominable words
as no Christian ear can endure to hear.
—WILLIAM SHAKESPEARE, 2 HENRY VI, 4.7

What follows is no tight theory of grammar, just definitions useful for the terms in this book. Where the text discusses something at length, I refer you to those pages. If you want to do a quick review to get started, read the entries on SUBJECT, SIMPLE SUBJECT, WHOLE SUBJECT, and VERB.

Action: Prototypically, action is expressed by a verb: *move, hate, think, discover.* But actions also appear in NOMINALIZATIONS: *movement, hatred, thought, discovery.* Actions are also implied in some adjectives: *advisable, resultant, explanatory,* etc.

Active: See p. 58.

Adjectival Clause: Adjectival clauses modify nouns. Also called RELATIVE clauses, they usually begin with a relative pronoun: *which, that, whom, whose, who.* There are two kinds: RESTRICTIVE and NONRESTRICTIVE. See pp. 17–19.

Restrictive	The book **that** *I read* was good.
Nonrestrictive	My car, **which** *you saw,* is gone.

Adjective: A word you can put *very* in front of: *very old, very interesting.* There are exceptions: *major, additional,* etc. Since this is also a test for ADVERBS, distinguish adjectives from adverbs by putting them between *the* and a noun: *The* **occupational** *hazard, the* **major** *reason,* etc. Some nouns also appear there—*the* **chemical** *hazard.*

Adjective Phrase: An ADJECTIVE and what attaches to it: *so* **full** *that it burst.*

Adverb: Adverbs modify all parts of speech except NOUNS:

Adjectives	**extremely** large, **rather** old
Verbs	**frequently** spoke, **often** slept
Adverbs	**very** carefully, **somewhat** rudely
Articles	**precisely** the man I meant, **just** the thing I need
Sentences	**Fortunately,** we were on time.

Adverb Phrase: An adverb and what attaches to it: *as* **soon** *as I could.*

Adverbial Clause: This is a kind of SUBORDINATE CLAUSE. It modifies a VERB or ADJECTIVE, indicating time, cause, condition, etc. It usually begins with a SUBORDINATING CONJUNCTION such as *because, when, if, since, while, unless:*

> **If you leave,** I will stop.   **Because he left,** I did too.

Agent: Prototypically, agents are flesh-and-blood sources of an ACTION, but for our purposes, an agent is the *seeming* source of any action, an entity without which the action could not occur: ***She*** *criticized the program in this report.* Often, we can make the means by which we do something a seeming agent: ***This report*** *criticizes the program.* Do not confuse agents with SUBJECTS. Agents prototypically are subjects, but an agent can be in a grammatical OBJECT: *I underwent an interrogation by* ***the police.***

Appositive: A noun phrase that is left after deleting **which** and **be:** *My dog,* ~~which is~~ ***a dalmatian,*** *ran away.*

Article: They are easier to list than to define: *a, an, the, this, these, that, those.*

Character: See pp. 52–58.

Clause: A clause has two defining characteristics:

1. It has a sequence of at least one SUBJECT + VERB.
2. The verb must agree with the subject in number and can be made past or present.

By this definition, these are clauses:

> She left   that they leave   if she left   why he is leaving

These next are not, because the verbal forms cannot be made past tense nor do they agree in number with the putative subject:

> for them to **go**   her **having gone**

Complement: Whatever completes a VERB:

> I am **home.**   You seem **tired.**   She helped **me.**

Compound Noun: See p. 68.

Conjunction: Usually defined as a word that links words, PHRASES, or CLAUSES. They are easier to illustrate than define (the first two are also categorized as SUBORDINATING conjunctions):

| adverbial conjunctions | because, although, when, since |
| relative conjunctions | who, whom, whose, which, that |

sentence conjunctions	thus, however, therefore, nevertheless
coordinating conjunctions	and, but, yet, for, so, or, nor
correlative conjunctions	both X and Y, not only X but Y, (n)either X (n)or Y, X as well as Y

Coordination: Coordination joins two grammatical units of the same order with *and, or, nor, but, yet:*

same part of speech	you **and** I, red **and** black, run **or** jump
phrases	in the house **but** not in the basement
clauses	when I leave **or** when you arrive

Dangling Modifier: See p. 64.

Dependent Clause: Any CLAUSE that cannot be punctuated as a MAIN CLAUSE, one beginning with a capital letter and ending with a period or question mark. It usually begins with a subordinating conjunction such as *because, if, when, which, that:*

why he left   because he left   which he left

Direct Object: The NOUN that follows a TRANSITIVE VERB and can be made the SUBJECT of a PASSIVE verb:

I found **the money.** → **The money** was found by me.

Finite Verb: A verb that can be made past or present. These are finite verbs because we can change their tense from past to present and vice versa:

She **wants** to leave. ↔ She **wantED** to leave.

These are not finite verbs because we cannot change the INFINITIVE to a past tense:

She wants to **leave.** → She wanted to **leaveD.**

Fragment: A PHRASE or DEPENDENT CLAUSE that begins with a capital letter and ends with a period, question mark, or exclamation mark:

Because I left.   Though I am here!   What you did?

These are complete sentences:

He left because I did.   Though I am here, she is not!   I know what we did.

Free Modifier: See pp. 140–141.

Gerund: A NOMINALIZATION created by adding -*ing* to a VERB:

When she **left** we were happy. → Her **leaving** made us happy.

Goal: That toward which the ACTION of a VERB is directed. In most cases, goals are DIRECT OBJECTS:

I see **you.**   I broke **the dish.**   I built **a house.**

But in some cases, the literal goal of an action can be the SUBJECT of an ACTIVE VERB:

I underwent an interrogation.   **She** received a warm welcome.

Grammatical Sentence: See pp. 226–227.

Hedge: See pp. 118–121.

Independent Clause: A CLAUSE that that can be punctuated as a grammatical sentence.

Infinitive: A VERB that cannot be made past or present. It often is preceded by the word *to: He decided to **stay.*** But sometimes not: *We helped him **repair** the door.*

Intensifier: See pp. 118–121.

Intransitive Verb: A verb that does not take an OBJECT and so cannot be made PASSIVE. These are not TRANSITIVE verbs:

He **exists.**   They **left** town.   She **became** a doctor.

Linking Verb: A VERB with a COMPLEMENT that refers to its SUBJECT.

He **is** my brother.   They **became** teachers.   She **seems** reliable.

Main Clause: A main or independent clause can be punctuated as an independent sentence:

I left.   Why did you leave?   We are leaving.

A SUBORDINATE or DEPENDENT CLAUSE cannot be punctuated as an independent sentence. These are incorrectly punctuated:

Because she left.   That they left.   Whom you spoke to.

Main Subject: SUBJECT of the MAIN CLAUSE.

Metadiscourse: See pp. 63–64.

Nominalization: See p. 36.

Nonrestrictive Clause: See pp. 17–19.

Noun: A word that fits this frame: *The* [   ] *is good.* Some are concrete: *dog, rock, car;* others abstract: *ambition, space, speed.* The nouns that most concern us are NOMINALIZATIONS, nouns derived from VERBS or ADJECTIVES: *act → action, wide → width*

Noun Clause: A noun clause functions like a noun, as the subject or object of a verb: *That you are here* proves *that you love me.*

Object: There are three kinds:

1. DIRECT object: the NOUN following a TRANSITIVE VERB:

   I *read* **the book.**   We *followed* **the car.**

2. PREPOSITIONAL object: the noun following a preposition:

   in **the house**   *by* **the walk**   *across* **the street**   *with* **fervor**

3. INDIRECT object: the noun between a VERB and its direct object:

   I *gave* **him** a tip.

Parallel: Sequences of coordinated words, PHRASES, or CLAUSES are parallel when they are of the same grammatical structure. This is parallel:

   I decided to work hard and do a good job.

This is not:

   I decided to work hard and that I should do a good job.

Passive: See pp. 58–59.

Past Participle: Usually the same form as the past tense *-ed: jumped, worked.* Irregular VERBS have irregular forms: *seen, broken, swum,* etc. It follows forms of *be* and *have: I have* GONE. *I am* FOUND. It also serves as a modifier: FOUND *money.*

Personal Pronoun: Easier to list than define: *my, mine, our, ours, your, yours, his, her, hers, their, theirs.*

Phrase: A group of words constituting a unit but not including a SUBJECT and a FINITE VERB: *the dog, too old, was leaving, in the house, ready to work*

Possessive: *my, your, his, her, its, their* or a NOUN ending with *-'s* or *-s': the* **dog's** *tail*

Predicate: Whatever follows the whole SUBJECT, beginning with the VERB PHRASE, including the COMPLEMENT and what attaches to it:

He **[left yesterday to buy a hat]** _{predicate}.

Preposition: Easier to list than to define: *in, on, up, over, of, at, by,* etc.

Prepositional Phrase: The preposition plus OBJECT: *in the house*

Present Participle: The *-ing* form of a VERB: *running, thinking*

Progressive: The PRESENT PARTICIPLE form of the VERB: ***Running** streams are beautiful.*

Punctuated Sentence: See pp. 226–227.

Relative Clause: See pp. 17–19.

Relative Pronoun: *who, whom, which, whose, that* when used in a relative clause.

Restrictive Clause: See pp. 17–19.

Resumptive Modifier: See pp. 138–139.

Run-on Sentence: A PUNCTUATED SENTENCE consisting of two or more GRAMMATICAL SENTENCES not separated by either a COORDINATING CONJUNCTION or any mark of punctuation this entry illustrates a run-on sentence.

Simple Subject: The simple subject is the smallest unit inside the WHOLE SUBJECT that determines whether a VERB is singular or plural:

[The **books** _{simple subject} that are required reading] _{whole subject} **are** listed.

The simple subject should be as close to its verb as you can get it.

If **a book** is required reading, **it** is listed.

Stress: See p. 95.

Subject: The subject is what the VERB agrees with in number:

Two men *are* at the door.   **One man** *is* at the door.

Distinguish the WHOLE SUBJECT from its SIMPLE SUBJECT.

Subjunctive: A form of the VERB used to talk about events that are contrary to fact:

> If he **were** President . . .

Subordinate Clause: A clause that usually begins with a SUBOR-DINATING CONJUNCTION such as *if, when, unless,* or *which, that, who.* There are three kinds of subordinate clauses: NOUN, ADVERBIAL, and ADJECTIVAL.

Subordinating Conjunction: *Because, if, when, since, unless, which, who, that, whose,* etc.

Summative Modifier: See pp. 139–140.

Topic: See pp. 79–80.

Topic String: The sequence of TOPICS through a series of sentences.

Transitive Verb: A VERB with a DIRECT OBJECT. The direct object prototypically "receives" an ACTION. The prototypical direct object can be made the SUBJECT of a PASSIVE verb:

> We **read** the book. → The book **was read** by us.

By this definition, *resemble, become,* and *stand* (as in *He stands six feet tall*) are not transitive.

Verb: The word that must agree with the SUBJECT in number and that can be inflected for past or present:

> The book **is** ready.   The books **were** returned.

Whole Subject: You can identify a whole subject once you iden-tify its VERB: Put a *who* or a *what* in front of the verb and turn the sentence into a question. The fullest answer to the question is the whole subject:

> The ability of the city to manage education is an accepted fact.
> Question: **What** is an accepted fact?
> Answer (and whole subject): the ability of the city to manage educa-tion

Distinguish the whole subject from the simple subject:

> The **ability** of the city to manage education **is** an accepted fact.

SUGGESTED ANSWERS

You will almost certainly come up with answers different from these, many probably much better. Don't worry whether your answer is word-for-word like mine; focus only on the general principle of the lesson and exercise.

EXERCISE 3.4

1a. Verbs: *argue, elevate*. No nominalizations.

1b. Verbs: *has been*. Nominalizations: *speculation, improvement, achievement*.

3a. Verbs: *identified, failed, develop, immunize*. Nominalizations: *risk*.

3b. Verbs: *met*. Nominalizations: *attempts, defining, employment, failure*.

5a. Verbs: *resulted in*. Nominalizations: *loss, share, disappearance*.

5b. Verbs: *discover, use, teach*. Nominalizations: *instruction*.

7a. Verbs: *fail, realize, are, protect, adjust*. Nominalizations: *life*.

7b. Verbs: *have come, are*. Nominalizations: *understanding, increases, resistance, costs, education*.

EXERCISE 3.5

1b. Some educators have speculated whether the family improves educational achievement (helps students achieve more).

3b. Economists have attempted but failed to define full employment.

5a. When domestic automakers lost market share to the Japanese, hundreds of thousands of jobs disappeared.

7b. Colleges understand that they can no longer increase tuition yearly because parents are strongly resisting the soaring cost of higher education.

EXERCISE 3.6

1. Lincoln hoped to preserve the Union without war, but when the South attacked Fort Sumter, war became inevitable.

3. Business executives predicted that the economy would quickly revive.

5. Because the health care industry cannot control costs, the public may decide that Congress must act.

7. Several candidates attempted to explain why more voters voted in this year's elections.

9. The business sector did not independently study why the trade surplus suddenly increased.

11. The CIA is uncertain whether North Korea intends to cease missile testing.

13. If the data contradict each other, you must explain why.

15. They performed the play enthusiastically but did not stage it intelligently.

EXERCISE 3.7

There are many plausible alternatives here, depending on the characters we invent.

1. Although we use models to teach prose style, students do not write more clearly or directly.

3. If members depart from established procedures, the Board may terminate their membership.

5. To implement a new curriculum successfully, faculty must cooperate with students to set goals that they can achieve within a reasonable time.

EXERCISE 4.1

1. Historians have reassessed the place of Columbus in Western history because they have interpreted the discovery of America in new ways.

3. To write more coherently, trace the transitions in a book or well-written article.

5. Networks are aware that they must revise their programming because viewers are watching network TV less and rental DVDs and cable more.

EXERCISE 4.2

1. Those on welfare become independent when they learn skills valued by the marketplace. [I like the passive here in order to stress "marketplace."]

3. In this article, I argue that the United States fought the Vietnam War to extend its influence in Southeast Asia and did not end it until North Vietnam made it clear that it could be defeated only if the U.S. used atomic weapons.

5. Bierce presents the first section of . . . dispassionately. In the first sentence, he describes . . . but he takes all emotion away from them . . . In paragraph 2, he describes . . . but betrays no feeling because he uses neutral and unemotional language. He presents this entire . . . even though he fills it with details. [Some will object here that the repeated use of "Bierce/he" is monotonous. Two points: first, most of us never notice when subjects are repeated, and second, we can make more changes: "Even though this section is devoid of emotion, it has many details." Again, the question is *not* which is the correct revision, but how we think about it and decide what we like best. That means going beyond simply repeating the rule, "write in the active voice."]

EXERCISE 4.3

1. We believe that students binge because they do not understand the risks of alcohol.

3. We suggest that Russia's economy has improved because it has exported more crude oil for hard currency.

5. In Section IV, I argue that the indigenous culture overcultivated the land and thereby exhausted it as a food-producing area.

7. To evaluate how the flow rate changed, the current flow rate was compared with the original rate on the basis of figures collected by Jordan in his study of diversion patterns of slow-growth swamps. [This sentence technically has a dangling modifier, but it is so common that no reader of technical prose would balk. That last clump of nominalizations is acceptable because it is a technical term.]

EXERCISE 4.4

1. We analyzed your figures to determine their accuracy. We will announce the results when we think it appropriate.

3. When the author treats the conspiracy theories, he abandons his impassioned narrative style and adopts a cautious one, but when he picks up the narrative line again, he invests his prose with the same vigor and force.

5. For many years, courts have ignored federal regulations concerning wiretaps. Only recently has the Department of Justice imposed tighter restrictions on the circumstances that warrant it.

7. We wrote these directives as simply as possible to communicate more effectively with employees who do not read well.

EXERCISE 4.6

1. The committee on standards for plant safety discussed recent announcements about regulating air quality.

3. The main goal of this article is to describe how readers comprehend text and produce protocols about recall.

5. This paper investigates how computers process information in games that simulate human cognition.

7. The Social Security program guarantees a potential package of benefits based on what individuals contributed to the program over their lifetime.

EXERCISE 5.1

1. When the president assumed office, he had two aims—the recovery of . . . He succeeded in the first as testified to by the drop in . . . But he had less success with the second, as indicated by our increased involvement . . . Nevertheless, the American voter was pleased by vast increases in the military . . .

EXERCISE 5.2

1. Except for those areas covered with ice or scorched by continual heat, the earth is covered by vegetation. Plants grow most richly in fertilized plains and river valleys, but they also grow at the edge of perpetual snow in high mountains. Dense vegetation grows in the ocean and around its edges as well as in and around lakes and swamps. Plants grow in the cracks of busy city sidewalks as well as on seemingly barren cliffs. Vegetation will cover the earth long after we have been swallowed up by evolutionary history.

3. In his paper on children's thinking, Jones (1985) stressed the importance of language skills in the ability of children to solve problems. He reported that when children improved their language skills, they improved their ability to solve nonverbal problems. Jones thinks that they performed better because they used previously acquired language habits to articulate the problems and activate knowledge learned through language. We might therefore explore whether children could learn to solve problems better if they practiced how to formulate them.

EXERCISE 5.3

1. Though modern mass communication offers many advantages, it also poses many threats. If it were controlled by a powerful minority, it could manipulate public opinion through biased reporting. And

while it provides us with a knowledge of public affairs through its national coverage, it may accentuate divisiveness and factionalism by connecting otherwise isolated, local conflicts into a single larger conflict when it shows us conflicts about the same issues occurring in different places. It will always be true that human nature produces differences of opinion, but the media may reinforce the threat of faction and division when it publishes uninformed opinion in national coverage. According to some, media can suppress faction through education when it communicates the true nature of conflicts, but history has shown that the media give as much coverage to people who encourage conflict as to people who try to remove it.

3. When Truman considered the Oppenheimer committee's recommendation to stop the hydrogen bomb project, he had to consider many issues. Russia and China had just proclaimed a Sino-Soviet bloc, so one issue he had to face was the Cold War. He was also losing support for his foreign policy among Republican leaders in Congress, and when the Russians tested their first atom bomb, the public demanded that he respond strongly. It was inevitable that Truman would conclude he could not let the public think he had allowed Russia to be first in developing the most powerful weapon yet. In retrospect, according to some historians, Truman should have risked taking the Oppenheimer recommendation, but he had to face political issues that were too powerful to ignore.

EXERCISE 6.1

1. [One can imagine different rationales for different stresses.] In my opinion, at least, the nation is most threatened by the judiciary's tendency to rewrite the Constitution.

3. In large American universities the opportunities for faculty to work with individual students are limited.

5. College students commonly complain about teachers who assign a long term paper and then give them a grade but no comments.

EXERCISE 6.2

1. During the reign of Queen Elizabeth, the story of King Lear and his daughters was so popular that by the time she died, readers could find it in at least a dozen books. Most of these stories, however, did not develop their characters and were simple narratives with an obvious moral. Several versions of this story must have been available to Shakespeare when he began work on *Lear*, perhaps his greatest tragedy. But while he based his characters on these stock figures of legend, he turned them into credible human beings with complex motives.

3. Because the most important event in Thucydides' *History* is Athens' catastrophic Sicilian Invasion, Thucydides devotes three-quarters of his book to setting it up. We can see this anticipation especially in how he describes the step-by-step decline in Athenian society so that he could create the inevitability that we associate with the tragic drama.

5. Revenues changed as follows during July 1–August 31: Ohio and Kentucky, up 73 percent from $32,934 to $56,792; Indiana and Illinois, up 10 percent from $153,281 to $168,651; Wisconsin and Minnesota, down 5 percent from $200,102 to $190,580. [The important thing here is to get the sequence of items in a regular order. I could imagine an argument insisting that the percentage be at the end of sentence.]

EXERCISE 6.3

The second sentence best introduces the themes of turmoil and disputed succession to the throne because it is that sentence that announces those themes in its stress.

EXERCISE 7.1

1. Critics must use complex and abstract terms to analyze literary texts meaningfully.

3. Graduate students face an uncertain future at best in finding good teaching jobs.

5. Most patients who go to a public clinic do not expect special treatment, because their health problems are minor and can be easily treated.

7. We can reduce the federal deficit only if we reduce federal spending.

9. A person may be rejected from a cost-sharing educational program only if that person receives a full hearing into why she was rejected. *Or:* An agency may reject a person from . . . only when that agency provides a full hearing into why it rejected her.

11. If we pay taxes, the government can pay its debts.

13. Catholics and Protestants will reconcile only when they agree on the Pope's authority.

EXERCISE 7.3

1. Recent research has applied schemata theory to the pedagogy of solving mathematical problems. [Sounds dull to me, but who knows?]

3. Because of their methodological differences, American and British historians have interpreted what caused the War of 1812 in radically different ways. [Sounds significant.]

5. Egyptian and Greek thought influenced scientific thinking. [Sounds banal to me.]

7. Birth order relates to academic success. [Seems signifcant.]

EXERCISE 7.4

1. On the other hand, some TV programming will always appeal to our most prurient interests.

3. One principle governs how to preserve the wilderness from exploitation.

5. Schools transmit more social values than do families.

EXERCISE 8.1

1. Proponents of workfare have not yet shown it is a successful alternative to welfare because they have not shown evidence that it can provide meaningful and regular employment for welfare recipients. Therefore, it is premature to recommend that all the states fully commit themselves to it.

3. We could prevent foreign piracy of videos and CDs if the justice systems of foreign countries moved cases faster through their courts and imposed stiffer penalties. But we cannot expect any immediate improvement in the level of expertise of judges who hear these cases.

5. The music industry has ignored the problem of how to apply a rating system to offensive lyrics broadcast over FM and AM radio. Until it does, stations are unlikely to improve their public image, even if they were willing to discuss such a system.

7. Young people will not be discouraged from smoking just because the film and TV industries agree not to show characters smoking.

9. When Congress voted funds to construct the Interstate Highway System, it did not anticipate inflation, and so the system has run into financial problems.

11. "Reality" shows are the most popular shows on TV because they appeal to our voyeuristic impulses.

13. If carbon monoxide continues to be emitted, world climate will change.

EXERCISE 8.2

1. Many school systems are returning to the basics, basics that have been the foundation of education for centuries. / . . . a change that is long overdue. . . . / trying to stem an ever rising drop-out rate.

3. For millennia, why we age has been a puzzle, a puzzle that only now can be answered with any certainty. / . . . a mystery that we can answer either biologically or spiritually. / . . . hoping that one day we might stop our inevitable decline into infirmity and death.

5. Both scientists and laypeople have been troubled by the ethical issues of test-tube fertilization, issues that require the most delicate balancing between religion and medical hope. / . . . an event that has changed the way we think about what it means to be human. / . . . finding in them inevitable conflicts between self-interest and religious values.

7. In the Renaissance, greater affluence and political stability allowed streams of thought to merge, streams that originated in ancient Greece, in the Middle East, and in Europe itself. / . . . a historical development that both undermined the dominance of religious authority over knowledge and laid the groundwork for everything that we know about the world. / . . . bringing together knowledge and modes of thought that resulted in a new vision of humankind's potential.

EXERCISE 9.2

1. Those who argue stridently over small matters are unlikely to think clearly about large ones.

3. We should pay more attention to those politicians who tell us how to make what we have better than to those who tell us how to get what we don't have.

5. Some teachers mistake neat papers that rehash old ideas for great thoughts wrapped in impressive packaging.

EXERCISE 9.3

1. If we invest our sweat in these projects, we must avoid appearing to be working only for our own self-interest.

3. Throughout history, science has progressed because dedicated scientists have ignored the hostility of an uninformed public.

5. Boards of education can no longer expect that taxpayers will support the extravagancies of incompetent bureaucrats.

EXERCISE 10.1

As the Illinois Commerce Commission has authorized, **you** will have to pay . . . **You** have not had to pay . . . , but **you** will now pay rates that have been restructured consistent with the policy of the Public Utilities Act that lets us base what **you** pay on what it costs to provide you with service.

As the Illinois Commerce Commission has authorized, **we** are charging you . . . **We** have not raised rates . . . but **we** are restructuring the rates now . . . so that **we** can charge you for what **we** pay to provide you with service.

EXERCISE 10.2

Your car may have a defective part that connects the suspension to the frame. If you brake hard and the plate fails, you won't be able to steer. We may also have to adjust the secondary latch on your hood because we may have misaligned it. If you don't latch the primary latch, the secondary latch might not hold the hood down. If the hood flies up while you are driving, you won't be able to see. If either of these things occurs, you could crash.

EXERCISE 10.3

There are forty nominalizations in the speech: Para 1: *appearing, address, statement, expiration, declarations, contest, attention, progress, hope, prediction* (1:13); Para 2: *thoughts, address, saving, effects, negotiation* (1:20); Para 3: *interest, interest, cause, interest, enlargement, cause, conflict, conflict, triumph, result, aid, assistance, wringing, prayers, offenses, offenses, offense, slavery, offenses, providence, offense, departure, toil, judgments, firmness* (1:18). The opening paragraph is highly nominalized. Then it tapers off quite a bit until the passage beginning with *offenses for it must needs be* through *providence*, in which he concentrates six nominalizations in thirty-five words, the highest in the speech. This is clearly the most philosophical section of the speech.

EXERCISE 10.4

Nine mentions of *war* occur in paragraph two, with all of them except the last one an object of some kind. In the last sentence of paragraph two it becomes an acting subject. It becomes an object again, but mostly as an instrument of God.

EXERCISE 10.5

This is a hard question to answer. The difference is that Lincoln had good intentions; the others did not. But do good intentions justify such stylistic sleights of hand?

Exercise 10.7

The last part of the Declaration topicalizes *we;* the middle part *he;* and the first part abstractions. It is so regular that Jefferson had to have something in mind. I suspect it was this: in the first part, he systemically subordinated the colonist/revolutionaries to abstractions such as duty, prudence, and so on, making them the constrained objects of higher principles. They have no choice in the matter: necessity forces them to revolt. But once he is past the philosophical foundations of his argument, he can introduce the evidence ("Let facts be submitted . . .") focusing on King George, and then at the end, he can focus on "we" as the dispositive agents who are now entitled to act on their own.

Exercise A.1

I can write a different kind of punctuated sentence: it would be a sentence that I could not break into shorter sentences merely by replacing commas and semicolons with periods; it would be a sentence consisting of several subordinate clauses: they would all depend on one main or independent clause—it would be a sentence like this one that you have almost finished, but it would probably feel longer than that sentence in the previous paragraph, yet it is shorter.

Exercise A.3

Here are the two passages, first with the least punctuation I can imagine, and then with much more.

1. Scientists and philosophers . . . precise, as if those . . . disagree. But in fact scientific language . . . believed. It too is subject to . . . understanding. Moreover, new theories or arguments are rarely if ever constructed by way of clear-cut steps of induction, . . . falsification. Neither are they defended, rejected or accepted in so straightforward a manner. In practice scientists combine . . . of intuition, aesthetics commitment. The importance . . . generally acknowledged. . . . But the role of . . . less visible. The ways in . . . common experiences, on extensive practice . . . taken for granted. Only when we step out of such a "consensual domain," when we can stand out . . . the unarticulated premises, mutual understandings and assumed practices of the group. Even in those subjects . . . to quantification, discourse depends heavily on conventions and interpretation, conventions that are acquired over years of practice and participation in a community.

   Scientists and philosophers of science . . . were intrinsically precise, as if those who use it . . . meaning, even if they disagree. But, in fact, scientific language . . . commonly believed: it, too, is subject to imprecision and ambiguity, and hence to imperfect understanding. Moreover, new theories, or arguments, are rarely, if ever, constructed by way of clear-cut steps of induction, deduction, and verification or falsification; neither are they defended, rejected, or accepted in so straightforward a manner. In practice, scientists combine the rules of scientific methodology with a generous admixture of intuition, aesthetics, and philosophical commitment. The importance of what are, sometimes, called extra-rational, or extra-logical components of . . . law is generally acknowledged . . . But the role of these extralogical . . . frequently discussed, partly because they are less visible. The ways in which the credibility, or effectiveness, of an argument depends on the realm of common experiences, on extensive practice . . . a common language, are hard to see precisely, because such commonalities are taken for granted. Only when we step out of such a "consensual domain," when we can stand . . . language, do we begin to become aware of the unarticulated premises, mutual understandings, and assumed practices of the group. Even in those subjects . . . quantification, discourse depends heavily on conventions and interpretation, conventions that . . . participation in a community.

2. In fact of course, the notion of . . . been an illusion. But it is an illusion fostered . . . else that is true. We are not today . . . man's experience. We know that we are ignorant. We are well taught it. And the more surely and deeply we know our own job, the better able . . . pervasive ignorance. We know . . . men at all. But knowledge rests on knowledge. What is new is . . . known before. This is a world . . . from most of them. Perhaps this sense was not so sharp in the village, that village which . . . not understand too well, the village of slow change . . . full comprehension. Perhaps in the villages men were not so lonely. Perhaps they found in each other a fixed community, a fixed and . . . single world. Even that we may doubt. For there seem . . . , endless and open.

    In fact, of course, the notion of universal knowledge . . . illusion, but it is an illusion . . . view of the world, in which a few great, central truths determine, in all its wonderful and amazing proliferation, everything else that is true. We are not, today, tempted to search . . . and of man's experience: we know that we are ignorant; we are well taught it; and the more surely and deeply we know our own job, the better able . . . pervasive ignorance. We know that these are inherent limits, compounded, no doubt, and exaggerated by . . . men at all. But knowledge rests on knowledge: what is new is meaningful, because it departs, slightly, from what was known before. This is a world of frontiers, where even the liveliest . . . of the time, from most of them. Perhaps, this sense was not so sharp in the village, that village which we have learned a little about, but probably do not understand too well—the village of slow change, and isolation, and fixed culture, which evokes our nostalgia, even if not our full comprehension. Perhaps in the villages men were not so lonely; perhaps they found in each other a fixed community, a fixed and . . . single world. Even that we may doubt, for there seem . . . and places, vast domains of mystery, if not unknowable, then imperfectly known—endless and open.

ACKNOWLEDGMENTS

D. H. Lawrence, *Studies in Classic American Literature*. New York: The Viking Press, 1961.

Norman Mailer, *Armies of the Night*. New York: The New American Library, Inc., 1971.

From *Science and the Common Understanding* by J. Robert Oppenheimer. Copyright © 1954 by J. Robert Oppenheimer, renewed © 1981 by Robert B. Meyner. Reprinted by permission.

From "The Aims of Education" in *The Aims of Education and Other Essays* by Alfred North Whitehead. Copyright © 1929 by Macmillan Publishing Co., Inc., renewed 1957 by Evelyn Whitehead. Reprinted by permission.

From Strunk, William Jr. & White, E. B. *The Elements of Style* 4/e. Copyright © 1999 by Pearson Education. Reprinted by permission.

INDEX